ANTICIPATORY DEMOCRACY

People in the Politics of the Future

ANTICIPATORY DEMOCRACY

People in the Politics of the Future

EDITED BY CLEMENT BEZOLD

INTRODUCTION BY ALVIN TOFFLER

Vintage Books

A Division of Random House, New York

VINTAGE BOOKS EDITION, October 1978

First Edition

Copyright © 1978 by Clement Bezold

Library of Congress Cataloging in Publication Data
Main entry under title:
Anticipatory democracy.
Includes index and bibliographical references.
1. Political participation—United States—Addresses,
essays, lectures. 2. Forecasting—Addresses, essays,
lectures. I. Bezold, Clement.
JK1764.A53 1978   309.2'12'0973   77-90318
ISBN 0-394-72402-X

Manufactured in the United States of America

Acknowledgments

All books, including this one, bear fruit from the labor of many. Alvin Toffler and others in the Committee for Anticipatory Democracy encouraged me to write this book and reinforced my initial feelings about its importance. Much of the credit for the content of this book belongs to the contributors, many of whom took time away from developing anticipatory democracy techniques in order to write about them. My own learning has benefited from several sources, and I would like to acknowledge and thank those responsible. The Center for Governmental Responsibility, particularly its director Jon Mills, schooled me in how the government does work, and allowed me to explore how it might work. My research at the Center was made possible in part through funds provided by Michael McIntosh and the McIntosh Foundation. William Birenbaum, president of Antioch University and a member of the Committee for Anticipatory Democracy, and Edgar Cahn, co-dean of Antioch School of Law, allowed me to start the Institute for Alternative Futures in the challenging setting provided by the many units and faces at Antioch University. For their enthusiasm, incisiveness, and persistence in the production of the book, I would like to thank Diane Sherwood and the Finders, Anne McCormally, and Betsy Amster and Anne Freedgood of Random House. Finally, I'd like to express my thanks and affection to the editor whose comments, understanding, and support were invaluable, Rosemarie Philips.

Contents

Introduction On Future-Conscious Politics

BY ALVIN TOFFLER

In a world governed by obsolete political dogmas, in which terms like "left wing," "right wing," "liberal," and "conservative" are still bandied about freely as though rich in meaning, it is refreshing to come upon a new idea that cannot be shoved into a convenient ideological cubbyhole. This book is about such an idea —anticipatory democracy—and I am proud to have had something to do with bringing it to birth.

Anticipatory democracy will appeal to people from every position on the political spectrum, not because it offers everything to everyone, like a desperate politician, but because it deals with *process* as distinct from program. Thus this book does not propagandize for increased minimum wages, full employment, environmental controls, or cuts in the military budget; nor does it tell us to hang on to the Panama Canals of the future, to slash welfare, or to cut corporate taxes.

Instead, it urges us to look at the very process by which we arrive at our political choices—*whatever* those choices may be. Anticipatory democracy, in this sense, deals not with politics, but with meta-politics.

The basic idea is simple. I spelled it out and termed it "anticipatory democracy" in the final pages of *Future Shock* and subsequently in many speeches and essays. Others have said many of the same things, often with more eloquence and impact. But not until now has there been a book devoted to elaborating the concept, examining its ramifications, and reporting on how people are putting it into action. For anticipatory democracy is more than an intellectual concept: It has become the basis for a new activist movement that could radically alter American political life.

Hundreds of thousands, indeed millions of Americans—and many thousands in other countries as well—have already been touched by this movement, and I believe we shall hear much, much more about it in the tense political years that lie immediately ahead.

The simplest definition of anticipatory democracy (or A/D, as some of us have begun to call it) is that it is a process for combining citizen participation with future consciousness. As such, it goes far beyond the usual notions of "participatory democracy." And it directly challenges the idea that long-range goal-setting is best left to politicians, planners, or professional futurists. A/D is, to put it another way, the fusion of freedom and futures.

Behind this deceptively simple, even naïve-sounding concept lies a set of fundamental and, I think, startling assumptions about the politics of the future.

My own espousal of A/D sprang, for example, from the recognition that our political institutions and processes, the mechanics of representative government, the entire apparatus of "democracy" as we know it—including voting, elections, parties, parliaments, and the like—are expressions not of some undying mystical human commitment to freedom but of the spread of industrial civilization that began in England 200 to 300 years ago.

This industrial civilization took the idea of representation (which like most ideas had rudimentary precedents in the ancient past) and merchandised it around the planet as the latest, most efficient, most humane form of government imaginable. As the industrial way of life spread, representative government, denatured or otherwise, spread with it. In fact, using shorthand, one might declare representative government—whether "capitalist" or "socialist" in form—to be the key political technology of the industrial era.

This era is now screeching to a halt. Industrial civilization is now in a state of terminal crisis, and a new, radically different civilization is emerging to take its place on the world stage. This does not mean that we are about to plunge ourselves voluntarily or simplistically back into some pre-technological way of life. Rather, it means that we are swiftly entering a new, more sophisticated stage of evolutionary development based on far more *advanced* yet more *appropriate* technologies than any known so far. This leap to a new phase of history is bringing with it new energy patterns, new geopolitical arrangements, new social institutions, new communications and information networks, new belief systems, symbols, and cultural assumptions.

Thus, it must also generate wholly new political structures and processes. I fail to see how it is possible for us to have a technological revolution, a social revolution, an information revolution, moral, sexual, and epistemological revolutions, and *not* a political revolution as well.

All this suggests that we need a fresh way to think about the political breakdown—the crisis of governmental competence—that we see all around us: the paralysis of parliaments, the ineptitudes of the giant governmental bureaucracies, the wild swings of political attention, focusing now here, now elsewhere, before any problem has been adequately understood, let alone solved. The erratic and ineffectual behavior of governments in the industrial world cannot be explained in conventional terms.

It is not because politicians and bureaucrats are stupid. It is not because of a conspiracy of the so-called right or left. It is not because greedy, rich people are corrupting and controlling our political institutions, though heaven knows they would like to. Nor does the crisis of ineffectuality arise because greedy, poor people are demanding too many "entitlements" from the system, as "neo-conservatives" would have us believe. Nor yet, for that matter, is it because we are witnessing the "general crisis of capitalism" that Marx predicted. Rather, it is because we are in the first stages of the "general crisis of industrialism" of which capitalism and socialism are both offshoots.

In this sense the breakdown of government as we have known it—which is to say representative government or parliamentary democracy or "indirect democracy"—is chiefly a consequence of obsolescence. Simply put, the political technology of the industrial age is no longer appropriate technology for the new civilization taking form around us. Our politics are obsolete.

To grasp why, let us for the moment lay aside all the other characteristics of political life (drama, ritual, struggle over power and resources, for example) and consider our present political system solely as a technology for the manufacture of collective decisions. This system—regardless of who runs it—is now, in my view, structurally incapable of making competent decisions about the world we inhabit.

A decision system suitable for one kind of environment may be totally ineffective or irrelevant in another—like a Seiko wristwatch in the midst of a pre-historic band of nomads or an Exxon oil refinery in a world without fossil fuels.

The industrial age produced a specific decisional environment —one based on social homogeneity. The industrial revolution generated tremendous cultural, political, and technological pressures that converged to create uniformity in language, values, machines, work methods, architecture, political views, and life styles in general. If it did nothing else, the industrial revolution produced "mass society."

Yet the revolution gathering momentum today is carrying us precisely in the opposite direction. We are fast becoming far more socially, culturally, and politically diverse than ever before. We use more varied resources and tools, we fill more varied occupations and roles, we live more varied life styles than during the heyday of industrialism. Regional, sectoral, ethnic, and subcultural differences are looming into greater political importance as society, rapidly differentiating, moves away from homogeneity and toward heterogeneity. In short, we are shifting from a "mass society" to a "de-massified society"—and this has truly revolutionary (though largely misunderstood) implications for politics.

Thus it is becoming harder and harder to achieve consensus even locally, let alone nationally. Demands now pour in to the political decision-makers from a much wider range of special interests than before. Instead of having to deal with a few well-established mass constituencies, they now face political demands from a kaleidoscopic, continually changing set of temporary mini-constituencies. Instead of a few widely voiced, class-based slogans calling, say, for jobs or housing or social security, the political decision-maker today faces a clamor of competing, often contradictory demands from gay activists, ethnic sub-sub-minorities, regional power blocs, feminists, cultural and linguistic groups, gray panthers, Panama Canalers, anti-nuclear campaigners, single parents, solar freaks, and Sun Myung Moonies. In short, the decisional environment has been transformed.

Our political decision-making machinery, however, both legislative and executive, was never designed to cope with such high levels of diversity. It was designed, instead, to produce uniform, basically repetitive decisions for a much less differentiated environment, a simpler, more comprehensible and manageable environment. Designed to respond to mass movements, mass opinion, mass media, and large flows of relatively simple information, the system is now struggling against a tidal wave of de-massified mini-movements, de-massified opinion, increasingly de-massified communications media, and torrents of specialized data pouring in through fast-multiplying channels.

It should hardly surprise us if the result of this mismatch between our decisional technology and the decisional environment is a cacaphonous confusion, countless self-canceling decisions, noise, fury, and gross ineptitude.

If, moreover, our legislative and executive policy-makers are overloaded, what about those who implement their decisions in the civil service bureaucracy? Here the effects of our transformation from a mass to a de-massified society are even more explosive.

Take, for example, the "tax revolt" now raging in the United States. This revolt aims its attack at bureaucrats and government on the assumption that "government is doing too much," as though the entire problem were simply quantitative. But there is a far deeper reason for the tax revolt. For if we look at the huge government bureaucracies that were established during the industrial era, we discover that they, too, were designed to operate in a more homogeneous, repetitive, and predictable mass society. They were to the service economy what factories were to the goods economy: a tool for mass production.

As consumers have grown more diverse in the past twenty years or so, industry has responded through what executives term "product differentiation." Companies have competed to turn out different models, sizes, types, and styles for the increasingly segmented marketplace. Whether this product variation is good or bad, whether the differences are real or trivial are issues that can be explored elsewhere. Here it is only necessary to note that while goods producers responded quickly to growing social diversity, and service producers in the private sector did the same —witness the proliferation of different "package tours" in the travel industry—government bureaucracies have been far less adaptive. Constrained by anachronistic political boundaries, by well-intended but simplistic notions of "equality," by organizational ossification and rigidity, lacking even the spur of competition, the great government "service factories" are still, even now, pumping out essentially uniform services for an increasingly non-uniform population. Not surprisingly, the gap between what people need or want and what they get from government has grown to monstrous proportions.

The problem, therefore, is not simply that government does "too much"; the problem is that much of what it does is also simply wrong or too late. People who desperately need help don't get it. People in no need at all receive lush benefits. Programs designed in the nation's capital are not adequately tailored for local needs. Old programs that should have been slashed years ago continue to grind out whatever it is they grind out, while new ones proliferate beyond the ability of anyone to manage them. And instead of customized services for real individuals, the government service factories churn out their mass product for dehumanized "clients."

The crisis of government ineffectuality, in short, is qualitative as well as merely quantitative. Once again, in the bureaucracy as in the legislative and executive centers, we see a collision between decision structures designed for the old mass society and a civilization that is rapidly de-massifying.

This by itself would be enough to account for many of our gravest difficulties. But this is by no means all that is meant by saying that our present political system is obsolete. For just as decision systems are designed to handle different levels of diversity, they are also designed to operate at quite different speeds. And if we add to the pressures generated by diversity those that arise from the acceleration of change, we drastically scale up the intensity of the decisional crisis.

Clearly, we no longer live in a world in which it might take a week for a congressional decision to get from Philadelphia to New York or Ohio. We now live in a communications net so tight that the slightest political sneeze in Zaire touches off instantaneous coughs, sniffles, or paroxysms in Peking, Paris, Brussels, or Washington, not to mention Moscow or Havana. Decisions that might have taken weeks to make in the past must now be made in hours. Experts are brought in. Computers are set to chattering. But the pressure for accelerated decision-making slams up hard against the increased complexity and unfamiliarity of the environment about which the decisions must be made. It is not as if the world were stable, routine, and predictable. It is surrealistic, with extremely complex events firing off at high speed. The result is that our political decision-makers swing wildly back and forth between doing nothing about a problem until it explodes into crisis and, alternatively, racing in with ill-conceived, poorly pre-assessed crash programs.

Any decision system is ultimately capable of handling only a given "decision load." The load gets heavier as needed decisions multiply, grow in complexity, or speed up. At some point the decision load is greater than the system can handle. At this point the fuses blow. And that, I think, is precisely what is happening to the political decision systems of all the high technology nations.

What we are witnessing is crushing decisional overload—in short, political future shock.

A political system is more than just a decision system, but if the decision system is malfunctioning, it becomes increasingly impossible to deal intelligently with the crucial issues of the day, from ecology and human rights to war, poverty, or relations with the nonindustrial world. Unless we can design an appropriate process for making collective decisions, one that fits the requirements of the new decisional environment, we face ultimate disaster.

A new decisional process, however, will not suddenly leap from the drawing board of social or political engineers. It will emerge, after repeated trial and error, from innovative experiments conducted by political activists. This, then, brings us back to the concept of anticipatory democracy.

There are essentially two contrasting ways to approach the crushing decisional overload at the center: one way is to attempt to further strengthen the center of government, adding more and yet more politicians, bureaucrats, experts, and computers in the desperate hope of outrunning the acceleration of complexity; the complexity; the other is to begin reducing the decision load by sharing it with more people, allowing more decisions to be made "down below" or at the "periphery" instead of concentrating them at the already stressed and malfunctioning center.

One leads to ever-greater centralization, technocracy, and totalitarianism; the other toward a new, more advanced level of democracy, and there are quite hard-headed, nonaltruistic reasons for preferring the latter. For it is an obsolete myth that centralist or totalitarian decision-making is "efficient" while democracy only "muddles through." Looked at dispassionately, from the point of view of information or decision theory as distinct from political philosophy, democracy has marked virtues that the centralist or authoritarian decision system lacks.

Thus while czar or dictator may be able to act swiftly because he need not put up with opposing views, this proves to be an advantage only if his decision is intelligent or appropriate in the first place. Not only reward but risk is amplified in such a system, and risk in today's world can be shattering. Unchecked by democratic dissent and unrefreshed by new ideas from "below," the actions of any "czar" become increasingly error-prone, dangerous, self-amplifying—and often self-defeating.

By contrast, increasing channels for feedback, and especially negative feedback, between citizens and government decision-makers decreases the risk of error. It also means that errors, once made, can be more quickly and cheaply corrected. The less democratic feedback (and feedforward), the more decisions become divorced from reality, and the greater the danger that errors will go uncorrected until they escalate into crisis. Democracy, in this sense, is not just theoretically "nice"—it is highly "efficient."

This argument for participation, however, is not enough, since there is also a time factor at work. For citizen participation to be effective, it must concern itself increasingly not merely with "here and now" decisions but with those more basic decisions that influence the long-range future. In fact, participation without future consciousness is not democracy at all; it is a mockery of democracy. In leaving the long-range issues to others by default, citizens groups wind up participating—if at all—in the making of purely implementary decisions, squabbling over how to carry out the long-range designs of others.

This is why anticipatory democracy insists on fusing citizen feedback and future-consciousness. A perceptive observer of the movement will no doubt notice within it an uneasy tension between those who are essentially "participationist" (but not very future-oriented) and those who are "futurist" (but not very participationist). The essence of anticipatory democracy, however, is the recognition that one without the other is either foolish or futile, if not actively dangerous.

It should be clear by now that this emphasis on the future has nothing in common with those technocratic planners who think we need a "master plan" for the next quarter century or who hanker for consensus so we can all "get behind" a single vision. Both of these attitudes are holdovers from the mass society of the past. In fact, what counts most for those involved in A/D is not the formulation of some specific set of goals for city, state, or nation but the creation of a new decision process in which all goals, no matter whose, are continually reevaluated in the light of accelerating change. The essence of A/D is not the goal but the process by which we arrive at it.

Anticipatory democracy, therefore, does not promise that decisions made by ordinary citizens (even when these are aided by experts, as is often the case) will necessarily be "correct." It does not assert that citizens are capable of understanding technical matters without education or expert help. It does not necessarily seek to form, let alone compel, consensus. It does not lend itself easily to the rhetoric of either the so-called right or left. What it *does* do, however, is build a constituency for the future, and nothing could be more important.

It creates a large number of active citizens who—whatever other differences they may have—recognize that the time horizons of political life must be extended beyond the next election if we are all to survive.

This constituency for the future frees intelligent politicians and public administrators to do a better job even with the present inadequate decision tools. It frees them to speak openly and intelligently about long-range needs without sounding like kooks or cranks. It provides a base of support for far-sighted policies. It also promotes consideration of imaginative options and alternatives—including visionary pathways into the future—that normally are squeezed out of view by political polarization. In all these ways it improves the decision process.

The A/D movement has already made concrete changes in existing political institutions. Its friends in the U.S. Congress, for example, have succeeded in making the exercise of "foresight" and the application of "futures research" a new and formal obligation of many committees in the House of Representatives. The Committee on Anticipatory Democracy is directly responsible, in considerable measure, for the creation of what is in effect an A/D caucus on Capitol Hill: the Congressional Clearinghouse on the Future. This new organization, backed by scores of members of Congress, bombards members and staff alike with news of futures research, with seminars on long-range trends, with bibliographies, technical discussions, and other material dealing with *both* foresight and increased citizen participation in the decision process.

But while the A/D movement has made distinct efforts to improve democratic decision-making, even with the obsolete tools of today, its more fundamental purpose is to question these tools and to help us face the deep questions about the future of representative government itself. If the political technology of the industrial age is increasingly obsolete, the A/D movement is helping us to begin thinking about new, more appropriate decision structures.

Thus one may view the various experiments described in this book as efforts not merely to reform or adapt the political technology of industrialism but to create new models more appropriate to the civilization now emerging to take its place. All sorts of questions flow from this.

Should citizens organized to formulate long-range goals simply advise their elected representatives? Or are some A/D organizations in reality para-parliaments, embryonic political structures of the future that rely not on election alone, as such, but on random sample surveys, on selection by lot, on electronic polling, on computer networking, and on other such methods? What should a Parliament or Congress look like in the year 2000? How shall we redefine the very definition of "representation?" A/D also compels us to ask how, when, and by what process today's increasingly obsolete constitutions must be rewritten. It forces us to ask how the Bill of Rights must be expanded to fit the needs of the new civilization.

Outside the formal political sphere, anticipatory democracy raises equally potent questions. To what extent can "experts" and "citizens" be brought back together in a nonadversary relationship? What is the relationship between democracy and education? (The Swedes, in a significant anticipatory democracy experiment, combined education and political goal-setting on a nationwide basis.) Can A/D help us devise something we now lack—broad, citizen-approved strategies for technological development? (The Berger inquiry in Canada, which invited not only various experts but also ordinary citizens, including Native Americans, to pre-assess the long-range impact of a projected pipeline, suggests we could do much more to democratize technological decision-making.)

A/D also forces us to face profound questions about control of the workplace and, indeed, the very functions of work. Whether one urges a "capitalist" model or a "self-management" model, A/D clearly implies that employees have a right to participate in making not merely short-range decisions about their working conditions and safety but longer-range decisions about which products to make, which investments to encourage, and the like. Though wrapped in obsolete Marxist rhetoric, the highly imaginative A/D actions taken by the Lucas Aerospace workers in Britain (described below by Clem Bezold), suggest a wide range of innovations in the economic decision system.

Anticipatory democracy is no panacea. At a time when our entire civilization is undergoing rapid and wrenching transformation, when the technology of representation is increasingly incapable of making competent decisions for the present, let alone the distant future, the movement for anticipatory democracy is not going to solve all our political problems. Indeed, seen against the enormity of the dangers that face us, A/D may seem to be a small and partial response. It is undramatic. It neither kills nor kidnaps its opponents. It threatens no coup d'état. It is decent and democratic in spirit. Yet it would be a mistake to underrate the power and significance of this new political force.

For it cuts much deeper into the core of today's political crises than most of the more publicized activist and militant movements, and it *could* play an absolutely pivotal role in the future. If our present political technologies are failing, it is long past necessary

Preface

In 1970 Alvin Toffler, describing the political implications of future shock, noted that:

Acceleration produces a faster turnover of goals, a greater transcience of purpose. Diversity or fragmentation leads to a relentless multiplication of goals. Caught in this churning, goal-cluttered environment, we stagger, future-shocked, from crisis to crisis, pursuing a welter of conflicting and self-canceling purposes. No vision—Utopian or otherwise—energizes our efforts. No rationally integrated goals bring order to the chaos."[1]

Toffler's prescription for the ills accompanying future shock was *anticipatory democracy,* the blending of future consciousness and genuine popular participation:

Two crucial problems endanger the stability and survival of our political system today.

First: Lack of future-consciousness. Instead of anticipating the problems and opportunities of the future, we lurch from crisis to crisis. The energy shortage, runaway inflation, ecological troubles—all reflect the failure of our political leaders at federal, state, and local levels to look beyond the next election. Our political system is "Future-blind." With but few exceptions, the same failure of foresight marks our corporations, trade unions, schools, hospitals, voluntary organizations, and communities as well. The result is political and social future shock.

Second: Lack of participation. Our government and other institutions have grown so large and complicated that most people feel powerless. They complain of being "planned upon." They are seldom consulted or asked for ideas about their own future. On the rare occasions when they are, it is ritualistic rather than real consultation. Blue-collar workers, poor people, the elderly, the youth, even the affluent among us, feel frozen out of the decision process. And as more and more millions feel powerless, the danger of violence and authoritarianism increases.

[1] *Future Shock* (New York: Bantam Books, 1970), p. 471.

Moreover, if this is true within the country, it is even more true of the world situation in which the previously powerless are demanding the right to participate in shaping the global future.

Anticipatory democracy (A/D) is a way to tackle both these critical problems simultaneously. It connects up future-consciousness with real participation. Thus the term "anticipatory" stresses the need for greater attention to the long-range future. The term "democracy" stresses the need for vastly increased popular participation and feed-back.

There is no single or magical way to build a truly anticipatory democracy. In general, we need to support any program or action that increases future-awareness in the society, while simultaneously creating new channels for genuine, broad-based citizen participation. This means, among other things, an emphasis not on "elite" or "techno-cratic" futures work, but on mass involvement. We certainly need experts and specialists; they are indispensable, in fact. But in anticipatory democracy, goals are not set by elites or experts alone. Thus, where futures activity exists, we need to open it to all sectors of society, making a special effort to involve women, the poor, working people, minority groups—young and old—and to involve them at all levels of leadership as well. Conversely, where participatory activities exist at community, state, or federal levels, or within various corporate or voluntary organizations, we need to press for attention to longer-range futures.[2]

Since Toffler first coined the term "anticipatory democracy," a wide variety of experiments and activities attempting to incorporate both a conscious orientation toward the future and the active participation of the citizenry have taken place. Many of these efforts are documented in this volume.

This volume is intended to present a variety of cases, to raise questions, and to develop theories. The articles are diverse in their outlook and are at times in disagreement with one another. They were chosen to illustrate examples of major A/D projects, to set out approaches for citizen activism for A/D, and to present the ideas of some of the leading thinkers in the field. It is hoped that by examining the results of various A/D experiments as well as the various viewpoints held by those who practice and encourage anticipatory democracy, the reader will review his or her own life to see if there are opportunities for democratic experimentation in inventing and choosing the future.

This book grows out of the concerns of the Committee on An-

[2] "What is Anticipatory Democracy?," *The Futurist*, The World Future Society, Washington, D.C. (December 1975).

ticipatory Democracy, a group of over fifty futurists, professional planners and future-oriented citizens formed by Alvin Toffler in 1975 to encourage the spread of A/D groups and the implementation of the foresight provision, an addition to the House Rules stipulating that congressional committees must consider the future on a continuing basis, in the U.S. House of Representatives. The Committee has sponsored a variety of activities, including the first legislative conference on futurism, called "Outsmarting Crises: Futures Thinking in Congress," in September 1975. Appendix I lists the original members of the Committee, and two items that grew out of its work; first, a proposal by Senator John C. Culver for federal support of A/D groups, and second, a description of A/D opportunities. Toffler and other members of the Committee, including myself, agreed that enough A/D activity had taken place around the country to warrant attention in an anthology such as this. Many of the articles in the book were written by members of the Committee.

My own interest in anticipatory democracy grew out of the discontent I experienced while working in political campaigns. Campaigns seldom result in greater public wisdom or a significantly better-informed electorate. In spite of my interest in how to address questions concerning the future in a campaign, I came to recognize that most campaigns cannot really invite voters to explore the future—instead, voters are told how the candidate will play his or her part (usually much smaller than implied in campaign literature) in shaping the future by specific policies. But the proposed policies seldom are directed toward a coherent vision, much less toward the development of a situation in which citizens can play a conscious role in shaping such a vision.

As a result, the nature of policy-making—by both elected and nonelected officials—and the role citizens might play in the policy-making process became of greater concern to me. This interest, coupled with my work on the congressional foresight provision for the Center for Governmental Responsibility and my doctoral dissertation, led me to discussions with Alvin Toffler and involvement with the Committee on Anticipatory Democracy.

I have since become the director of the Institute for Alternative Futures, a unit of Antioch University located at its School of Law in Washington, D.C. Alvin Toffler and Antioch President William Birenbaum established the Institute in 1977 to act as a center for encouraging the development of A/D processes. Readers of this volume are invited to share their experiences with anticipatory democracy and to receive further information by writing to me at the Institute for Alternative Futures, Antioch School of Law, 1624 Crescent Place, N.W., Washington, D.C. 20009 (Tel.: 202–265-0346).

As advanced industrial societies tremble on the edge of an uncertain future, with the spaceship earth growing increasingly out of control, we are forced by necessity to evolve ways to create some kind of manageable order. Only through more conscious awareness of the range of alternative futures and their implications can citizens make better-informed decisions, and only through more effective citizen involvement is the future likely to provide social and economic justice.

Such involvement of the citizenry in what should be our major collective concern—our common future—would be a realization of the optimistic, Jeffersonian principles on which our country was founded.

Clement Bezold
Director
Institute for Alternative Futures

March 1978
Antioch School of Law

I

Anticipatory Democracy in Cities, States, and Regions

Anticipatory democracy as an identifiable socio-political phenomenon has surfaced in state and local goal-setting programs and in "Tomorrow" and "Year 2000" groups. David Baker, director of Illinois 2000, begins the book with an overview of more than forty local, state, and regional groups involved in some form of citizen definition of the future. He points out the value of these processes in educating citizens and politicians and in developing new information, policy alternatives, and community spirit.

Some A/D projects focus on a range of alternative futures, others on specific goals. As Hawaii 2000 was becoming the first state-government futures project, Governor Jimmy Carter was developing the first state-level goals project—Goals for Georgia. When Jimmy Carter ran for Governor, he was clearly a farmer outside the circle of the ruling elite of the state. Carter wanted to let citizens play a more direct role in the policy-making of his administration, yet he was operating in a state whose history of participation was low. Goals for Georgia was one of his attempts to rouse the state's citizenry. In Chapter 2, Newt Gingrich, a professor at Georgia State College involved in state politics and in A/D activity, describes Carter's efforts and the program itself.

In Chapter 3, Robert Bradley, a political scientist at the University of Texas at Dallas, gives a history and critique of Goals for

Dallas, the oldest and most copied example of a municipal goal-setting project.

The most sophisticated A/D process yet developed at the state level took place in Washington. Robert Stilger, director of the Northwest Regional Foundation, an educational organization aimed at helping people take a more active and responsible part in preparing for the future, reviews the Alternatives for Washington (AFW) program in Chapter 4. While the program met with political opposition from the state legislature it was able to develop scenarios of alternative futures for the state and see to it that at least some A/D policies were successfully incorporated into the decision-making process.

The articles in this section give some of the flavor of A/D exercises and the complexity of the political and social settings with which they must contend. They provide a sense of how citizens can be involved in shaping the future. The cases represent a first step toward realizing the ideal of genuine participation in a policy process that is effectively conscious of the future.

CHAPTER ONE

State, Regional, and Local Experiments in Anticipatory Democracy: An Overview

BY DAVID E. BAKER

In the last decade, the anticipatory democracy process has become a reality in such states as Hawaii and Washington, in such cities as Dallas and Seattle, and in such regions as the New York metropolitan area, the Great Lakes, and the South. In these and other jurisdictions, public and private groups have ventured boldly into the world of forecasting possible futures and defining goals for public policy.

Citizen response to many of these programs has been remarkable, given the popular image of an apathetic and ill-formed American body politic. In Washington State, over 60,000 people out of the state's population of 3.5 million participated directly in the year-long Alternatives for Washington program. They were at once the authors and critics of a blueprint of alternative state growth policies for the next ten years. Politicians, planners, and citizen leaders are now using the result of their efforts as the basis for long-range policy planning.

In Massachusetts the humble, unfunded Legislative Commission on Patterns of Growth and Quality of Life in the Commonwealth inspired legislation that has led 300 of the state's 350 towns to carefully examine their growth-related problems and goals, and to report their findings to the state.

In Charlotte, North Carolina, the city government already has adopted 20 percent of the 105 policy-related goals set in 1973 by Dimensions for Charlotte-Mecklenburg. A task force of 119 citizens chosen from all segments of Charlotte's society defined these goals.[1]

Anticipatory democracy groups have grown out of a spreading discontent within American politics in recent years. Citizens and politicians alike have begun to feel that change is occurring so quickly that governmental institutions can only react, not initiate. Yet they realize that economic, environmental, and social problems must be approached with long-range purposes in mind; and that people outside government must have the opportunity to share in the shaping of general goals and policies. There is growing mistrust of government. Consistent with recent national polls, a Minnesota poll conducted in July 1976 indicated that 69 percent of the adult population doubted the veracity of state government and the media.[2] Low voter turnout in both national and local elections is yet another potent indication of citizen mistrust and apathy.

A major purpose of the anticipatory democracy (A/D) groups is to involve a wide range of citizens and government officials in a comprehensive analysis of the current problems and future options of a given state or locality, and a subsequent definition of goals. By encouraging widespread participation in the process, leaders of these experiments have aimed to reduce the sense of isolation from government that citizens have felt and to benefit from the creativity provided by the diverse opinions of a wide range of people. Further, these programs usually seek to extend the planning process beyond the normal cycles of elections and budget years, and across the jurisdictions of agencies and neighboring governments to provide a more holistic view of policy issues.

Since the pioneering programs of California Tomorrow in 1961 and Goals for Dallas in 1965, over forty major A/D projects have been developed.[3] Of these identified, eighteen have taken place in seventeen states (two in Massachusetts), six at the multistate regional level, two at the substate regional level, and eighteen at the local level. In addition, many other states and localities have launched similar programs dealing with long-range issues of growth and development, land use, the environment, and others.[4] However, this article concentrates on the major example of A/D projects, because of their special concentration on the involvement of citizens and officials alike in the goal-setting and futures-planning process. All forty-four projects are listed in Table 1. Chart 1 contains more detailed comparative information on fifteen of these.

Let us look now at the new processes these A/D groups offer

TABLE 1. **Major Anticipatory Democracy Projects in the United States**

GROUP	DATE OF INCEPTION
The States	
California Tomorrow	1961
New Hampshire Tomorrow	1969
Hawaii Commission on the Year 2000*	1970
Massachusetts Tomorrow*	1971
Goals for Georgia*	1971
Goals for Louisiana	1971
North Carolina Board on Goals and Policy	1971
Iowa 2000	1972
Vermont Tomorrow*	1972
Commission on Minnesota's Future*	1973
Massachusetts' Special Legislative Commission on the Effect of Patterns of Growth on the Quality of Life in the Commonwealth*	1973
Commission on Maine's Future	1974
Delaware Tomorrow Commission	1974
Alternatives for Washington*	1974
Idaho's Tomorrow	1975
Commission on Connecticut's Future	1976
Alaska Growth Policy Council	1977
Illinois 2000	1977
Multistate Regions	
Federation of Rocky Mountain States*	1965
Choices for '76: Regional Plan Association (New York, New Jersey, Connecticut)	1973
Commission on the Future of the South*	1974
Great Lakes Tomorrow	1975
Delaware Valley Regional Planning Commission	1975
Critical Choices for the Upper Midwest	1976

Substate Regions

Willamette Valley: Choices for the Future (Oregon)	1972
Central Virginia Tomorrow (Lynchburg)	1974

Localities

Goals for Dallas	1965
Los Angeles Goals Program	1965
Greater Hartford Process	1969
Fort Worth Sector Planning Program	1969
Goals for Raleigh-Wake (North Carolina)*	1972
Seattle 2000	1972
Boulder Growth Study Commission (Colorado)	1972
Dimensions for Charlotte-Mecklenburg (North Carolina)*	1973
Goals for the Greater Akron Area*	1973
Austin Tomorrow*	1973
Kansas City (Missouri) Alternative Futures	1973
Goals for Corpus Christi	1974
Nashville Citizen Goals 2000 Committee	1974
Norwich, Citizens Unlimited (New York)	1974
Santa Barbara, ACCESS (California)*	1974
Clarinda Citizens' Involvement (Iowa)	1976
Greater Philadelphia Partnership	1976
Atlanta 2000	1977

(Note: This list was compiled from reports cited in Footnote 3. Some programs may have been inadvertently left out because their activities did not reach the attention of researchers or were started after these lists were compiled.
* See pages 10–14.

states and localities, the structures and strategies previously employed, and the routes taken by some of the experiments to reach the public and policy-makers. Obviously, future efforts must build on the varied experiences of these pioneer groups.

ALTERNATIVE PLANNING AND POLICY
TOOLS OFFERED BY A/D GROUPS

If government officials have to appropriate funds to set up an A/D process, they must first be convinced that it will provide innovative and *needed* institutions and tools to improve the long-range planning process. The following list defines some of the tools A/D programs can offer.

1. *Agenda Setting.* A newly elected governor or mayor can benefit from the A/D group's role as a goal-definer and agenda-maker for the jurisdiction. By adjusting his/her own legislative and administrative agendas to relate more closely to those goals identified by citizen groups, the executive can broaden the base of support for long-range actions that might not be ordinarily acceptable.

2. *Long-Range Issues Analysis and Legislative Planning.* An A/D project can provide three new and extremely important functions for state and local legislative bodies. First, it can analyze issues that have a long time horizon, generally beyond the purview or abilities of understaffed standing committees of the legislatures.

Second, the project, if requested, may forecast the long-term effects and unintended outcomes of current laws and legislative proposals.

Third, and perhaps most important, the members and staff of the A/D group can develop alternative approaches to the major policy issues relating to growth and the quality of life.

3. *Institutional Reforms.* By struggling with issues that extend across normal agency jurisdictions and by virtue of its position outside the normal bureaucracy, the A/D group is able to identify areas for government reform or reorganization to make agencies and programs more attuned to changing conditions and public preferences.

4. *An Avenue for Citizen Participation and a Wider Expression of Values.* Governments at all levels encourage some types of citizen input. Most input, however, comes as programs are being implemented rather than when they are chosen or designed. The A/D group, using the media and the newest techniques for polling, surveys, and workshops, provides direct and informed feedback from the people on the policy issues under consideration.

5. *A Constituency for Long-Range Policies.* Politicians often cite a lack of citizen concern as a reason for the failure to anticipate

A SURVEY OF SELECTED STATE GOALS AND FUTURES GROUPS

by David Baker, Illinois 2000, with Keith Alan Bea, Congressional Research Service

States

GROUP	YEARS OF ACTIVITY	METHOD OF ESTABLISH-MENT	LINKAGE TO POLICY-MAKERS	MAJOR PURPOSES	PRINCIPAL METHODS OF IMPLEMENTATION	AMOUNT OF FUNDING	SOURCE OF FUNDING	USE OF MEDIA	OUTPUTS
Hawaii Commission on the Year 2000 (follow up to Governor's Conference on the Year 2000)	1970–Onward	State law	Annual report to governor, legislature	Examine trends; Recommendations on goals and policy; Coordinate and promote futures activities	Nine-member commission, task forces; Educational program in schools; State conferences	$46,000 (1976)	Legislative appropriation; Business & labor contributions	Newspaper articles; TV	Task force reports on future of economy, judiciary; Students trained in futures research
Goals for Georgia	1971	Gubernatorial directive	To governor via Georgia Planning Ass'n	Citizens set goals and policy recommendations for state programs; Assess cost trade-offs	State/regional conferences; Survey of citizens	$225,000 (estimated total)	U.S. Dept of Commerce; Georgia Planning Ass'n; Local funds	Statewide TV broadcasts with phone-in questions from citizens	Statistics on citizen preferences and support for state programs; State reorganization
Massachusetts Tomorrow	1971–Onward	Organized by concerned citizens	Indirect via educational programs	Educate citizens on futures-issues, alternatives	Conferences; Workshops; Publications	$56,000 (1976)	Massachusetts Foundation for Humanities & Public Policy; Private gifts	Newsletter	*Massachusetts Tomorrow* (a book on values and alternative life styles, sustainable economy)

Vermont Tomorrow	1972–Onward	Grass-roots*	Informal education of legislators through publications and personal contact	Press for optimum use of resources/ self-reliance for Vermonters	Demonstration projects; Surveys; Conferences, workshops	$50,000 (1976)	Title I, U.S. Higher Education Act; Vermont Council on Humanities; Citizen Involvement Network	Newsletter	1977 survey results on Vermonters' views of the future; Citizens' guide to community development
Commission on Minnesota's Future	1973–1977	State law	To governor via state planning agency; Legislators serve on commission; Minnesota Horizons presentation to legislature	Assess state growth/development issues; Report on future trends; Assess role of state agencies in Minnesota's growth	Forty-member commission plus regional planners, legislators; Regional workshops	$160,000 (1976–1977)	Legislative appropriation	News coverage of regional meetings	Recommendations for state action in eight issue areas; Description of current situation and future options through Minnesota Horizons
Massachusetts Legislative Special Commission on Patterns of Growth and the Quality of Life in the Commonwealth	1973–1977	Joint resolution	To governor via planning agency; To legislature via legislative members of the commission	Outline major growth-related issues for legislative action	Fifteen-member commission with subcommittees; Local growth-policy committees	None	(Used staff from state agencies, universities, volunteers)	News articles on local growth-policy committees	Drafted Massachusetts Growth Policy Development Act, anticipate state growth policy based on local growth-policy committee reports

GROUP	YEARS OF ACTIVITY	METHOD OF ESTABLISHMENT	LINKAGE TO POLICY-MAKERS	MAJOR PURPOSES	PRINCIPAL METHODS OF IMPLEMENTATION	AMOUNT OF FUNDING	SOURCE OF FUNDING	USE OF MEDIA	OUTPUTS
Alternatives for Washington	1974–1977	Gubernatorial directive	To governor via planning office; 11 legislative members	Involve citizens in long-range budgeting and planning process; Assess costs of major proposals	150-person state task force/four major state conferences; Regional conferences; Surveys; Cost trade-off teams	$750,000 (1974–1976)	Governor's planning funds; Pacific Northwest Regional Commission; HUD; Dept. of Commerce	11 educational television shows on alternatives; Newspaper surveys	1975 legislative package of governor based on eight issue areas; 1977 report to legislature on costs of implementation
Regional Groups									
Federation of Rocky Mountain States, Inc.	1965– Onward	Organized by governors, educators, and businessmen from Colorado, Montana, New Mexico, Utah, and Wyoming	The five governors make up board (state legislators may also serve)	Increase the states' ability to manage policy and program developments and regional economic growth; Test futures-oriented technology on a regional basis	Board of the government acts on recommendations of coordinating council for allocating regional resources; Supported by issues councils representing business, government, academic, private	$110,000 (1976) plus $1,000,000 in grants contracts	State government dues; Business donations	Newsletter	Policy recommendations and statements; Stimulation of regional economic activity; Coordination of large-scale economic growth of region
Commission on the Future of the South	1974–1975	Charter of Southern Growth Policies Board	15 commission members appointed by governors; Four governors chaired committees; Governor Carter, chairman	To attempt to manage and direct the South's growth for the benefit of all Southerners	Commission research; Committee reports	$200,000	National Science Foundation; Private foundations; Southern Growth Policies Board	Little or none	Four topical final reports

Goals for the Greater Akron Area	1973–Onward	Formed by mayor and civic leaders	Direct interaction at all levels of government—local, state, and federal	Establish and implement alternative plans and goals; Maximize citizen participation in process	Neighborhood meetings on citizen interest; State conference on goals; Task forces on implementation	$50,000 (1976)	HUD 701 program; City; Private contributions	Newspaper coverage; Television (3½ hour shows); Radio shows	Task force reports to public; Final report on goals
Dimensions for Charlotte/Mecklenburg	1973–1976	Mayor urged private individuals to organize	Informal ties to community agencies	Education of citizens on growth alternatives; Form plan for area's future	24-member policy board; 119-member task force on goals; Achievement committees; Feedback ballots from citizens	$75,000	City and county; Private gifts	Television broadcast; Newspaper ballots; News coverage	20 percent of goals have been attained, final report published
Clarinda Citizens' Involvement, Inc.	1976–Onward	Clarinda Industrial Development Corporation; Town leaders	Public officials participate equally with citizens	Involve as many citizens as possible in designing the image of the future for the city	Neighborhood meetings; Issue task forces and conferences	$20,000 (1976)	Citizen involvement network; CETA grant; Individual donations	Newspaper & radio coverage	Goals determined by citizens Implementation and monitoring of goals

GROUP	YEARS OF ACTIVITY	METHOD OF ESTABLISH-MENT	LINKAGE TO POLICY-MAKERS	MAJOR PURPOSES	PRINCIPAL METHODS OF IMPLEMENTATION	AMOUNT OF FUNDING	SOURCE OF FUNDING	USE OF MEDIA	OUTPUTS
Goals for Dallas	1965–Onward	Created by mayor	City administrators work with task forces; Mayor present on board of trustees; State officials on task forces	Develop a comprehensive plan for growth; Encourage high level of citizen participation	Task forces; Goals conferences; Public consideration of goals	$175,000 per year	Private foundations; Individuals; Businesses	Newspaper coverage and publication of ballots; Radio & TV; Editorial support	75 percent of original goals have been achieved; New goals submitted to public for their consideration
Goals for Raleigh/Wake	1972–Onward (temporarily inoperative)	Grass-roots	City council accepts goals suggestions; Mayor on board of directors; Contacts with chamber of commerce and county commissioners	Involve citizens in planning process; Establish forums for debate; Provide history of Raleigh development	Issue/goals study groups; Surveys; Workshops and forums on goals	$28,000 (1976)	North Carolina Humanities Committee; City and county funds	Newspaper ballots for survey responses to TV program	Goals for the community; Publications; Transportation and housing reports
Austin Tomorrow	1973–Onward	Created by city council	Direct relations with city planning dept., city council, and other major offices; Voice in city budget	Formulate and update city master plan; Monitor progress towards goals	Citizens' committee; Multi-media public education program; City assembly; Neighborhood meetings	$100,000 (1976)	HUD 701 planning funds; Local funding	Radio and television, newsletter	Statement of goals published 1975; Advisory reports to city officials

emerging problems, particularly where solutions might require some personal discipline or cost to citizens. A/D groups can sensitize citizens to the need for current action and help create the constituency necessary for long-range policies.

6. *Demographic Information in Policy Planning.* Accurate demographic data is fundamental to an understanding of growth trends. A/D projects focus the need for this data and, working with state statistical offices, can improve its availability, examine its implications, and interpret its significance to policy-makers and the public.

7. *Long-Range Budgetary Decisions.* Until recently, state and local plans for capital improvement either followed rough growth projections or were drawn up in response to haphazard growth patterns. The A/D group can analyze both past trends to see how budgetary decisions have been tied to growth, and ways in which future decisions regarding growth patterns and other policies can be rationalized.

8. *Assessment of the Impacts of Federal and Private Sector Decisions.* External economic and political decisions can have a tremendous effect on local plans, yet there is no effective way for states or localities to register concern or challenge the federal government or private industry on growth-related decisions. By first setting and publicizing goals for the jurisdiction, and by assessing the effects different events might have, A/D projects can alert their corresponding governments to the implications of federal and private actions.

ORGANIZATIONAL PATTERNS

A review of the structures and strategies of A/D groups shows that they have combined old, familiar models for citizen participation, such as commissions, task forces, and area hearings, with modern approaches—electronic balloting systems, television call-in programs, and sophisticated survey techniques. Below is a summary of the dominant organizational patterns chosen by the groups. (Chart 1 provides more complete information for each group listed.)

A *commission or council* appointed by the executive or legislative branch or both, made up of a variety of experts, government officials, and citizen representatives: Hawaii (1970), Massachusetts (legislative commission) (1973), Minnesota (1973), Federation of Rocky Mountain States (1965), Commission on the Future of the South (1974).

A *private, educational group* emphasizing conferences and publications to educate citizens: Massachusetts Tomorrow (1971) and Vermont Tomorrow (1972).

A *state- or city-level conference approach,* generally preceded by task force exploration of major issues or local and regional conferences: Georgia (1971), Washington (1974).

City or regional task forces supported by neighborhood meetings and public opinion surveys, some media involvement, and balloting on goals: Dallas (1965), Raleigh, N.C. (1972), Charlotte, N.C. (1973), Akron (1973), Austin (1973), Clarinda, Iowa (1976).

ASSESSING THE A/D GROUPS

A/D projects have been organized to allow individuals the opportunity to assess options and shape the future of their city or state, and to insure that the information developed is communicated to policy-makers. The objectives of the projects fall primarily into four categories: education of the participants, the general public, and policy-makers concerning futures issues; generation of information both about futures issues and citizen attitudes; design of alternative policies; and development of consensus opinions on the issues to relay directly to the policy-makers.

How have A/D projects approached these various objectives? The experience of various projects will be used to illustrate the possibilities:

THE EDUCATION PROCESS

Hawaii 2000

The Governor's Conference on the Year 2000 was the first major government-sponsored state-level effort to involve citizens in active pursuit of goals and alternative futures. George Chaplin, editor of the Honolulu *Advertiser,* was the principal architect of the Hawaii 2000 experience. He felt that Hawaii would be an excellent testing ground for a citizen government project on the future of the state because of its geographical isolation, its recent experience of rapid change, and its vulnerability to rapid economic growth and environmental deterioration.

With the blessing of the governor, the legislature, and state funding, Chaplin and an advisory task force organized a statewide conference to discuss reports from special research teams of citizens and experts on ten subject areas, such as people and life styles in the year 2000, the natural environment, housing, and transportation. Development and presentation of these reports became the focus for the education both of task-force members and of participants in the Hawaii 2000 Conference. Over a five-month period, the members analyzed projections and alternative scenarios of the future developed by resource people on each task force to come up with their vision of the state thirty years hence. For instance, the Housing and Transportation 2000 task force settled on two key solutions for survival of the Hawaiian spirit and sense of community: movement to clustered neighborhoods surrounded by open spaces permitting retention of a wide variety of natural vegetation; and institution of an inexpensive, intra-island water ferry system to protect both the mountains and remaining shoreline areas from additional road construction.

The draft task-force reports were then shared two weeks in advance of the conference with all participants and speakers. The issues the reports raised provided the main source of comment and focus for many of the speakers and were the basis of thirteen workshops during which a wide range of participants critiqued and modified the proposals.[5]

The Hawaii 2000 experiment succeeded in reaching the Hawaiian people and in mobilizing a large number of participants who became deeply involved in the futures-planning process. The conference report of the experience, published later as a book, also provided valuable lessons for other programs.[6] These lessons suggested that:

First, focus on the year 2000 turned out to be arbitrary and restrictive. Use of "Hawaii Futures" was suggested as an alternative.

Second, the selection of independent, sectoral task forces limited the education process and caused difficulties in integrating the materials later.

Third, although the participants could define goals for the islands, they had difficulty in developing ideas for a practical transition program.

Fourth, the task forces were ill-equipped to develop more than one or two feasible alternatives in their problem areas.

Responding to the directions set by the conference, the legislature set up and modestly funded the Hawaii Commission on the Year 2000, which is still active.

Alternatives for Washington (AFW)

The Alternatives for Washington (AFW) program focused more time and money on the training and education of its 150-person task force than any program to date.* George Chaplin and Alvin Toffler both encouraged the Washington planners involved to maximize the citizen education and involvement process. Governor Dan Evans, a committed environmentalist, also gave his full support to the planning effort and enabled the AFW program to launch its extensive effort through strong state funding and staff support.

Assisted by John Osman and a team from the Brookings Institution, the state conducted a program of classroom sessions, interchanges, workshops, and "futures-creating sessions" for the task-force members. Governor Evans chose the members from a list of four thousand individuals from all walks of life who had been nominated by political leaders and major state organizations. Fifteen hundred additional citizens participated in regional conferences that reviewed the findings of the task force.

The personal energy and commitment of its chairman, Dr. Edward Lindaman, president of Whitworth College in Spokane, held the AFW process together. "The greatest benefit of the program," said Lindaman "was in the transformation of the typical citizen, when exposed to the futures-invention process, into a regular addict for futures planning. After two hundred hours of work over the course of a year, seven out of ten members of the task force were totally committed to the futures-planning process."[7]

Nicholas Lewis, who directed the AFW program for the State

* See Chapter 4 on Alternatives for Washington.

Planning Division, stressed the importance of participant involvement in the Alternatives experiment. He said:

The Alternatives program has been an effort on the part of state government to reinvolve the people in a public decision-making process. The participants determined what government *ought* to do. The technicians in the planning office were then charged with a more appropriate role of figuring out how to translate citizens' goals into program recommendations.[8]

One group left out of Phase I, however, was the state legislature. Their negative reception of the first set of recommendations is detailed below.

In 1976, AFW carried out Phase II of the program, in which planners, citizens from the task force, policy-makers, and outside experts examined the alternatives and policy recommendations in terms of their potential costs and the trade-offs required among them. This unique educational process has forced the citizens to place their general goals for society into the real world of Washington politics and fiscal constraints.

The Commission on Minnesota's Future

The Commission on Minnesota's Future began in 1973 as a joint effort of the state's progressive young governor, Wendell Anderson, and Bruce McLaury, president of the Ninth Federal Reserve Bank in Minneapolis. In February 1973, at a conference preceding the Commission's creation, Governor Anderson said:

All of us profess grave concern for the future. Yet, far too often the future loses out to the present. Immediate needs take up our time and our attention.

If we were truly thinking about the future, we would never have allowed a coal-burning power plant to be built on the St. Croix, one of the most magnificent rivers anywhere in the United States.

We would not have permitted urban sprawl to begin its creeping hold upon a metropolitan area that now spreads throughout seven counties.

Nor would we have built expensive elementary classrooms, for which there is now little need, and state college dormitory facilities that already have three thousand empty beds.[9]

To begin the process of assessing present conditions, the commission's forty citizen members, joined by twelve legislators and thirteen regional planners, worked on one of four general sub-committees: Natural Environment, Man-Made Environment, Human Environment, and Government Environment.

By the fall of 1974, however, the Commission decided that these areas were too general and did not permit sufficient integration of issues, so they adopted a format that encompassed more prosaic issues of government concern: housing, health care, education, employment and income, environment, recreation, leisure and culture, and governance. Staff members of the state planning agency and consultants carefully researched specific issues within these areas which they then presented to the Commission members in weekend workshops held every six weeks. The Commission members considered the proposed alternatives and voted on recommendations.

During the final weekend sessions the staff and Commission members identified the major themes that controlled or affected the more specific areas. These included the depletion of vital resources, particularly energy resources as Canada withdraws her petroleum from the U.S. market; the rising costs of consumer goods and services, engendered primarily by increased resource costs; the pressure for the redistribution of wealth through reduction of higher incomes instead of simply increasing all incomes; a modification of the definition of high living standards as material goals become less attainable in a society based on scarcity; and a heavy stress on human development to meet the challenge of reduced resources and higher costs.

In summary, A/D groups have taken a variety of approaches, but in each case a cadre of direct participants has come to learn a great deal about the future—the future of the state, including its major problems and the interactions among issues.

The next step for A/D projects, after analyzing the issues and developing draft goals and recommendations, is to seek the reaction and recommendations of the general public. Unfortunately, small budgets—usually $10,000 to $80,000 per year—have severely limited the education process.[10]

In order to reach the public, underfunded groups have either raised the funds to underwrite large-scale television and newspaper coverage or have attempted to involve the media directly in the planning and execution of the projects, thus gaining free air time and newspaper space for items deemed newsworthy.

Goals for Georgia and Television

The Goals for Georgia program, set up in 1971 by then Governor Jimmy Carter to involve Georgians in setting priorities for government action, reached about 5,000 individuals through area conferences.* Eight television broadcasts then presented the findings and goals to perhaps 250,000 more Georgians, 5 percent of the state population.[11] The Georgia Planning Association cooperated closely with television stations in the state in order to reduce production and air costs. The programs featured the Governor and other state officials discussing the findings of the area conference and responding to audience and viewer questions. Experts then met in eight statewide conferences to analyze and focus the citizen recommendations.

Choices for '76: The Regional Plan Association's Televised Town Meetings

In 1973 the Regional Plan Asssociation, a private, nonprofit professional organization that conducts urban planning studies for the New York Metropolitan Region, developed a unique program to educate the region's twenty million inhabitants on the major growth-related choices facing the region in the coming decade.[12] Their design called for five televised town meetings; each would focus on one major issue such as housing, environment, or transportation. The fifty-one "Choices for '76" proposed by the Regional Plan Association have been published in paperback and distributed throughout the region. Newspapers cooperated by providing free space for the announcements of programs, news supplements, and ballots for citizen response on the choices.

The RPA actively sought cooperation from the eighteen commercial and educational television stations serving the tri-state area, all of which ultimately agreed to participate. Many of them donated free air time. The town meetings were then broadcast in different half-hour time slots over a consecutive three-day period throughout the spring.

* See Chapter 2 for more information on Goals for Georgia.

For an investment of $2 million, raised from foundations, corporations, and government, the Regional Plan Association made an impressive dent on the consciousness of the region. Based on Nielsen ratings and back-up surveys, approximately 600,000 people watched each of the five shows. An average of 26,500 individuals cast their ballots on each of the five "Choices for '76" clusters. These responses were tabulated and presented to regional and state policy-makers and were used in subsequent legislative planning and decision-making.[13]

Iowa 2000 Capitalizes on Media Involvement

Under the guidance of then Congressman John Culver, Governor Robert D. Ray, and University of Iowa President William Boyd, the people of Iowa participated in a state goals-setting program in 1974. Realizing that their $70,000 budget could not possibly cover purchased air time for a special program to introduce the Iowa 2000 project, the project directors went to the electronic and print media to gain their guidance and cooperation. As a result, fifteen commercial stations and the one public TV station donated prime time for Iowa 2000's introductory program, hosted by Harry Reasoner.

The *Des Moines Register* cooperated by providing background material for the Reasoner telecast through a door-to-door poll. The pollsters asked Iowa citizens questions on population trends and favored levels of total population for Iowa, distribution of population between rural and urban Iowa, farm policy and goals for pollution control, land-use planning, energy use and conservation, and social welfare. The *Register* printed the same questions in its Sunday papers the day of the telecast so that the viewing audience could compare their own responses to the poll's results as reported by the *Register* and Harry Reasoner.

In all, fifty thousand people or almost 2 percent of the state's population participated directly in the telecast, the local and regional workshops that followed, or the state conference on Iowa 2000.

While television continues to provide the opportunity for these A/D groups to reach large segments of the population, they face the universal difficulty of measuring actual information retention and impact on the viewers. Further, costs of production and prime-time air space far exceed the budgets of most futures groups: the $2 million spent on television by the Regional Plan Association for "Choices for '76" was a clear exception. The entire purpose of "Choices for '76" was to reach a large viewing audience through the media, and the RPA spent $100,000 just to raise the $2 million television budget. Most programs will have to rely on the Iowa model of gaining early and inexpensive support of the media. Project staff must show the media that A/D programs raise crucial issues that require full public airing. For instance, the Commission on Maine's Future widely publicizes its meetings and then invites the media to telecast them. The majority of the Commission's formal meetings have been broadcast.

Many futures and goals groups, particularly the "Tomorrow" groups in California, Massachusetts, and Vermont, organized largely to overcome the unwillingness or inability of public policy-makers to consider long-range and multidimensional planning as a necessary and serious enterprise. This education of policy-makers remains the most monumental difficulty for A/D projects, although some have had considerable success in the ongoing task of making specific recommendations to the government.

Minnesota's Commission on the Future inaugurated two special mechanisms to insure continuing education of policy-makers. First, the statute creating the Commission called for a twelve-member legislative review committee to periodically assess the Commission's work. The legislators on this review committee have since become full participants in the Commission's deliberations.

Second, the Commission, in cooperation with the State Planning Agency and the legislature, put on "Minnesota Horizons," a three-day program before a special joint session of the legislature in January 1975. The program was given considerable advance notice and was televised statewide on public television. It reviewed the first year's activities of the Commission; outlined trends in population, economics, and the environment; and suggested the major issues for future legislative consideration. Reactions were very positive. One legislator stated:

I was especially thrilled for the new members, who received the most terrific briefing possible for a group of freshman legislators going into their first session. They'll be able to ask the kinds of hard questions that will result in good legislation.[14]

The Horizons program was repeated in January 1977 and called "Horizons II." This time the legislators received an update on Minnesota's growth patterns from the staff of the State Planning Agency, and then the final report of the Commission on Minnesota's Future through an audio-visual presentation conducted by eleven members of the Commission. The Horizons programs are unique and excellent examples of open and direct communication and education among citizens and policy-makers.

In 1973 the Alternative Futures Program in Kansas City (Missouri) cooperated with the city's Development Department to distribute to one thousand selected citizens a series of Delphi-type questionnaires on policy issues facing the metropolitan area.* A task group of one hundred persons as well as members of the City Council and Development Department staff sifted the answers. In this way, those charged with the development of policy became intimately involved with data and ideas generated by the public, well before they might be presented with a glossy report destined for the oblivion of a dusty shelf.

A/D GROUPS GENERATE NEW INFORMATION FOR FUTURES-ORIENTED DECISION-MAKING

Much of the popular dismay with government activities over the last twenty years derives from the inability of governments at all levels to project the consequences of specific actions, or to interpret correctly the sentiments of the people. Many A/D groups have attempted to correct this situation by:

1. bringing to light hidden or forgotten government research that might otherwise be disregarded;
2. promoting studies to identify and analyze the consequences that available studies have ignored;

* A Delphi survey, mentioned throughout this book, is usually a series of questions asked of a panel (often experts in a particular field). The results are analyzed and distributed to the panel so that members can refine their original answers and discuss the implications of certain choices. Originally developed for use in forecasting the availability of aerospace technologies, it is called "Delphi" in reference to Greeks seeking wisdom from the Delphic oracles.

3. using popular media to inform citizens of the range of future options, then polling them for their preferences;
4. presenting the above in usable and accessible formats.

Although most population projections are still quite inadequate, many mistakes could be avoided if leaders understood and anticipated major trends, such as shifts in the school-age and the aging populations, changing job and housing needs, and rural-urban population changes. Better forecasting techniques and consideration of the side effects of public decisions on the communities' growth might prevent repetition of the planning errors of the 1950s and 1960s.

In 1975 State Senator David Huber, a member of the Commission on Maine's Future, noted:

The demographic and statistical work of the Commission is its most important work to date. The staff is beginning to develop accurate estimates of population change which will in turn generate the questions about growth and change that should be asked. If it does nothing else, the Commission will have developed the basic demographic information-gathering systems to support meaningful policy decisions in the future.[15]

The new Commission's system, based on driver's license applications and information from utilities and telephone hookups, should be a great improvement over the data now available by giving a more precise awareness of the shifts in the age and location of the state's population.

The A/D groups' final reports form another major source of new information, although their distribution is somewhat limited. The Goals for Georgia report brought together the opinions and ideas of five thousand Georgians in a very readable form.[16] The tables in the report gave policy-makers a quick view of public attitudes on a wide range of proposed policies, showing where consensus was the greatest.

The Georgia program also asked respondents to indicate which changes they were willing to finance through increased taxes, adding a link to reality in the goal-setting process that is absent from many other programs. The report reveals, for example, that 78.8 percent of the people surveyed felt that spending more for colleges and universities is important, but only 28.5 percent considered it important enough to raise taxes. Agreed by 92.7 percent was that medical aid to the elderly is important, and 60.7 percent thought it important enough to raise taxes. A majority of the respondents also favored spending more of the state's revenues on physical and mental health, education, and the environment. The relevance of such statistics to the planning process is obvious; new surveys should seriously consider adding this element.

Goals for Dallas and Seattle 2000 represent two of the most well-funded and extensive city-wide A/D groups. Each program published paperback books describing its findings, thereby providing policy-makers and citizens alike with a blueprint for future action.[17] The reports describe current activities in each issue area and citizen opinion, then offer sets of related goals for consideration by the city government.

A/D GROUPS DESIGN ALTERNATIVE FUTURES

One of the more imaginative aspects of A/D projects is designing alternative futures for the area. One of the most challenging tasks then becomes specifying appropriate policies to achieve the preferred future. The process of developing policy goals based on preferred futures, comparing these goals to current situations, assessing available resources and institutional capabilities for action is essential to more effective policy-making. The failure to consider a range of alternative futures precludes certain options and shows itself in the form of empty schools, freeways cluttering and destroying inner cities, rivers lost forever to dams and industrial wastes, and farmlands permanently converted to suburbs.

The experience of the A/D groups in meeting this challenge has been mixed for three reasons. First, there are very few successful examples to emulate. Second, most of the programs have not had the staff nor the funds to carry out intensive research on available choices in order to present them to citizen members. Finally, each of the alternatives carry political assets and liabilities that cause politicians to resist open consideration of them. Let us now look at the experiences of some of the groups in attempting to develop alternative futures.

Two basic approaches to design of alternatives have been tried: first, creation of holistic scenarios for the area, and second, focusing on particular topics or issues around which to develop goals.

Alternatives for Washington again provides the best example of an attempt to develop genuine alternative futures, or scenarios, for the state. According to Chairman Edward Lindaman, "Much of the initial purpose of the task force program was to bring people together from all walks of life and encourage them to create the future."[18] As the process continued, trends and clusters of ideas emerged and task-force members formulated eleven alternative "Washingtons." When the state's citizens were later polled on their preferences, the largest number of respondents, 23 percent, favored "Agricultural Washington," 20 percent approved "Balanced Washington," and the fewest citizens, less than 2 percent, favored "Urban Washington."

While setting the mood for future discussions, the alternative scenarios did not yield the immediate pay-off expected in terms of policy recommendations. Lindaman indicated that most people preferred some combination of the alternatives, and despite the tremendous investment of time in their development, the alternative Washingtons remained in fairly generalized form. Citizens were asked not only their preferred future but also their preferences within different areas of government policy. In its second phase the whole Washington program shifted to analysis of the trade-offs among specific policy issues, using as background the general preferences the citizens revealed when polled about the eleven alternatives.

The Boulder Area Growth Study Commission experimented in another way.[19] Citizen researchers chose four different rates of population growth as the basis for four scenarios of the future. Economic growth, housing needs, shifts in land use, pollution, public utility costs, and social issues were keyed to the population growth rates. The model builders then suggested alternative policies to deal with the issues the scenarios raised. These alternative futures, although extremely educational, ran into serious political trouble when more growth-oriented city executives came into office.

The Commission on Minnesota's Future is searching systematically for alternatives within public policy areas. For instance, a consultant prepared an exhaustive report on the future of postsecondary education, including demographics, geographic dispersion, and quality of education in the state, given current patterns and continuation of current trends. The report developed four public policy alternatives for review by the Commission and the legislature. Because some of these plans called for considerable cutback of underused facilities, they aroused public controversy and demonstrated to the Commission the political risks involved in an open analysis and publication of all alternative solutions.

The lack of success in developing useful alternatives that other futures groups have experienced may lie in the basic part-time, nonexpert nature of the participants. Each policy path requires extensive research, original thinking, and review for consistency and practicality. Commission members and part-time task-force members do not have the time to carry out such investigations, but they may well be able to react sensitively to the alternatives created by staff work. It is possible that the mobilization of university research-center teams of students, public-interest groups, and responsible state-agency staff could lead to more exacting exploration of alternatives. Again, the cost of this work is often a limiting factor.

A/D GROUPS DEVELOP AND COMMUNICATE CONSENSUS RECOMMENDATIONS TO THE POLICY-MAKERS

The A/D groups designed to affect policy have been operating for too short a time to permit full evaluation. Lack of political support and lack of funds have hampered them. Nonetheless, these groups are constantly working to improve their design and operation and are increasingly better suited to affect policy change. Consider the following examples.

1. The Goals for Georgia program provides an example of the usefulness of the goal-setting experience. The goals supported in the Governor's project were used in a variety of ways. They were considered in the reorganization of state government. The Governor prepared a "Blueprint for Action" to guide legislators. State sources indicate that of the sixty-one new programs underway in the state, many were based on the Goals' recommendations.

2. With the Alternatives for Washington program, the concept of direct organized citizen input into the policy-making process received its most complete test so far. Describing the experience, Nicholas Lewis, the ranking state planner involved with the program, explained:

In December 1974, an all-day meeting was held between Governor Evans and the 25-member drafting committee of the Task Force. The Task Force had spent the fall collating raw data from the surveys and conferences into eight policy areas. The Governor sat and listened to the recommendations which were based on the Task Force's one-year effort. These citizens had obviously done their homework and this session was the payoff.[20]

Governor Evans used the material from the session in his *State of the State* speech and integrated the material into twenty-five of his thirty pieces of legislation recommended to the legislature in 1975.

Unfortunately, Governor Evans, a liberal Republican, found a Democratic legislature unwilling to consider his proposals. In addition, they considered the AFW program too closely tied to his administration and did not give credence to the preliminary findings. Governor Evans had financed the 1974 program out of his discretionary planning funds and federal grants and had not come to the legislature for approval or appropriations. Therefore, they did not have a stake in the outcome or follow-up, and would not provide appropriations for 1975–76 when requested.

Despite the setbacks the Evans Administration continued to work with the AFW material in an effort to shape executive policy and future state programs. The Phase II process—formulating trade-offs among the policy recommendations of Phase I—was completed for the 1977 legislative session. This represents the first major attempt by an A/D group to test each recommendation for its practicality and to weigh benefits against costs.

3. Dimensions for Charlotte-Mecklenburg has been one of the more successful local A/D groups, having obtained positive action on goals it identified. Using a citizen task force (119 citizens picked by eleven original board members) to define 105 goals for policy consideration, the program was far more direct in its approach to policy-makers. Instead of publishing an overall report and relying on policy-makers to take up the issues, task-force members visited the community agencies to outline the goals and discuss implementation, then monitored the agencies' responses.[21]

According to the staff, almost 20 percent of the goals have been reached. Some of these include: establishment of an independent environmental health agency, appointment of a full-time director of the Council on Aging, and development of a cultural-activities coordinating agency. Among the most satisfying results has been the increase in citizen interest and participation after their original apathy and the willingness of interest groups to compromise to support the goals of the citizen task force.[22]

4. The Massachusetts Legislative Commission on the Effects of Growth Patterns on the Quality of Life in the Commonwealth has had considerable organizational difficulty because of lack of staff and funding. However, in 1975 the Commission's leadership, including Co-Chairman State Representative Robert Wetmore and Land Use Committee Chairman Senator Robert Saltonstall, decided to focus the activities of the Commission on land use/growth issues.

A bill, drawn up for the Commission by an MIT professor and student interns, became law in late 1975 as the Massachusetts Growth Policy Development Act. Although the bill carried no formal requirements nor provided any funds, 300 of Massachusetts's 351 towns responded to it by setting up local growth-policy committees of officials and citizens, which answered complex questionnaires on their perception of growth and development issues. So far, the growth-policy reports of the towns have been of surprisingly good quality and evidently done in good faith. When reviewed and analyzed they will provide the Office of State Planning and the Commission with valuable insights into the towns' perceptions of growth, land use, and intergovernmental issues. The Commission will make recommendations in 1977 for statewide land-use-related legislation based on the reports.

ELEMENTS IN DEVELOPMENT OF AN EFFECTIVE A/D PROGRAM

1. *Obtain Adequate Funding*

Organizers of an A/D program must evaluate the possibilities of obtaining sufficient funding prior to launching their project. Experience indicates that at least one full-time staff director and secretary are required for an effective program. In addition, funds are required for meetings, per diem, travel, telephones, postage, printing, and consultants. Public education, balloting, and surveys also add considerable cost. Programs supporting this basic budget generally require a minimum of $70,000 to $100,000 per year.

Federal funds such as Housing and Urban Development Planning grants (701 Program), Economic Development Administration grants, Coastal Zone Management Program grants, and staff aid under the Comprehensive Employment and Training Act (CETA) have assisted A/D groups in the past. But without a real funding commitment by the station or locality, the commission is in serious jeopardy from the start.

Programs can exist and function without funding, as in Massachusetts where volunteers developed and implemented a major piece of legislation, but this route is difficult and less effective. A key to survival is to have one paid staff member or an activist chairperson who can write grants, line up volunteer assistance from other agencies, and make informal contacts with policy-makers.

2. *Face Political Realities*

Even when dealing in the future tense, the activities of A/D groups must relate directly to the essentials of the political process: allocation of scarce resources; balancing of competing interests; resolving conflicts; and scoring political points to ensure re-election. Futures and goals activities that have been the pet project of either the governor or the legislature, or of one party or the other, despite intentions and actions to involve every interest group, tend to be regarded by opponents as political grandstanding. This was part of the reason why the legislature did not support Alternatives for Washington. In Minnesota, on the other hand, the Governor suggested the commission idea, and it won strong bipartisan support from both houses and was launched with a solid political footing.

Further, many politicians have a strong bias against long-range planning and organized citizen participation from the start, and feel that projections, goal-setting, and current sacrifices for future goals do not fit the nature of the American political system. They cannot win elections based on decisions that will reap public benefits in ten to twenty years. Commissions and futures groups must, therefore, concentrate on both short-range—two to five years—as well as long-range efforts. In the end, assisting policy-makers in assessing the impact of current proposals may be as important as developing far-reaching plans or generalized scenarios for the future.

3. *Decide on the Major Research/Goals Topic Early*

The state or locality's future can encompass many areas of concern. Therefore, an A/D group must grapple first with the issues it can address reasonably, given time, funding, and information restraints. Struggling with a very broad mandate ("to prepare a proposed state growth and development strategy"[23]), the Commission on Minnesota's Future redefined its areas of consideration twice, and was barely able to deal with eight issue topics in three years. It was unable to integrate the issues. The staff director had to spend an enormous amount of time re-examining the different areas to find common threads.

Many A/D groups, including North Carolina's Board on Goals and Policy, Iowa 2000, and the Conference on Hawaii 2000, experienced frustration over the magnitude of the issues they had to deal with and the superficiality with which they had to address them. Focusing on goals alone can lead to this frustration. Time must be taken to develop alternative strategies and to examine the interrelationships between approaches.

4. *Build Ties with the Bureaucracy*

Information and statistics on governmental operations are expensive to develop, especially for a group that is underfunded from the start. An effective A/D group must cultivate relationships within existing agencies to encourage an open flow of information and staff assistance. Interns examining the development of a futures commission in Connecticut have discovered a large number of reports on futures-related issues carried out by state agencies, then shelved. These data represent months of staff work and are available for immediate use.

More important, the recommendations of an A/D group will never be implemented if the bureaucracy opposes both the group and the ideas. All factions of any bureaucracy are jealous of their prerogatives, and strong leadership from the governor or mayor may be necessary to gain full cooperation.

5. *Design and Implement a Process that Involves Policy-Makers from the Start*

As noted earlier, there are many models to choose from for an A/D group. Usually, groups have a core staff and board, a citizen's task force, and a plan to involve much larger numbers of citizens. They often disregard development of a strategy that allows policy-makers to review progress periodically and to make recommendations of their own.

The ultimate test of an A/D group is its ability to transmit citizen goals, objectives, and alternatives to the policy-makers and thereby influence and improve the decisions made. If the policy-makers do not read or act on reports of citizens' groups or commissions, then other avenues must be found to transmit the information. Some groups have tried hearings, informal sessions with the leaders, major media events such as the "Minnesota Horizons" program, and statutory inclusion of policy-makers on the commission or council.

6. *Present Findings Early and Throughout the Life of the Project*

By presenting results over the last year of activity, staff and task-force members will be able to answer questions, meet with politicians, and testify on legislation deriving from the recommendations.

A FINAL NOTE

This review of the experiences of A/D groups should provide those considering development of groups in their communities with both heartening and sobering thoughts. First, the programs have been extremely successful in discovering a new energy among citizen participants and the general public which they have reached. People have willingly spent enormous amounts of time *gratis,* attending meetings, deliberating over goals, and working out recommendations. Second, the A/D groups have assembled new information for use by policy-makers and presented it so that it is readily accessible. Third, several of the groups have succeeded in providing new alternative solutions to problems in their jurisdictions. And much of this has been accomplished on inadequate budgets with minimal staff support.

Equally important, however, these experiences show that A/D groups must respect and develop links to the established political system in order to be able to share their findings and enter into the policy-making dialogue. The process has started in such places as Georgia, Washington, Minnesota, Maine, and Massachusetts. Advocates of the anticipatory democracy process should watch carefully as the findings of these groups are presented to legislatures and executives.

CHAPTER TWO

The Goals for Georgia Program

BY NEWT GINGRICH

The 1971–72 Governor's Goals for Georgia Program was one of the earliest state-level anticipatory democracy efforts—it pioneered state participatory activities in the South. It deserves examination as an innovative program developed at a crucial point in Georgia's history. It also has particular importance because it was a key part of Jimmy Carter's governorship and offers some insights into what his operating style may continue to be as President.

In the late 1960s Georgia wavered between the styles of the Old and the New South. Lester Maddox, an eccentric small businessman and extreme advocate of segregation, served as governor from 1967 to 1971. Maddox was an ineffective administrator but a shrewd political comic who stayed on the front pages of Georgia newspapers through a variety of stunts. He worked hard for prison reform, public education, and the quiet hiring of a considerable number of black state employees. But he also maintained the rhetoric of segregation politics, engaged in antiwhite Washington diatribes, and allied himself closely with George Wallace and other advocates of segregation.

Georgia was still sufficiently racist and amused by Maddox to elect him lieutenant governor in 1970, when the state constitution still prohibited an individual from serving consecutive terms as governor. As lieutenant governor, Maddox spent four years in a running feud with Governor Carter on nearly every issue. The constant attacks from the lieutenant governor (who in Georgia has considerable power as presiding officer of the state senate and in Maddox's case had additional power through an alliance with key senators) seriously hindered Carter's efforts at reform.

Georgia's continued affection for the Old South ran far beyond its support of Lester Maddox. In the 1968 presidential race George Wallace had carried the state, while Richard Nixon ran second. Hubert Humphrey ran third, receiving the support only of Georgia's black population and of a very small percentage of white liberals.

The Georgia legislature was, if possible, even more reactionary during this period than the state as a whole. In spite of a special redistricting required by the U.S. Supreme Court, in 1965 the traditional rural power structure dominated the legislature. Throughout Carter's governorship, this traditional rural clique continued to exercise more power than the urban and suburban legislators.

In the late 1960s Georgia had a more progressive image than neighboring Alabama or South Carolina because cosmopolitan Atlanta was the gateway to, and the capital of, the state. Yet most of Georgia was more inclined to be hospitable to George Wallace than to Julian Bond.

Although Atlanta's cultural and progressive attitudes did not extend deeply into the state, its economic power dominated Georgia. Rural legislators dominated state government, but they were in turn greatly influenced by the Coca-Cola Company and the large Atlanta banks.

It was the members of the Atlanta managerial elite who kept the Georgia public schools open in the early 1960s. It was their money and effort that kept Atlanta throughout the 1960s a "city too busy to hate." In 1962 they had successfully backed Carl Sanders, then a young state senator, for governor; he became one of the most progressive southern politicians in a generally reactionary decade. In the 1970 gubernatorial race, most of the establishment again backed Sanders in hopes that he could return order after the calamitous years of the Maddox Administration. However, a few key members of the monied community chose instead to work for Jimmy Carter, a young populist from South Georgia with innovative ideas.

Jimmy Carter had been running for governor ever since 1966, when he had finished a close third in the Democratic primary. After that, he spent four years speaking and visiting around the state, emphasizing populist issues and his background as a farmer. In addition to carrying on his campaign activities, Carter co-founded the Georgia Conservancy (an aggressive environmental group comprised largely of upper-middle-class urbanites), and he helped to found and then served as the first president of the Georgia Planning Association. His quiet appeal to key black leaders during this period eventually earned him what many considered to be a surprising share of the black vote against Sanders.

Carter was in many ways as much an enigma when he became governor as he would be six years later on becoming President. He was a farmer, technocrat, and nuclear engineer from a conservative, small town, fundamentalist Baptist background, and an advocate of planning whose appeal extended to both rural segregationist whites and urban blacks.

Carter's four-year campaign taught him a great deal about Georgia politics. He knew that he and his supporters were not members of the political and economic elites of the state. However, instead of trying to become a part of the elite, he decided to open up the Georgia power structure so that average citizens could participate in government. He stated the case most clearly in a December 1970 *Atlanta Magazine* interview shortly after his election:

Carter: Georgia has the lowest voter participation of any state in the nation. The reason is that . . . interested citizens, and those who are not quite so interested, have been deliberately excluded from having a viable voice in their own affairs, in the Democratic party processes, and in the affairs of government. I'm determined during the next four years to completely democratize the Democratic party, to return control of it to Georgia Democrats, and open up all functions of government to the limit of my ability . . . to those Georgians who don't seek any selfish advantage from government participation, who just want to see us have a good state. . . .

Atlanta Magazine: What you are calling for is participatory democracy. I'm going to assume that you believe in it.

Carter: I do.[1]

It is difficult to overstate the daring quality of these statements in 1970. Georgians had never before had a governor committed to opening up politics to every citizen. Their surprise increased as they learned that he was deeply committed to planning as well as to participation.

Carter came to the governorship determined and prepared to make an impact. He had served as chairman of his county and regional planning commissions. During his campaign he had sought expert advice on every major phase of government operations. With his engineering background and as a former president of the Georgia Planning Association, Carter believed deeply in the efficacy of careful plans and programs. In that same *Atlanta Magazine* interview he asserted that:

This may be the most important contribution I can bring to state government: to involve in a complete way the principles of planning, with which I'm fairly familiar. . . . Planning *does* work, it *has* worked.[2]

The new Administration intended to focus first and foremost on reorganizing state government. Not since Richard Russell in the early 1930s had anyone systematically reviewed and restructured the government of Georgia. The challenge appealed to Carter's energy, planning instincts, and sense of history. It would be a way to make his mark upon the state.

Focusing on the massive task of reorganization absorbed a lot of the new governor's time and political capital. However, he did not allow it to diminish his interest either in anticipating the future or in involving more people in the process of self-government. He set the tone in his inaugural address, January 12, 1971:

With wisdom and judgment we should take future actions according to carefully considered long-range plans and priorities. . . . William Jennings Bryan said, "Destiny is not a thing to be waited for, it is a thing to be achieved". . . . No group of elected officials, no matter how dedicated or enlightened, can control the destiny of a great state like ours. . . . This control rests in *your* hands, the people of Georgia.

In a democracy, no government can be stronger, or wiser, or more just than its people.[3]

The essence of Carter's political philosophy is to be found in these few lines. He blends the technocrat's trust in planning, the historical beliefs and roots of a southern Democrat quoting a populist hero, and the Jeffersonian belief in trusting people to make decisions about their own lives. It is this political philosophy which prompted him to launch his Goals for Georgia Program—one of the earliest state-backed efforts to encourage citizen participation in planning and decision-making.

Carter was not alone in his interest in popular participation and planning. Other Georgians had worked on forerunners of the governor's anticipatory efforts. In April 1969, for example, the State Board of Education had appointed a twelve-member advisory committee to conduct an intensive study of Georgia's goals for education. This committee produced a brief, 49-page report entitled *Goals for Education in Georgia* in December 1969. However, the committee made its real effort with its 537-page book, *Focus on the Future of Georgia 1970–1985*.[4] Published by the Georgia State Department of Education, this work remains the most thorough effort ever made to analyze Georgia's future. It incorporates the efforts of academicians, government employees, and business representatives in chapters on the economy, population, religion, race relations, ecology, and a variety of other topics.

The book's twenty-one authors and twenty-seven critics were either in influential positions or experts in their fields, and they offered a wide range of recommendations about Georgia's future, calling for more vocational education; greater use of nurses in health care; and the reorientation of education toward the teaching of values, alternatives, and thought processes. They warned that an increase in social disorganization, greater pluralism in religious beliefs and practices, and an increasing complexity of state government were likely prospects. Dr. Morris Collins, in his essay on "Structure of Government in Georgia," predicted that "there will be considerable increase in participatory democracy in the years ahead."[5]

Yet, while the *Goals for Education* effort had some impact on the state educational system, there is no evidence that it played any significant role in the development of the governor's Goals program. It was published and apparently shelved in the nearest library.

The business community was similarly involved in anticipating the future. Maynard Smith, then chairman of the board of the

Georgia Business and Industry Association, proposed a *Goals for Georgia in the 1970s* project in June 1970. He asked Harold McKenzie, vice-president of the Georgia Power Company, to recruit a committee of twenty key young leaders to formulate goals for the future. McKenzie went to work, and within a brief time the project was underway. The committee met once a month in all-day sessions. Each meeting had four to six speakers and focused on a single theme. The problems and opportunities analyzed at these sessions included education, public finance, social relations, environmental planning, and crime. In the spring of 1971 the committee submitted twenty-five pages of recommendations to the association's board of directors. These were approved and released to the public.[6]

Both the State Board of Education and the Georgia Business and Industry Association projects were closed and elitist. While both looked at the future, neither involved significant public participation. In contrast, the governor's Goals for Georgia Program put heavy emphasis on involving the public, although, as is noted below, it put less emphasis on long-range than on short-range issues. In this sense, it marked a dramatic shift from the earlier studies.

The funding for the Goals program came from a variety of sources. While Governor Carter was willing to use part of his emergency fund to finance the program, that budget was not large enough to finance the project on the scale he envisioned. Nor would borrowing personnel from as many state agencies and universities as possible fill the gap between his dream and fiscal realities. Therefore, the Administration turned to the Coastal Plains Regional Commission for help. This federal agency distributes development grants to state and local governments within its jurisdiction. The proposal submitted to the Commission in March and April 1971 resulted in $225,000 in federal money. In addition, the state government allocated $115,430 in funds, and the University of Georgia donated $5,550 in staff time and $1,768 in travel expenses. Thus over 60 percent of the program was dependent on federal funding.

Once funded, the program began to develop rapidly. Kirby Winters, a young staff member of the Bureau of State Planning and Community Services, was loaned to the program as director. He developed a schedule that called for tightly controlled projects culminating in preliminary reports to the governor by December 1971.

Governor Carter called on the Georgia Planning Association to sponsor and coordinate the program. Then State Representative (later United States Senator) Sam Nunn, who had succeeded Carter as president of the association, became chairman of the program. He worked closely with Winters in developing the schedule and implementing it. In many ways, much of the program's success can be attributed to Nunn's ability to ride herd on the staff and to get the governor's attention on key issues.

The schedule was truly backbreaking, and included the following steps:

> Georgia Planning Association Development Conference—March 1971
> Provided eight major areas for the development of goals
>
> Georgia Planning Association Statewide Conference—April 1971
> Raises questions regarding the goals in the eight areas
>
> Attitude survey—summer and fall 1971
> Provided representative cross section to Georgia's citizens' responses to Goals questionnaire
>
> Regional conferences—summer 1971
> Sponsored by the Area Regional Planning and Development Commissions
> 61 meetings involved more than 6,000 Georgia citizens
>
> Statewide television broadcasts—summer-fall 1971
> Eight programs on the Goals topics, viewed by as many as 250,000 citizens
>
> Statewide conferences—October 1971
> One about each of the eight topics where leaders refined the issues
>
> Goals for Georgia reports—January 1972
>
> Governor's use of Goals results in his proposal for legislation and the state budget—March 1972

The Georgia state archives now has the executive branch files for the Carter Administration. They reveal the intensity, tight planning, and even tighter management that have become a Carter trademark. One of the documents included in the files is an internal memorandum on May 14, 1971, outlining the goals of the governor's program. Entitled "The Challenge: Active Participation by Citizens of Georgia in Determining State Directions, Goals, and Priorities for the Coming Year," the memo focused on the task of getting citizens to participate in the program so they could develop goals for the immediate future. There was little effort to increase citizen awareness for long-range options or to create a dialogue about alternative futures. Instead the emphasis was on creating a dialogue about managing state government and meeting short-term goals. As the memo outlined it, the program was designed to:

1. Identify issues (problems) that face the state of Georgia.
2. Determine alternative directions (solutions) to alleviate the problem.
3. Set priorities (rank) among the most important or critical issues to be solved.
4. Establish goals for the state in the next biennium.
5. Develop realistic state programs to reach the desired goals statewide.[7]

These objectives fit Carter's determination to bridge the gap between people and their state government. His two statewide campaigns had convinced him that there was a "great desire of Georgia people to participate in government—to feel a part of the processes that make the laws by which we live." It was his hope that "the active involvement of individual citizens in the political processes will help to relieve frustration and tension."[8]

The Carter Administration worked hard to bring people into the Goals for Georgia Program. There were sixty-one local and regional conferences sponsored by the various Area Planning and Development Commissions. APDCs are a Georgia invention designed to bring together local governments in a single area planning agency. Their funding comes largely from federal and state grants. Each APDC is governed by a committee of representatives from the local governments. Increasingly, however, these agencies and their staffs are becoming more autonomous. They have been more and more willing to create area-wide projects when county and city governments fail to act on their recommendations. They were the logical organization to sponsor conferences about goals for Georgia.

These conferences were well advertised with press releases, written invitations, and local radio spots in which the governor invited local citizens to participate. There was a concerted effort to ensure that every interested person knew about the meetings.

At each conference officials explained the concept and schedule of the governor's Goals for Georgia Program. State officials explained key topics and answered questions. Then the participants were asked to discuss various issues and to fill out workbooks. Some conferences lasted all day. Others occupied afternoons or evenings only.

Response varied widely. It is difficult to compare levels of participation around the state because different APDCs developed different structures and formats for their conferences. One APDC hosted eleven meetings while another held only one. In the mountains there was an effort to hold a conference in each county. This led to many small meetings with as few as ten participants in one session. On the other hand, one urban meeting attracted 520 people. In all, approximately four thousand people attended the conference; this represents about one tenth of 1 percent of the state population.

For the most part, the participants were upper-middle-class elites. They were fairly representative of the sex and racial composition of the state but were on the average somewhat younger than the state's adult population. They were much better educated than the general population; while 15 percent lacked a high school diploma, the percentage of participants who were college graduates (46 percent) was nearly ten times the proportion of the state population having a college degree. Professional and technical occupations dominated the meetings, with 52.1 percent of the attendees in these categories. More than two out of three persons (69.2 percent) considered themselves white-collar workers. Government employees were the largest single group of participants, with 36.8 percent of the registrations (25.2 percent nonteachers, 11.6 percent in the public education system alone). It is, of course, likely that state and local government employees were strongly encouraged to attend the meetings. However, they were also the ones most likely to know about the Goals program and to be already involved in state and local planning. There was significant participation by business, labor, and farm groups and by the black community as well.

In addition to the regional conferences, which reached only a very small portion of the state population, a second effort to involve the public was made. During July and August, eight one-hour programs on public television focused on Goals for Georgia. Each program had several state officials explaining their role in the Goals program. The public was invited to call in to ask questions on the air. The first six programs were so successful that the last two shows were extended to ninety minutes.

Public participation in the Goals program culminated with a series of eight statewide Goals conferences that brought together experts, state officials, and the general public. Each conference focused on one of the major areas identified at the first Georgia Planning Association Conference on the Goals project: education, government, protection of persons and property, transportation, social development, economic development, natural environment, and physical and mental health. Thirty-five thousand Georgians received written invitations to the conference, and over two thousand attended.

It is difficult to determine exactly how many people actually took part in the entire Goals program. While over four thousand workbooks were returned, some fourteen thousand were distributed at the regional meetings and through civic clubs. Over twenty thousand information brochures were distributed and, in addition to the eight television programs, a twenty-minute film on Goals for Georgia was widely distributed. Governor Carter claimed that 250,000 people watched one or more of the public television programs. Interview programs on commercial stations increased the number of individuals with television exposure to the Goals program. For example, WMAZ-TV in Macon donated a half hour to Governor Carter and Sam Nunn immediately before the All-Star game on July 30. A considerable number of people probably saw at least some of that program.

While a great number of people may have seen all or part of the various television programs, a much smaller number responded with specific ideas. Goals for Georgia Program received approximately three hundred letters in response to the call for ideas. The progress report to the Coastal Plains Regional Commission estimated that there was an average of fifteen in-coming toll-free calls per day but does not mention for how many days. The television programs drew fewer than three hundred telephone calls in nine hours of programming.

The program staff developed some interesting efforts to broaden public use of the workbooks. For example, Ellis MacDougall, the state prison director, sent workbooks to one hundred inmates and asked them to respond. Newspapers often editorialized in favor of the program. The State Chamber of Commerce helped publicize each of the conferences.

None of these efforts, however, awakened a massive public response. Georgians were not used to being involved in their state government. They had grown up in a political tradition of indifference and cynicism. Now a governor was asking them to take government seriously and to believe that their political leadership had a sincere interest in decent government. It would have taken longer than the Goals program permitted to build this new spirit of participation.

WHAT THE GOALS PROGRAM REVEALED

The press release that announced the Goals program asserted that "this is your program; this is your chance to plan the future of state government."

Given this opportunity, what did the Georgia public want?

To illustrate the nature of the goals identified in the process, the following list includes those goals that received over 80 percent support from the citizens:

> The very best education should be provided for citizens of all ages and abilities.

> Teachers should be given the support and assistance they need to do an outstanding job of teaching.

> Policies and programs which help to improve education or extend its benefits should be endorsed or created.

> All Georgians are entitled to high standards of efficiency and economy in their local governments.

State government should help local governments to meet their responsibilities and to find better ways of serving the people.

The legal system must safeguard persons and property and must deal justly with the rights of the public as well as the accused.

Georgia laws should shield the uneducated and the unwary from unscrupulous businessmen and fraudulent business practices.

Public transportation should be operated, expanded, and modified with an eye toward enhancing the economic health of the state as a whole and toward providing social and economic benefits to both urban and rural communities.

Transportation by road, air, water, and rail should be planned, coordinated, and managed so that people and goods can move as efficiently and easily as possible throughout the state.

Essential social services should be quickly and easily available to all Georgians wherever and whenever they are needed.

Georgia's older citizens must have greater opportunities to live productive, comfortable lives.

Every citizen should be provided the essential means to satisfy basic human needs.

All Georgians should have a sound home in a decent neighborhood.

Georgians must continue to build a strong economy in the rural areas of the state as well as in the cities.

Well-planned, orderly economic growth should be initiated and encouraged by all state government agencies.

Healthy economic development throughout the state should be a mutual concern of private business and government.

Georgia's natural environment must have the best efforts of citizens and strong leadership from government to restore, improve, preserve, and protect it.

Every citizen should have the opportunity to enjoy natural beauty and outdoor recreation as a necessary and important part of his life.

A comprehensive, wide-ranging program of education for health should be part of the public school curriculum and should also be readily available to adults.

Qualified persons trained in health care services should be used more often to help bring care and treatment to more people and to allow health professionals to use their limited time more productively.

A complete array of coordinated public and private health services should be within easy reach of everyone who seeks prevention, diagnosis, or treatment of physical and mental health problems.[9]

The workbooks dealt with more specific goals as well, many of which have been acted on. For example, almost 93 percent of the respondents "agreed" or "strongly agreed" that Georgia needed social programs for mentally retarded children. Serious steps have been taken to develop those classes in every school system. Almost 83 percent agreed that there should be periodic evaluation of student performance, which is now done by the State Department of Education. Some 56 percent wanted more vocational training; a great deal of money has been spent to develop comprehensive high schools and vocational-technical schools. Approximately 88 percent favored teacher aides, and most school systems now use them. An overwhelming 94 percent favored stricter consumer protection laws, and Georgia now has an Office of Consumer Affairs. Almost three out of four Georgians favored the creation of a State Department of Transportation, which was developed shortly thereafter. The public indicated that they favored spending more on physical health, mental health, education, and the environment, in that order.

While the government has acted on many of the desires expressed by the workbooks, it has ignored or rejected many others. For example, 86 percent of the respondents favored statewide kindergartens, but they still do not exist. Four out of five citizens favored state revenue sharing with local government, but it has not been developed. Finally, some 92 percent favored the development of a senior citizen corps, similar to the one that is part of VISTA, to use the skills of the retired, but such a program has not even been proposed in the legislature.

The workbooks provided a flood of data on attitudes on specific issues and ideas. In addition, the Goals program commissioned a public-opinion survey to create a benchmark for comparing the attitudes expressed in the workbooks with those of the general population. This survey involved interviews with 723 citizens. Each interview lasted an average of seventy minutes. Dr. Tim Ryles, a political scientist at Georgia State University, developed the survey and analyzed it in *Citizen Perspectives on Goals for Georgia*.[10]

The survey indicated a range of problems between individual citizens and their government. Some 45.3 percent felt that the state courts give people a fair trial only "sometimes" or almost never. The statement that laws were written for the benefit of the rich men brought agreement from 56.8 percent of the whites and 82.2 percent of the blacks. Three out of four Georgians agreed that government and politics seemed so complicated that they could not really understand them. Over 56 percent agreed that they didn't have any say in their government. Three out of five believed that most public officials do not care about the public's opinions on issues.

The survey indicated that Georgia was wracked with more than simple alienation. There was a strong antibusiness mood in the state. Over half of the population favored stricter laws about commercial development. Nearly nine out of ten Georgians were willing to punish businesses that were polluting the environment. Four out of five favored stricter laws regarding farm use of pesticides. Nearly two thirds of the population favored higher corporate income tax if there had to be a tax increase (only a tax on alcoholic beverages received greater support in a list of seven possible taxes). Some 63.7 percent mentioned business as the primary group avoiding its fair share of taxes.

The survey showed not only that the public as a whole was skeptical of public officials and convinced that business was not carrying its fair share of the load, but also that Georgia was deeply divided along racial lines. Busing was an obvious point of difference—with 74 percent of whites opposed to it and 79 percent of blacks favoring it. Blacks and whites had differing perceptions of reality. Only 35.5 percent of whites believed that black schools are not as good as white schools, whereas 61 percent of blacks felt that their schools were inferior. While 55 percent of the whites expressed support for day care centers, some 91 percent of the black population endorsed the idea. Only 22 percent of the white population thought black employment opportunities were not as good as those of whites, and 15 percent thought blacks had better employment opportunities. In contrast, four out of five blacks thought that they did not have an equal opportunity to get a job. Whereas 45.3 percent of the state population thought the judicial process was sometimes or almost never fair, only one third of the white respondents felt that way, while among blacks the figure was 77 percent.

The alienation and racial disagreement shown in the survey were never broadly reported or publicized, and a planned second survey was canceled. The Goals program used only that part of the survey that was most relevant to the goals in the eight areas.

Although the Goals program was not without its faults, it has to be considered a substantial success. Its legacy was a tremendous agenda of legislative and administrative goals. It will take years for Georgia's government to digest all the advice and ideas developed in that brief nineteen months of interaction.

The eight statewide conferences established more coherent sets of goals and their requirements. For example, the Report on Mental and Physical Health indicates the range of ideas examined. This report recommended community health services for mental health and included alcohol and drug rehabilitation as mental health problems. For many Georgians in 1971 that was radical talk indeed. This was one of the first Georgia government documents to argue that alcoholism and drug abuse were not primarily legal problems. The report went on to advocate prenatal care for indigent mothers, family planning services, fluoridation of all drinking water, drug abuse and venereal disease programs in the schools, the use of certified medical assistants to help physicians, an increase in the practice of family medicine, the training of more licensed practical nurses, the use of pharmacists as health educators, and the creation of a state Office of Health Manpower Resources.

Many of these goals were reached during the Carter Administration. There has been considerable progress toward the creation of community mental-health centers. Indigent mothers can get pre-natal care. There has been a substantial increase in the practice of family medicine. There are now more licensed prenatal nurses.

Each of the other seven reports had a similar number of agenda items. These have created an enormous backlog of ideas for the government to examine. A second Goals program might have been redundant during Carter's Administration simply because the state had not completed its cycle of presenting, studying, and adopting or rejecting the proposals based on the first set of goals.

Committees of specialists developed the reports and prepared the conferences in October 1971. These meetings included speeches by significant figures in the field, workshop sessions led by experts, and intensive discussion on specific topics. The Natural Environment Conference, for example, was chaired by Joe Tanner (later Georgia commissioner of natural resources) and Walter Mitchell (then president of the Georgia Conservancy). Dr. Eugene Odum, of the University of Georgia Institute of Ecology, made the major address. Dr. William Nash, consultant to the governor on planning and a member of the Harvard faculty, later dean of the Urban Life School at Georgia State University, and Governor Carter also spoke. There were subcommittees on coastal resources: wildlife; environmental law and planning; aquaculture; the natural environment—air, water, soils; forestry; mining and mineral processing; parks and recreation; agriculture; tourism and historical preservation; and air, water, and solid waste. Each subcommittee made a report with specific recommendations.

One of the greatest advantages of the statewide conferences may have been the fact that they brought many knowledgeable experts together in all-day discussions. New ideas were generated with the benefit of cross-fertilization among disciplines, and alliances between state officials and public activists were formed.

ASSESSING GOALS FOR GEORGIA

Interviews in 1977 suggested that one of the primary benefits of Goals for Georgia was the opportunity for community leaders to learn from each other.[11] It was a rare chance for business and labor leaders to share meetings about the state's future. It was a chance for senior bureaucrats and local community leaders to share ideas and to learn about mutual problems. In many ways it set the stage for the state government reorganization effort, by making bureaucrats and citizens more aware of current problems.

The Goals program had some impact on the state legislature. Governor Carter appointed to the project eight state senators and eight state representatives to be legislative advisers—with the opportunity to attend various conferences and hearings. In their selection, Sam Nunn was invaluable in ensuring that key figures in the legislature were consulted. All legislators received copies of the reports of the program. Some used them to justify introducing various pieces of legislation and, in a few instances, a legislator became active on an issue because Goals' hearings had focused on it. Governor Carter was better at involving the legislature than was Governor Evans a few years later in Washington State.* There was no overt legislative hostility to the governor's Goals program, and some specific program recommendations were successfully implemented. On the whole, however, it is difficult to distinguish between legislative actions that were based on the Goals program and those developed independently by the governor, the legislators, or others.[12] Some actions—the creation of the Department of Transportation, for example—reflected both the Goals program and the governor's original legislative program. There is a consensus among interviewed legislators that the Goals program played a substantial role in increasing their awareness of state problems and in paving the way for Carter's program.

The 1971 Goals program was not truly anticipatory in the sense of exploring an array of alternative futures as Jim Dator describes in Chapter 19. There was no systematic effort to outline a wide range of options and to examine their implications. There was no effort to educate the citizenry about possible futures, the range of problems and opportunities that Georgia faces, or the process of more anticipatory and democratic participation. Public participation remained scattered and lacked any continuity. Most of the dialogue went from the state officials to the public rather than vice versa. Once the discussion and reporting at the conferences was over, the real decision-making reverted to the normal pro-

* Editor's note: See Chapter 4 on Alternatives for Washington.

cedures. There was no systematic effort to build public involvement and commitment as bases for future programs.

In this sense, there is a fundamental difference between the
Georgia Goals program and the Hawaii and Washington efforts to
develop alternative visions of the future. The Goals for Georgia
Program was clearly designed to take some initial steps in public
dialogue, to provide some advice for the Carter Administration as
it developed budgets, programs, and state reorganization plans, and
to make citizens aware that some officials cared about their opinions. Viewed within the context of those aims, it was an extremely
successful program. Politicians seldom think in ten- to twenty-five-
year time frames. The shorter one- to five-year horizon of the Goals
program is understandable. This time frame for a participatory
program in Georgia was a great step forward.

The governor's Goals program represented the work of Carter
the political theorist much more than Carter the planner. Clearly
he wanted to bring people closer to their government and to at
least begin the process of dialogue. However, he was not sure how
to do it and, in the long run, his engineering/planning interests
took up more and more of his time. State government reorganization became Carter's top priority, and while information developed
in the Goals program was used in the process, there was little direct
participation in the design phase of that effort.

When Carter moved into national politics, he left behind a
legacy of innovation and creativity that is a watershed in Georgia
politics. The Goals for Georgia Program has not been repeated,
which is unfortunate because the populace continues to be uninvolved in planning the state. Yet planning for the future will be
especially important during the next decade because Georgia has
an opportunity to anticipate its growth problems thereby avoiding
many of the mistakes of the northeastern and midwestern states.
However, there are four traditions in Georgia politics that make
anticipatory democracy difficult to develop.

First, Georgia politics is historically personality- rather than
issue-oriented, and the news media reinforce that bias; it is extremely difficult to develop a serious issue theme in the newspapers,
while rather easy to get coverage for spectacular stunts. Lester
Maddox riding a bicycle backwards represented more than the
antics of an eccentric man. Maddox had shrewdly adapted to a
news-media environment that kept serious issues on the editorial

page and scandals and trivia on the front page. Maddox consistently overshadowed more thoughtful and serious politicians.

In a personality- and scandal-oriented political system, anticipatory democracy is a radical development. To be effective, anticipatory democracy must rely on thematic dialogues over time in order to enable the individual citizen to understand the problems, and respond by helping to develop serious alternatives. Yet this kind of discourse requires a tradition of citizen concern which simply has not occurred in Georgia's political history.

Second, the political culture of Georgia is actively hostile to efforts to develop dialogue. Georgians generally do not want to be involved in politics:

Georgia is dominated by what Daniel Elazar characterized as a *traditionalistic political culture*. According to Elazar, government in such cultures is elitist, paternalistic, and seeks to preserve existing social relationships. Thus, on the surface, Goals for Georgia represents a more open style of political leadership, somewhat inconsistent with established customs.

. . . Insofar as the mass public is concerned, Georgia does not have a participatory political culture. No matter how one measures participation in government and politics, Georgia has one of the lowest participation rates in the nation.[13]

Measured against this tradition of alienation and disinterest, the governor's Goals for Georgia Program was a successful experiment with a fairly high level of response. This suggests that if a governor were willing to commit substantial amounts of his (or her) prestige, time, and budget to developing a permanent goals program, it might become an institution. Over time, it might develop a public willing to support it with time and energy. However, it will be an expensive and slow process to build such a constituency. It will take much more effort than state reorganization. Initially, it will produce fewer visible results. In a citizenry grown cynical about politics, there will be little applause for what may seem to be a quixotic effort.

Third, any further effort in Georgia will for a long time remain the governor's program because there are no groups of concerned activists to take over an anticipatory democracy program, though there are some possibilities. There is a small chapter of an Atlanta 2000 Project that has been set up to explore that city's future. The

Georgia Conservancy is small but is working toward its particular image of the future for the state. The Georgia Planning Association, sponsor of the first Goals for Georgia Program, has grown since 1971.

Yet the reality is that most citizen-activism is centered in Atlanta and even there it is not thoroughly entrenched. The need for a citizen leadership base for anticipatory democracy runs head-long into public apathy. Because there are relatively few civic (as opposed to special-interest) groups putting pressure on politicians, the latter continue to focus on such traditional issues as teachers' salaries, legalizing wider mobile homes, or reforming welfare. Because there is no strong cadre mobilizing public support, the average citizen remains uninvolved.

Fourth, the low level of citizen activism is likely to make any Goals program dependent on the life of the incumbent administration. Without a network of supporters within government capable of sustaining such a program, it is unlikely that even a public committed to participating in the planning process could have a serious impact on state government.

ANOTHER GOALS PROGRAM?

Georgia needs a new goals program.* Six years have passed since the original effort, and many other states have experimented in anticipatory democracy. Georgia has an opportunity to draw on its own experiences and those of other states to develop a more thorough and long-lasting program. Georgia is uniquely placed to initiate a new program because it has an incumbent governor who is almost certain to be re-elected in 1978. George Busbee has been a hard-working and systematic chief executive. His eighteen years of experience in the state legislature made him probably the best-prepared governor Georgia has had in recent times. He has brought that experience to bear in gradually trimming and remolding Georgia's government.

Since Busbee will probably serve for six more years, he has a real opportunity to create a goals program that would develop an

* Editor's note: Two participation exercises were begun in 1977 by Georgia ecologists, Georgia 2000 and Atlanta 2000.

on-going dialogue between the public, the experts, and government officials. If such a program were developed in spite of the political traditions working against its foundation, it might well become a model for other states to examine, and might provide some guidelines for Georgia's growth in the next quarter century.

Any thorough goals effort should be structured in a way that includes the commitment of the governor and the legislature but gives citizens the independence to develop alternatives. One approach is to ask the legislature to create an independent Commission on Georgia's Future. This commission could bring together appointees from the executive branch, the legislature, local governments, industry, labor, and key public-interest groups. It should serve for a limited period in order to keep from becoming a permanent bureaucracy. A three-year limitation would give it time to plan carefully, develop a serious dialogue, and prepare thorough reports. Such a commission should receive one dollar per year per citizen for a total budget of approximately $13,500,000 for the three years. This may seem extravagant to some, but it is time that advocates of anticipatory efforts speak frankly about the cost of maintaining a democratic and free society. This nation spends billions of dollars to implement programs while it refuses to spend even 1 percent of the cost of those programs to evaluate them. America is like an enormous ocean liner that spends massive amounts of energy on the engine room but refuses to buy radar or a steering wheel. True anticipatory dialogue is going to be expensive and it will not be successful until it has a competent staff, mass communication facilities, computerized record keeping, and sufficient time to allow local participation to become a habit.

A well-funded commission would be in a position to consider a variety of possibilities for bringing anticipatory ideas to the attention of the general public. The public utilities, for example, could be asked to enclose anticipatory material with their bills; if necessary, the commission could even pay any extra postage involved. Such mailings, with self-addressed post cards for responses, would bring an awareness of the need for anticipatory decision-making into homes that never watch public television or talk to politicians.

This kind of aggressive effort will require large amounts of accurate data and analysis. Much of the needed information about possible alternative futures is currently available but is too little known. The commission could take advantage of the expertise of public and private universities by developing consultative task forces to help build alternative models of the future for Georgia, and to identify those key areas in which decisions are likely to have long-range impact.

The commission could develop a series of television programs on Georgia's future. If possible, independent sponsoring should be obtained. For example, the Coca-Cola and Royal Crown Cola companies are Georgia natives, and among their top executives are futurists who might well be interested in participating in such an effort. Adequate financing might enable future-oriented programs to overcome the enormous gap that currently exists between the professional pace of commercial television and the slower, more stilted style of the state-produced public television programs. If the general public is to be attracted and educated with anticipatory programming, it will have to be as fast and professionally paced as prime-time commercial television. This kind of programming should be followed up with audience participation in the form of discussions and call-in shows. They should be reinforced and supplemented by newspaper surveys that give citizens the opportunity to outline their choices and their options. Radio stations should be used to build interest in both the television and newspaper programming, and to develop dialogues on their own call-in shows.

As the values and preferences emerge as a result of these media processes, more specialized and regional efforts should be undertaken. Each Area Planning Development Commission should create a local Commission of the Future that would function concurrently with the state effort, and be funded as part of that effort. These local commissions could use the local public television and radio stations as well as the newspapers to contribute to the development of the unique characteristics of their regions. It is possible, for example, that the South Georgia coastal plain could become a breadbasket to rival the Midwest. Atlanta's future will be substantially different. Some of the richest and most important dialogue and decision-making may well have to occur at a regional rather than a state level.

There will also have to be a great deal of work among specialists. Different professions and industries have different alternative futures. State planning has to be more than a series of value decisions among macro-systems or an examination of aggregate data. There has to be considerable concern for discrete areas of planning such as health care, education, recreation, the environment, industrial development, etc.

An ideal anticipatory system will combine expert data on probable developments and their potential effects with the concerns, values, and goals of the general public. Ultimately, the public should develop an informed set of values that provide guidelines within which professional planners design specific policies. The development of such an interactive information and decision-making system will require time, the development of new modes of communication, and considerable flexibility on the part of political leaders. But this type of working model of anticipatory democracy would be a tremendous legacy for an official to leave his or her state.

CHAPTER THREE

Goals for Dallas

BY ROBERT B. BRADLEY

Goals for Dallas is the largest and the oldest experiment in urban goal-setting attempted by the United States. It represents a well-organized and broadly based effort to involve citizens in the creation of Dallas's future. The Goals program has been examined closely and imitated in scores of communities across the country.

After a decade Goals for Dallas has realized both more and less than its early promise. Its experience deserves to be widely shared, and the following pages attempt to trace the direction and tenor of the Goals process as it has unfolded. However, the achievements and limitations of Goals for Dallas must be seen in the context of the city's unique social, economic, and political milieu. In particular, the timing of the Goals proposal, coming late in 1964 and after the Kennedy assassination, must be taken into account. Some of the experiences and lessons of the Goals program are necessarily unique to Dallas; but the Goals *process* offers several important lessons for communities interested in goal-setting and concerned with organizing themselves for the future.*

Copyright © 1978 by Robert B. Bradley. Grateful acknowledgment to Goals for Dallas for permission to reprint portions herein.
* I would like to thank Ken Orr for his invaluable efforts in data gathering. In addition, this paper has benefited from the comments of Carolyn Herrington and Paul Peretz.

THE SOCIAL, ECONOMIC, AND POLITICAL ENVIRONMENT OF DALLAS

Since the beginning of World War II, Dallas has experienced an explosive population growth. It has grown faster than the nation as a whole and faster than most large cities in the country.[1] In 1940 the population of the city was 294,734; by 1970 it had grown to 844,401. And while population growth slowed in the 1970s, the rapid earlier growth has had serious ramifications for the economic development of the city. The magnitude of the increase has spawned problems of increasing complexity and opportunities of considerable potential. The timing of this growth, coming well after the peak of the American industrial revolution, has bestowed its own legacy. Experts on urban growth have noted that the character of a metropolitan area's growth "depends on the technological premises of its formative development."[2] Dallas, from this perspective, is a "postindustrial" city, well beyond a reliance upon heavy industrialization for its growth.

Dallas was founded in the middle of the nineteenth century as a river-crossing point. By the turn of the century, and with the assistance of political influence in the state legislature, the city had become a regional transportation center. Its political base in the legislature encouraged and sustained Dallas's development as a regional trading hub. It also encouraged the location of ancillary economic activities in Dallas and made investment in the city quite attractive.

Between 1940 and 1960, Dallas's national ranking among cities rose to third in the nation in insurance activities, to eleventh in banking, to fourteenth in retail sales, and to tenth in the number of "million-dollar firms" headquartered in the city.[3] But Dallas did not become a manufacturing center; the amount of manufacturing activity in the area is substantially less than in most metropolitan areas in the country. Unlike older, industrial cities, postindustrial cities typically have small proportions of their work force in manufacturing. Such cities instead shift to service-sector employment.

Postindustrial cities differ from older, industrial cities in other ways as well. The older cities sealed their political boundaries long ago, while younger, postindustrial cities continued to annex land in the post-World War II period. Dallas, for example, increased municipal land area by 137 percent between 1950 and 1970.

Furthermore, whereas other inner cities of older metropolitan areas rapidly lost their young, employed population as income rose in the postwar period, postindustrial cities have been able to keep dynamic elements of their population in the face of considerable suburban pressures. In Dallas the average family income within the city in 1970 was higher than that of families in the suburban ring.[4] On balance, the citizens of Dallas proper are well off; its median income, the percentage of persons who have graduated from high school, the median years of school completed, the percentage of persons in white-collar jobs are all quite high when compared to cities nationwide.[5]

But such statistical averages effectively hide one of the major problems in Dallas: the condition of its minorities, of which the most significant group is the black population. Residential racial segregation in Dallas is severe; it ranks among the most segregated cities in the South.[6] In fact, between 1960 and 1970 the degree of concentration of the black community increased. The median family income of blacks is little more than half that of white families in the city. Black achievement in education lags well behind that of whites. The occupational differences between blacks and whites are substantial; blacks are underrepresented in white-collar occupations but make up most of the transport and service workers throughout the inner city. In short, blacks in Dallas face a situation, socially and economically, as bad as that in other urban areas.[7]

Politically, blacks in Dallas have experienced particular difficulties. The legacy of segregation stretched well into the 1960s. Until 1968 the city charter gave the city council authority to pass ordinances to provide for separate residential blocks, amusement areas, churches, schools, and places of assembly for members of the "white" and the "colored" races.[8] The desegregation of schools has proceeded only slowly. And it appears that the quality of the delivery of city services by the police, sanitation, and parks and recreation departments to the black community falls short of that provided to the white community. Indeed, blacks for the most part have not been among those hired to deliver many kinds of services; in 1974 less than 5 percent of the police force and the fire department were black.

Despite the magnitude and extent of black problems, their participation in and protest against Dallas politics has been muted.

In part, this may stem from the weak electoral position of blacks in the city; in 1970 only a quarter of the population was black. This percentage generally is not enough to elect black candidates without white support. However, numbers alone probably do not explain the position of blacks in Dallas politics. In the wake of *Smith v. Allwright* (1944)—the decision in which the U.S. Supreme Court declared the "white primary" system unconstitutional—blacks in Dallas, as everywhere, had the opportunity to participate in the political affairs of the city. But the extent of black political organization that followed this decision in so many southern cities was less pronounced in Dallas, due in part to the flexibility of the establishment in meeting the political demands of those parts of the black community that did become active.[9]

Over the years the city leadership has been both flexible and assertive. The most often-quoted example of its assertive character is an event that occurred during the difficult days of the Depression. Under the leadership of R. L. Thornton, Sr., Dallas managed to win the competition among Texas cities to host the Texas Centennial Exposition. The Texas legislature awarded Dallas the fair over cities whose histories were closer to the spirit of the exposition, which ultimately earned Dallas considerable prestige and revenue. The thirteen million visitors to the state-fair grounds not only gave the city invaluable publicity, but also helped to establish the city leadership's reputation for sound and decisive action. More than any other event, this experience catapulted the city's business community into position as the dominant and most dynamic element on the political scene. In 1937 the creation of the Dallas Citizens Council formalized the leadership structure.[10]

This coalition of business leaders was neither accidental nor transitory. In the mid-1960s, *Fortune* magazine noted, "The fact of the matter is that Dallas's business leadership has no parallel anywhere in the U.S."[11] Well into the mid-1960s, the leaders of the major banks—Mercantile National, Republic National, and First National—managed to sustain their early commitments to cooperation and community service. The business leadership was able to encourage the cooperation and support of other elements of the community through the sheer weight of their standing in the local society. Through a complex network of organizations and committees, the Citizens Council was able to exert enormous influence over all aspects of city life. The Charter Citizens Association

(CCA), a political arm of the council, selected slates of candidates of local office; the slates almost always won. Between 1969 and 1974, CCA candidates won 82 percent of all local council seats up for election.[12] In the years between 1939 and 1970, the CCA selected all but two mayors.

The very character of the local political institutions reinforced the influence of business. Dallas is the largest city in the United States using the council-manager form of local government. Its local elections are nonpartisan and, until 1974, council members were elected at large. This combination acted to keep political participation in local elections low and to diffuse the impact of small blocks of voters. "In the five Dallas city council elections held from 1965 to 1973, the average voter turnout was less than 55,000; this represented less than 15 percent of the registered voters and less than 10 percent of the adult residents of the city."[13] Despite substantial block voting by the black population in the years after 1959, it was not until 1969 that a black candidate was elected to the city council and even then only because he had the endorsement of the CCA.[14]

It would be unwise to conclude that the elite controlling Dallas has remained unchanged. Indeed, the strength of the leadership has flowed from its ability to anticipate and deal with changes in the city's character. Certainly the leadership deserves much of the credit for Dallas's strong economic position in the Southwest. But the leadership has been unwilling or unable to deal effectively with a range of problems. The belated inclusion of blacks in city government is symptomatic of the reluctance of the CCA to respond to the increasing numbers of blacks in the city.

The politically conservative leadership was slow to react to the social changes of the early 1960s—in fact, the pace of social and educational change led during the latter part of the 1960s to differences within the leadership.

The last ten years have been a period of change and adjustment for the business leadership. The pattern of family-owned businesses has given way to more impersonal forms of ownership. The large, downtown banks have expanded their horizons, looking beyond Dallas to Texas and the Southwest. In sum, the leadership in the mid-1970s is less coherent than at almost any time in recent history. Yet in spite of its shortcomings and the cracks in its cohesion, the business community still dominates governing circles to a degree not equaled in most other large metropolitan areas.

THE CONTEXT OF GOALS FOR DALLAS

In November 1964 the newly appointed mayor of Dallas, Erik Jonsson, proposed the Goals for Dallas program. He arugued, "As I have worked to fulfill my responsibilities as Mayor of Dallas, I have become increasingly aware of the lack of goals and plans for our city."[15] The Goals for Dallas program, as he envisioned it, "was a part of a systematic process of determining what was to be done, how we were to do it, when we were going to do it, and what tools and resources were available."[16] The program was designed to push the perspective of city planning into the future, to move beyond the cycle of thinking one year at a time. Jonsson hoped goal identification and clarification would make the city leadership less reactive, more anticipatory.

When I came to City Hall, I found that essentially we were living on a one-year basis. You presented to the council a one-year budget on August 15. On October 1 you accepted or rejected the final budget . . . and that was what you did in the succeeding year. That was no way to run a railroad or a city. If you simply react to strong protests, the council becomes one that responds to the squeaking wheel and puts grease on it and lets the other wheels of the wagon go ungreased. Sooner or later you buy an axle or a wheel or both because of that procedure. This isn't rational.[17]

When Jonsson proposed the project, it was widely regarded as the first municipally-inspired project of its kind.[18] Its philosophical basis might be traced to President Eisenhower's effort to catalog "Goals for America." Alternatively, Jonsson's own experience in goal formulation as chairman of the board of Texas Instruments might be viewed as the genesis of this innovative approach to local planning. Another view of the conception of the Goals program, however, emphasizes the unique context within which the proposal was made and the goals were framed.

The Dallas business leadership, which had contributed so much to the economic well-being of the city, had become, by the early 1960s, inbred and insensitive to a number of the city's social problems.[19] In particular it did not recognize, or else refused to recognize the full impact of the growing civil rights movement. Intellectual and moral conformity threatened the leadership; the elite structure appeared to be ossifying. Dr. Willis Tate, president of Southern Methodist University, characterized the situation in this manner:

The business and financial group has an enormous enthusiasm for the development of the city, but its dedication has often turned into fierce pride. Naturally, the business leaders have a vested background slanted more toward the economic and industrial aspect than the real health of the city. They have rarely accepted professional groups in their councils and have been unaware of the vacuum this has created. There just isn't any free flow of ideas.[20]

The assassination of President Kennedy in November 1963 underlined the magnitude of the problem, for suddenly Dallas's reputation for dynamic action and strong leadership was replaced by one that characterized the city as the "hate capital of the nation." The national press censured the business leadership severely for nurturing an atmosphere of intolerance and violence. Levi Olan, rabbi of Temple Emanu-El and a spokesman for the Jewish community, observed:

Fifteen years ago the business leaders were dynamic men. They not only dominated the community as they do now, they built it with vision and daring. To be sure, they had sort of a medieval, feudal approach. But they understood power. They understood it carries responsibility with it. The leaders today also seek to control, to dominate paternalistically. But they do not assume responsibility, they will not acknowledge the need for accountability. The business leadership rarely faces up to the real problems of the city.[21]

In the months following the Kennedy assassination, the Dallas leadership moved to counter the recriminations swirling around the event and to refurbish its national image. Earle Cabell, the city's mayor in 1963, resigned in January 1964 to run for the U.S. House of Representatives against Bruce Alger, the incumbent conservative congressman. The CCA appointed Erik Jonsson as interim mayor;

but Jonsson quickly established himself as much more than the ceremonial mayor posited in the council-manager form of government. Through decisive moves in the council chamber, as well as through symbolic gestures, Jonsson more than made up for his lack of staff or administrative authority. According to one source, "he was front-page news almost every day, visiting the city departments, calling on the council to prepare for the challenge of the future, appointing an 'emergency committee' on traffic safety, and urging the public to make Dallas great."[22] Over the next year, Jonsson was able to secure the resignation of Elgin Crull, the city manager of fourteen years. Jonsson brought to city government the research and analysis techniques that had served him well at Texas Instruments.

The choice of Jonsson as interim mayor was salutary in more than one respect. Unlike many in the Dallas leadership structure, "Jonsson was a wealthy and prestigious businessman who had come to Dallas from New Jersey during the Depression . . . Jonsson was a cosmopolitan."[23] He recognized that the community leaders were not tuned into the diverse needs of the Dallas area. He was able to see the truth in *Fortune* magazine's criticism that the "lack of running dissent has robbed Dallas of the tension it needs to become a truly great city."[24] He and a growing number of other city leaders recognized that a broadened membership was necessary to legitimize the existing leadership's continued role in the city. If nothing else, Jonsson's proposed Goals for Dallas envisioned an expanded participation in city decision-making.

From the outset, Jonsson was explicit in his desire to include a "broad spectrum of viewpoints and pursuits" in the Goals for Dallas project.[25] Jonsson set out to increase the types and amount of information available to the leadership and to introduce more flexibility and accountability into the leadership.

Besides being an outgrowth of the need for new, or at best varied, leadership, the Goals project proposed to tap the diverse skills and energies of Dallas's leading citizens as a way to discern citizen concerns. Goals for Dallas also met a heartfelt community need at a time when the city desperately needed an improved self-image. As one person involved with the program put it, "The community's self-guilt and self-pity [over the Kennedy assassination] shattered and preoccupied the Dallas leadership and other citizens. There was a need to look forward and to bring something to the community for them to react to and participate in."[26] Goals for Dallas provided a new focus for the city.

THE DESIGN OF GOALS FOR DALLAS

Erik Jonsson ran for mayor in 1965 on the Goals for Dallas program he had proposed the previous winter. His overwhelming victory at the polls—73 percent of the vote—was interpreted as a mandate for the program. Throughout the rest of 1965, Jonsson worked to build further support for the concept.

In December 1965, Jonsson enlisted the services of Dr. Bryghte Godbold, vice-president of the Graduate Research Center of the Southwest, to serve as staff director of the Goals for Dallas project. In addition, Jonsson assembled an influential group of twenty-three citizens (later twenty-six) to act as the planning committee for the project.[27]

Jonsson sketched the broad outlines of his proposal to the initial members of the group and presented specific recommendations for the early operation of the program. The members of the planning committee agreed to work for one year, and the program was established for that time period. As framed in January 1966, the Planning Committee was to have two major functions: 1) to raise funds for the program from private sources in the community, and 2) to provide leadership and supervision. The planning committee was charged with the initial selecting of issues of local concern to be considered in the Goals project. These issue areas were to be examined in commissioned essays, due by April 1966 at the latest. These essays were to identify needs and to establish criteria for further discussion.

In the early months of 1966 the Goals for Dallas Planning Committee met monthly for lectures from consultants summoned from across the United States to address issues relevant to the goals project. The planning committee then chose a larger group to help draft a preliminary set of goals. After having studied the initial essays, this larger group—consisting of the twenty-six members of the planning committee and sixty-one citizens representing a cross section of Dallas and several adjacent municipalities—met for three days in mid-June 1966. Eighty-seven individuals gathered in Salado, a hundred miles from Dallas, to discuss the question Erik Jonsson had posed months before, namely, "What are we trying to do with our community? What are we trying to be?"[28]

The retreat at Salado consisted of six three-hour work sessions. The participants were divided into four panels, which considered proposals within specified issue areas. The long hours of discussion and the retreat setting encouraged each panel to work toward fundamental consensus. Moreover, the members of each panel knew they would have to bring a report back to the group as a whole on the final day of the meeting; this created an additional pressure for consensus within each panel, but provided members with the opportunity to raise significant outstanding disagreements in another forum. In the end, the eighty-seven participants worked out a statement of goals.

The Salado conference resulted in ninety-eight goals in twelve general areas. For each issue area the participants wrote a general goal and then elaborated on this with a set of specific goals. The twelve general goals were: 1) the government of the city, 2) the design of the city, 3) health, 4) welfare, 5) transportation, 6) public safety, 7) elementary and secondary education, 8) higher education, 9) continuing education, 10) cultural activities, 11) recreation and entertainment, and 12) the economy of Dallas. These goals are shown in Table 1. An example of the detail of the specific goals is provided in Table 2, which lists the participants' elaboration of the general goal for the Dallas transportation system.

The Goals for Dallas organization published the entire set of goals (both general and specific), together with the essays prepared for the conferees, in a small book entitled *Goals for Dallas: Submitted for Consideration by Dallas Citizens*. This publication appeared in September 1966 and formed the basis for discussion at a series of meetings held late that year. Throughout Dallas, neighborhood meetings hosted by veterans of the Salado conference provided citizens and groups a chance to approve, revise, delete, and add to the proposed goals. These meetings resembled the format developed at Salado. Participating citizens were divided into subgroups that considered only two general goals and their elaborations. After a period of discussion, the general group was reconvened and votes were taken on the goals and on the changes recommended by the subgroups.

These meetings led to a revision of more than 60 percent of the original set of goals and the addition of fourteen more goals at a second Goals for Dallas conference convened in February 1967. At this conference, eighty participants considered the recommendations of the more than six thousand citizens who had participated in the local meetings. The results of this conference were published in *Goals for Dallas: Mutual Aims of its Citizens.*

TABLE 1. General Goals[29]

THE GOVERNMENT OF THE CITY

For the present, Dallas should maintain the Council-Manager form of government. With the rapid growth and changing complexion of our metropolitan area, we should seek a system which provides for consolidation and joint supervision of duplicated services and functions now provided by contiguous jurisdictions. Since our city is the largest in the nation under the Council-Manager form of government, we should frequently examine our government to assure that it is sufficiently representative and responsive to the needs of the area and its people.

THE DESIGN OF THE CITY

We demand a city of quality with beauty and functional fitness to satisfy both eye and mind. A series of studies and plans must be made which will become a continuing dynamic, living design for our city.

HEALTH

The physical well-being of its citizens is a major Dallas goal. Without health the individual cannot attain fully his potentials for his own benefit or the benefit of the community. The problems of health are complex and interrelated but their solution is a challenge we must meet to have the kind of city we envision.

WELFARE

Dallas must provide its indigent and needy with access to—and assure them at least minimum requirements for—food, clothing, medical care, professional counseling and housing through a social welfare program that is administered with compassionate respect for the dignity of man. An integral function of our welfare administration should be to identify and eliminate conditions which produce and perpetuate the need for welfare services. A further integral purpose of our welfare administration must be to make recipients self-reliant and thereby convert beneficiaries into contributors.

TRANSPORTATION

Dallas must recognize and improve its position as a major transportation and communications center. In order that we may continue to grow and compete successfully with other metropolitan regions, we should work constantly to improve transportation and communication facilities. Within the city and the region, people must be able to move rapidly, pleasantly, safely and economically from their homes to work, to schools, to shopping areas and to recreational and cultural facilities. Transportation of goods within the city and region should be efficient without interfering with the citizen's enjoyment of his city.

PUBLIC SAFETY

Each citizen must be assured the opportunity to enjoy life in our community in peace and free of fear. At the same time, we urge renewed recognition of the responsibilities of the individual in and to an urban society. We also seek wider understanding and appreciation for law and police authority as essential instrumentalities for living together. To meet constant challenges to public order and personal security inherent in rapid population expansion and increasing urbanization, we should strengthen each of those agencies charged with the responsibilities of assuring public safety.

ELEMENTARY AND SECONDARY EDUCATION

Every Dallas child should have the very best education possible to assure his development as a well-adjusted individual and responsible citizen. His interests, talents, and skills must be directed, encouraged, and developed to the end that he can pursue, if qualified, his education beyond high school and to enable him to enjoy a useful, fruitful and satisfying life in a school system which ranks with those of the highest quality in the nation.

HIGHER EDUCATION

Dallas and the North Texas area—possessing the necessary population, economic wealth, human resources and the nucleus of a university-college complex—can and must become one of the great educational centers of the nation. We should provide the intellectual atmosphere and programs to meet the higher educational needs of individuals, to expand knowledge through research at all levels, to strengthen our economy and to make our lives more meaningful and satisfying. All programs should be of high quality, with graduate programs reaching to become steeples of excellence.

CONTINUING EDUCATION

Our way of life is constantly being altered by technological and social changes. Increasingly, people seek educational opportunities to assist in obtaining employment, re-employment and job advancement and to keep up with developments in their fields of interest. Therefore, each person in our community, throughout his life and regardless of educational status, must have the opportunity to continue his education.

CULTURAL ACTIVITIES

To assure a heightened sense of the drama, beauty, and spiritual values of life, and a deeper appreciation for them, Dallas should provide a lively cultural environment for its citizens. We should continue to develop selected activities in the performing and fine arts, with the quality of cultural programs to be steadily improved, for excellence is our goal. To inspire greater appreciation of cultural activities, people should have the opportunity to know, understand and experience the pleasures of such pursuits.

RECREATION AND ENTERTAINMENT

Each person in our community should have access to a wide range of recreational activities. By day or at night, indoors and out, free and commercial, everyone must be able to find active or passive recreation as a spectator or a participant. Recreational facilities and programs adequate to satisfy the individual's needs should be accessible and reasonable in cost. Such programs are especially desirable to keep the young constructively occupied, satisfy the special needs of older people and to be enjoyed by families together.

THE ECONOMY OF DALLAS

Balanced economic growth which is the life blood of Dallas must be preserved. Both the human skills and physical resources of our community should be intelligently, imaginatively and boldly exhibited and employed in a continuing drive to attract new enterprise and develop existing resources and institutions.

Like the first set of goals, those formulated in early 1967 were broadly written and conceived without regard for their implementation. The question of how to implement the goals required yet another effort by the Goals for Dallas volunteers and staff. In April 1968, twelve task forces were formed under the leadership of

TABLE 2. **Specific Transportation Goals**[30]

TRANSPORTATION

1. Continue to expand and improve transportation service to other metropolitan areas and nations at reasonable rates.
2. Secure, with the support of other governmental units in the region, enabling legislation for a Transit Authority or Authorities which would:
    a. Serve as large an area initially as is practical and be designed ultimately for the entire metropolitan region. Membership would include representatives of the areas served.
    b. Study the technology of rapid transit to select the system or systems which can best satisfy our needs.
    c. Assume ownership and operation of the Dallas Transit System and extend its services to satisfy as many needs as the Authority can justify economically.
    d. See to it that Dallas and other municipalities protect and, if possible, preserve at today's price, right-of-way for future rapid transit.
    e. Consider subsidy of public transit by the metropolitan region.
3. Bring the Dallas–Fort Worth airport to its fullest potential as a regional and world air center. Develop more private aircraft and short-hop commercial facilities.
4. Maintain a perpetual list of the community's needs in communication and take effective action to assure postal, telephone and telegraph services which meet the needs.
5. Make available adequate taxi service in all parts of the city and at all hours.
6. Design transportation facilities and services to satisfy the needs of users without dissatisfying other people. For example, when transportation changes are needed, sufficient right-of-way should be acquired to protect adjacent land.

a Coordinating Committee headed by Les Potter. The 293 volunteers who worked on these task forces were charged with "[scheduling] activities to achieve each Goal; to identify the organizations public and private which should take part; to estimate the cost of the Goals when possible and to establish timetables for their attainment."[31] To accomplish this:

The work of each task force was divided among subcommittees whose members interviewed both local and out-of-town experts as well as

Dallasites who head public and private organizations which would bear the major responsibility for achieving the Goals. Based on these and other discussions with interested individuals and citizen groups, each task force reached consensus on the recommendations. These became the first drafts of proposals for achieving the Goals. Each task force was assisted by a part-time staff associate whose services were contributed by a Dallas business or educational institution. The Goals for Dallas staff, under the leadership of Dr. Bryghte Godbold, also provide support to facilitate the volunteers' work, but not to perform it or determine the substance.[32]

The task forces jointly constructed a questionnaire designed to monitor, as broadly as possible, citizen views on the relative importance of the specific goals within each general goal category. In the fall of 1968, at more than 450 neighborhood meetings, nearly twenty-five thousand citizens evaluated the Goals. The task forces used the results of these meetings in making their recommendations to the planning committee on the possibilities for implementing each of the goals.

Other committees processed the task forces' recommendations in order to check for clarity, feasibility, and consistency. They were then circulated among "scores of organization heads who would be directly involved in achieving the Goals."[33] Finally, a third review group headed by the task forces' chairmen approved the final wording of the proposals as they appeared in *Goals for Dallas: Proposals for Achieving the Goals.*

The third Goals for Dallas publication contained not only the goals that had emerged from the neighborhood meetings of 1966, but also a brief interpretation of each goal, its schedule for implementation, and any progress already made toward its fulfillment. This information was taken back to the citizens for review in the fall of 1969, when more than fifty thousand citizens took part in neighborhood meetings designed to answer four basic questions:[34]

1. Is the interpretation of the goal the right one?
2. Is the general approach for achieving the goal the best way to proceed?
3. Is the organization shown for achieving each step the appropriate one?
4. Is the time scale shown for achieving the goal reasonable?

The comments resulting from these meetings were compiled and used in yet another conference, convened in May 1970. At that time, "Considering the suggestions from the fall 1969 neighborhood meetings, the 175 (conferees) revised both the Goals and the proposals for their achievement accordingly. New priorities also were established in each Goal area."[35] This conference published its results in *Goals for Dallas: Achieving the Proposals*. The report contained 108 specific goals, their interpretations, and the general approach and timetable for implementing them.

In a sense, the goal-setting process ended at this point. But in order to achieve the goals and to sustain interest in the Goals process, twelve Goals Achievement Committees were organized. Each of these committees was charged with following the progress of goal fulfillment within one of the twelve general issue areas. Each committee was to encourage the relevant public and private agencies to undertake their particular responsibilities in implementing the specific goals; it was also to enlist and encourage public support of measures taken toward goal fulfillment. Yet there was no formal link between the Achievement Committees and the various agencies; the connections were strictly informal. The prestige of the Goals program together with the status and influence of the Achievement Committee chairmen acted to create strong bonds. In many cases, this bond proved ample.

The annual reports issued by the Achievement Committees provided additional incentives for cooperation between the Committees and the agencies. These reports helped to sustain community support for the Goals program by detailing the progress made toward achieving each goal. Table 3 shows the relative progress reported by the Committees in 1970 and in 1972.

In December 1972 the Goals for Dallas program was seven years old. By that time nearly 70 percent of the original goals had

TABLE 3. **Progress Toward Achieving Goals, 1970 and 1972**[36]

	1970	1972
Goals Achieved	—	27%
Substantial Progress	44%	43%
Moderate Progress	50%	28%
No Progress	6%	2%

been achieved or were well on their way toward being fulfilled; more than one hundred thousand people had participated in the program. The Goals process had involved a complex interaction of planning committees, conferences, and neighborhood meetings. Figure 1 gives a summary of the first seven years.

Early in 1973 the Planning Committee commissioned a group of more than twenty persons to evaluate the goals process and to consider its future. This group's report, completed in April, concluded that the Goals program should be continued but that it could benefit from increased involvement of media and action agency heads, broader-based community participation, more detailed and intensive monitoring of goal implementation, and greater attention to the relation between the priorities of the goals and the available information bearing on the goals.

These recommendations were not acted upon immediately. In fact, Goals for Dallas languished visibly. The next round did not really get underway until late in 1975. Under a restructured Goals for Dallas corporation, headed by a thirty-five-member Board of Trustees, a new set of task forces set out to identify the issues facing Dallas in the years ahead. Beginning in January 1976, sixteen task forces, consisting of approximately thirty people each (including college students), tackled the following sixteen issue areas: 1) citizen involvement, 2) continuing education, 3) cultural activities, 4) design of the city, 5) economy, 6) elementary and secondary education, 7) energy, 8) environment, 9) government, 10) health, 11) higher education, 12) public safety, 13) quality of the citizenry, 14) recreation and leisure time, 15) social services, and 16) transportation. In all, the task forces identified over 150 separate issues.

These issues formed the agenda for a discussion in mid-June of the problems facing the city. One hundred citizens met at Lake Texoma and proposed 170 new goals. To the original agenda they added seventeen new concerns and one major issue area—housing. A questionnaire provided citizens from all walks of life the opportunity to comment on the proposed goals in September and October 1976. The questionnaires were augmented by comments gathered at fourteen neighborhood meetings held in November and early December. On December 11 an all-day conference was held to bring together delegates from the neighborhoods, local high schools, area colleges, and various community organizations. At

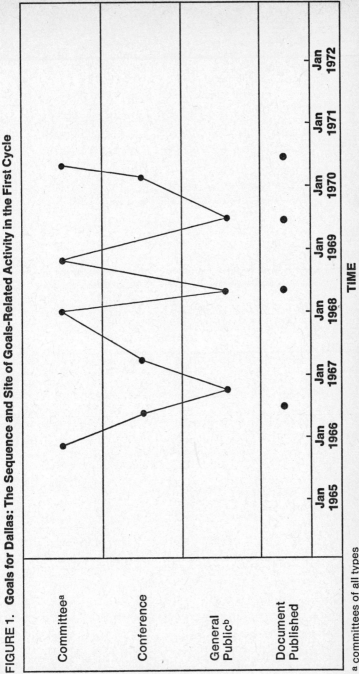

FIGURE 1. Goals for Dallas: The Sequence and Site of Goals-Related Activity in the First Cycle

a committees of all types
b mass meetings and questionnaires

year's end, the Goals for Dallas program was once again well underway. The second cycle had begun.

GOALS FOR DALLAS: AN EVALUATION
OF RESULTS

The Goals for Dallas program is now over a decade old. Since its
inception, an estimated one hundred thousand people have been
involved with some aspect of it.[37] For this reason alone, it might
appear that the Goals program has been an enormous success.
However, the program deserves a more thorough evaluation. David
Baker has argued that the experiences of goals groups can be considered in terms of four broad purposes that underlie their development.* He identifies these purposes as follows:

1.   Educating participants, the public, and policy-makers about
     the future-planning and goal-setting process and receiving
     citizen feedback;
2.   Generating new information for future-oriented decision-
     making;
3.   Designing alternative futures; and
4.   Developing and communicating consensus recommendations
     to policy-makers.

This section examines the Goals for Dallas experience in terms of
these general purposes.

1. EDUCATIONAL OBJECTIVES

The Goals program appears to have had an educational effect on
many of the task-force participants. One of the program's early
second-cycle projects was a questionnaire which asked if individual
participants in the several task forces had learned more about their
community, had changed their attitudes about community institutions, or had changed their views about other citizens as a result

* Editor's note: For an elaboration of this argument see Chapter 1 of this
volume.

of their experience. Hundreds of participants were polled on a range of issues. The results suggest that the Goals process had resulted in an "increase in knowledge" but had left attitudes unchanged. This conclusion is based on the decrease in the number of "no opinion" or "don't know" responses to the questionnaire.[38] According to this evidence, the greatest increases in knowledge occurred in areas such as culture, the economy, the environment, health, government, leisure, and social services.

Thus it appears that the participants of the task forces benefited from their involvement in the Goals process. However, their roles called for sustained involvement and allowed for considerable personal impact. (Figure 1 shows the continuing importance of such committees.) But what of the general public? Did the Goals program educate individual citizens?

There is no reliable information gauging the city-wide effects of the Goals for Dallas program. The anecdotal data on the subject are often at odds. For example, Bryghte Godbold has argued that the program has provided an educational process for the community. Dallas City Manager George Schrader "felt that the program also had a positive effect on the attitude of citizens toward the city. This was a result of the process itself—having extensive citizen participation in setting goals for the community."[39] But community leaders do not necessarily share this view. Rabbi Olan, a long-time leader in the community, does not believe that most citizens took the efforts seriously or that the program had much educational impact. He felt that apathy was pervasive and that the Goals program was largely a symbolic exercise, save for those who were personally involved.

But how many—and what types of people—were actively involved? Each of the large conferences explicitly included a range of interests and representatives from all parts of the community. Yet it appears that there was not really a diversity of participants. The results of the 1976 questionnaire of task-force members suggest that the typical participant may be described in the following way: white, married, Protestant, male, age forty-five, having a postgraduate degree, owning a home in North Dallas (the most affluent part of the city), working in the private sector of the economy, having a middle-management position within the city of Dallas and an annual *family* income in excess of $30,000.[40] In short, the task-force participants—who were the ones who felt that they had gained in knowledge about the issues—shared a generally high socio-economic status within the commuunity.

The poor, the minorities, and the disadvantaged were only marginally represented in the process. However, the leaders of the program are aware of this problem and have taken steps to increase the participation of these groups. According to Dr. Godbold, "There has always been a problem with a lack of participation from the poor. They are interested in immediate problems, such as food and jobs. Yet during the second cycle there has been more diversity in participation, minorities, and youth."[41]*

A major objective of the Goals for Dallas program has been the education of local policy-makers about planning and goal-setting in the community. The program itself is a private organization; its funding is from private sources and most of the participants from the private sector. Nonetheless the relation between the Goals program and local government agencies has been close. Erik Jonsson's role as founder and nurturer of the Goals program has ensured that its proposals receive a fair hearing in governmental circles. As mayor for nearly eight years, he provided a vital link between the public and private sectors.

The current Board members of the Goals for Dallas organization include Jonsson and George Schrader, the current city manager. The presence of such officials does not ensure that the recommendations of the Goals program will be turned into public policy. However, according to Dr. Godbold, their participation and support is a necessary precondition for implementation of the individual goals. City officials have taken a generally favorable attitude toward the Goals program: "According to the Assistant City Planner, Goals for Dallas has been an important tool in helping the Planning Department to carry out its responsibilities. First, the planners were more aware of the desires and priorities of the

---

* Editor's note: The neglect by Goals of Dallas of the interests of the black community led to a realization on the part of some black leaders in the city that they would have to assert themselves. They therefore established the Goals for Black Dallas Program, whose purpose is to formulate specific goals for the black community. Eddie Bernice Johnson, a state representative and leader of the Goals for Black Dallas, said that Goals for Black Dallas is not in conflict with the original Goals program, which has—in its second round—included black activists who have succeeded in bringing some of the concerns of the Goals for Black Dallas into the original Goals program.

citizens, and second, City Council granted the department more money to work toward the achievement of the goals."[42] George Schrader attributes an even greater role to the Goals program; according to him, the "Goals for Dallas was to some degree responsible for the more sophisticated city budget, the better information system, and the overall improved management system. The city . . . was forced to make these improvements in order to respond to the goals set by the citizens."[43]

2. INFORMATIONAL OBJECTIVES

The Goals program has generated much new information. This information takes many forms. For policy-makers, the program provides signals about the preferences of different parts of the community. Perhaps even more importantly, the Goals process reflects the interests of the leadership group.

But the Goals program has resulted in yet another kind of information. Very early in the first cycle, it was recognized that "accurate data about the resources available to achieve the Goals" were necessary.[44] Indeed, one of the specific goals evolved during the first cycle read as follows:[45]

Develop a comprehensive system of research in the field of regional science embracing economics and related sciences. Research should build upon existing private and public facilities, with the development of new ones as required to assure continued evaluation of the short- and long-term economic potentials and problems of the city and region.

To achieve this goal, the Goals organization applied for and received a grant from the Ford Foundation to assemble a data base on the community and to develop a projection system. The Institute of Urban Studies at Southern Methodist University together with the National Planning Association (NPA) produced the *Dallas Economic Potential Handbook.*

The *Handbook* met two basic objectives. First, it designed an indicator system to identify the kinds of social, economic, and demographic data necessary to the goals-planning process. The indicator system gathered and compiled information on six major factors: population characteristics, work-force characteristics, wealth and investment characteristics, attitudes, public sector resources, and economic activity characteristics. The second objectives met by the *Handbook* was developing projection techniques. Using historical data and a sophisticated methodology, NPA made projections for several socio-economic indicators through the years 1975 and 1980.

3. ALTERNATIVE FUTURES

The Goals process is predicated on the notion that citizens share enough common ideals and aspirations to create an atmosphere in which these ideals can be forged into a common vision of the future. In a sense, the Goals is meant to design a future.

But the program does not address the fact that there are many futures. Unlike other anticipatory democracy programs, Goals for Dallas did not generate alternative scenarios. The proceedings of conferences and task forces within the Goals process were marked by the discussion of alternative plans for countering specific problems. But the purpose of these discussions was to evolve a single objective or a rather specific set of steps that might lead to achieving an objective.

As a result, the Goals program has a particular legacy. Once it was decided that a set of goals was to be determined and that they were to be implemented in a certain fashion, the Goals organization foreclosed the possibility that other views of the future of the city could be explored under its aegis. Justifiably, the organization fell prey to charges that it was serving one set of community interests over others. The inclusion of greater numbers of community meetings or citizen conferences in the process could not resolve this dilemma, although it did blunt the criticism. The numerous neighborhood meetings in the fall of 1969, together with the conference held in May 1970, theoretically afforded various interests another opportunity to impact upon the Goals process. However, these meetings were based on the same implicit assumption as the initial goal-setting, namely, that the various interests did not conflict in so fundamental a way as to preclude arriving at a single set of common goals and implementing tactics. For the poor or otherwise disadvantaged in Dallas, this assumption simply did not hold true.

This is a dilemma from which the Goals program cannot escape. Although it has no way of implementing its aims, the Goals organization has an inherently dynamic design. Rather than offering alternatives or constructing alternative futures to be evaluated by the public officials or citizens in the community, the Goals program acts as an advocate for a narrow range of insufficiently explored alternatives. It is constructed to involve the leadership of the community, public and private, in a process where mutual concessions can be extracted and decisions jointly made. This enables the Goals organization to take resolute stands on pressing community problems and to make recommendations with high probabilities of being implemented. On the other hand, it means that those least able to voice their interests in the Goals process are likely to be neglected; they are also the ones least likely to share in the "common" vision to emerge from the process. In the first cycle, for example, three of the twelve general goals were directly concerned with education. Yet none of the specific goals were designed to meet the problems of school desegregation and educational equality. Similarly, the first round did not address itself at all to housing—a problem of great concern to the poor. As early as 1968 Dr. Sanford Kravitz of Brandeis University criticized the program for devoting "insufficient attention to the plight of the poor."[46]

In the second cycle of the Goals process, some efforts have been made to increase participation and to incorporate problems of the disadvantaged and minorities (housing was added to the list of issue areas). According to Dr. Godbold,[47]

In 1976 the Goals are more comprehensive and specific and deal squarely with problems such as desegregation. We are more system-oriented and emphasize problem interdependence. We are placing more concern on the DBD [Downtown Business District]. We have more diversity in participation, particularly minorities and youth. In 1966 the Goals for Dallas was predominantly composed of "middle-class" people and interests. There was a more prevalent feeling that the Goals for Dallas was a facade for special interests.

However, it is still too early to tell whether such efforts will prove meaningful. In any event, the process itself retains its basic features in that it depends on consensus and communication around specific goals without a broad scanning of the range of alternative futures for the city. The Goals program will be able to overcome the suspicions of those parts of the community which it has generally ignored only to the degree that it broadens its concerns and allows for greater participation at all stages of the process. It will become necessary to accept the fact that decisions about the future will have to be based on a wide range of alternatives.

4. CONSENSUS AND COMMUNICATION OBJECTIVES

The Goals for Dallas Program has placed considerable importance on developing consensus among the participants and in the community on the aims of the city. According to Dr. Godbold, "The Goals are blueprints and promote understanding of each other and our diverse views."[48] Nonetheless there has also been an explicit realization within the Goals leadership that "no one involved agrees on all the goals." Rather, the people involved in an active way developed a respect for each other. The experience promoted an attitude which Dr. Godbold has typified as "you're a good guy, I'm a good guy . . . Let's cooperate."[49] For the participants, the many hours of working together produced an "alumni feeling."[50] Philosophical differences—to the extent that there were any—are likely to remain, but participants continued to communicate and work with one another long after their stint in the Goals process was over.

While the Goals process depended on consensus in order to go about the business of establishing goals and steps by which to fulfill them, it may be that the communication fostered in reaching these ends has been the most important by-product of the enterprise. Thinking back to Rabbi Olan's comments in *Fortune,* this observation takes on new meaning. He, along with Willis Tate, suggested "there just isn't free flow of ideas";[51] he has also argued that "everything that happens in Dallas will happen regardless of the Goals for Dallas."[52] Such comments ignore the fact that the Goals program introduced a new dynamic into city leadership and that the program played a crucial role in promoting communication among community leaders.

The Goals program formed an excellent vehicle for introducing new ideas and new personnel into the city's governing circles in the early 1960s, when the leadership structure had become rigid and self-contained. The Goals format demanded that a diversity of leaders participate in the process. Of course, this involved the entrenched business elite of the city, but it also meant that other community leaders were included, allowing individuals who had been at the periphery of local decision-making entry into Dallas's governing circles. The Goals for Dallas program opened new avenues for many community leaders and fostered the exposure of new ideas.

Although there is no direct evidence to substantiate the effects of the Goals program, Dallas made a remarkable comeback from the doldrums noted in *Fortune* in 1964. Economically, the city leaped ahead; endowed with resources flowing to cities in the "Sunbelt," Dallas made real many aspects of the vision imparted to the Goals program by Erik Jonsson and others. The Dallas–Ft. Worth airport is but the most visible manifestation of this effort. Politically, the Charter Citizens Association diversified its membership and adapted to changing circumstances sufficiently to sponsor and elect a black council member in 1969.

The changes that have taken place in Dallas, however, are not solely attributable to the Goals program. In the last ten years, Dallas has changed politically. In the years since Erik Jonsson has left office, the political control of the CCA has declined. This is due, in part, to a court-ordered shift in the structure of elections, from at-large elections to single-member districts. Under the single-member district plan, minorities, residentially concentrated, have greatly increased their political clout. But there are other manifestations of the decline of CCA power. The mayor's office slipped from the control of the CCA after 1971. A coalition led by local environmentalists defeated one of the favorite projects of the CCA leadership and a significant component of the Goals program, the canalization of the Trinity River. Commenting on the situation, the new mayor Robert Folsom had this to say:[53]

In January [1975] a group of us went to Acapulco to talk about the way the city was going. None of the men were involved in politics. We were concerned because the business community was losing interest in trying to guide the city. Business leaders in the past took an interest in the city; that's the reason we have such a fine town. But we saw the mayor and city council positions becoming political stepping stones for other jobs instead of being looked on as civic responsibilities.

WAS GOALS FOR DALLAS GOOD FOR DALLAS?

Rabbi Olan believes the Goals program has been merely symbolic. But the symbolic aspect of the program has had very real benefits for many in the community, not just—although perhaps primarily —for the leadership group. The prestige and import of the program was actively promoted by its leadership. Over time, participation in the program, the goals themselves, and implementation procedures sanctioned by the Goals process acquired community consequence. Special interest groups and citizens in the community cited the Goals to further their own concerns. As Dr. Godbold explained, the Goals are used as rallying points by various groups in presentations to the city council and elsewhere. For example, community groups pressing for more "open space" used the Goals effectively to support their case throughout the city. "The Goals take on the effect of a charter for the City. Special interests use the Goals as leverage."[54]

Both Dr. Godbold and George Schrader have cited the Goals program as influential in the success of large bond referenda in 1967 and 1972. According to one source,[55]

Schrader felt that the citizens had agreed to items in that vote that they would not have agreed to without the increased awareness of the needs of the city resulting from Goals for Dallas. Several of the programs passed in the bond issue were long term and very future-oriented, e.g., the redevelopment of the core area of the city. Goals for Dallas, he said, seemed to have given the citizens more confidence in their city at a time when confidence in cities generally was at a very low point.

The city also profited from the future orientation of the Goals program and the leadership of Erik Jonsson. Planning of all sorts, neighborhood as well as regional, has been initiated from the Dallas metropolitan area. The budgeting procedures and the information-acquisition facilities of the city have increased significantly.

Numerous other goals have been achieved. In addition to the Dallas–Ft. Worth airport, the Dallas floodway system is nearly completed; a comprehensive noise-control ordinance was developed and enacted in 1971; the amount of green space in the city has been greatly increased; the Dallas Community College program has been expanded greatly; the public library system has been improved. The list of goals achieved is long.

However, it is difficult to credit the Goals organization and process directly for the many achievements. Because the Goals program has no implementation authority, Erik Jonsson offered the following caution:[56]

We make no outlandish claims about the program. Surely, good things, important to Dallas, would have been achieved without Goals for Dallas. Neither do we suggest that as a result of the program all our problems are being completely, perfectly, and permanently solved. We did not expect all our urban ills to yield to instant solution.

GOALS FOR DALLAS: A SUMMARY COMMENTARY

The Goals for Dallas program has been imitated in many cities throughout the United States. Numerous cities in Texas—Corpus Christi and Austin, for example—have profited directly from the Goals experience and leadership. In 1973, Goals for Corpus Christi was founded at a luncheon of thirty-nine community leaders addressed by Dr. Godbold.[57]

The Goals organization has long been aware of the example it has provided for other American cities. Its advice to other municipalities interested in goal-setting stresses the need for 1) strong, committed leadership; 2) a small, full-time staff; 3) adequate, independent funding; 4) wide-scale support from the major community institutions and groups; 5) citizen involvement and feedback throughout the process; 6) freedom from dominance by any single community interest. This is, of course, the rhetoric of the ideal. The program has been both more and less than it set out to be.

In Dallas the Goals program provided a useful mechanism by which to forge a purposeful consensus among the leadership groups within the city. It helped revitalize the leadership and acted to invigorate the community in the wake of the Kennedy assassination. It involved large numbers of citizens in thinking about Dallas's future, and it helped elevate planning as an idea of importance on the local policy agenda.

Many of the positive aspects of the Goals program can be directly linked to its inherently dynamic design. It was designed not only to formulate goals but to press for their implementation. This format had its own logic. It required the participants in the goal-setting process to identify a single future for the city and then to represent this view to the agencies that were to act on this vision. This single-mindedness has had some genuine benefits. First, it required different elements of the leadership to work together, to share ideas, and to consider many of the city's problems. Second, it pulled many individuals into the goal-setting process who otherwise would have been neglected (even if it ignored some others). Third, it produced an extensive list of projects that the community might usefully pursue.

It is clear that Goals for Dallas was responsible for some major changes in the community. Even though many of the changes might have been undertaken without the program, there is general agreement that the program was helpful, and in some cases crucial, in achieving them. It is in any case questionable whether the same amount of change could have been achieved as quickly without the Goals program.

The program's successes should not blind us to its considerable shortcomings. There are two major failings of Goals for Dallas. The two are intimately related; the first concerns the design of the program while the second is related to the specific nature of the Dallas leadership at the time of the implementation of the program.

Goals for Dallas was designed to forge a single vision of the city's future. Its attempts to involve the citizenry through neighborhood meetings, questionnaires, and conferences were intended, in part, to help frame this vision. The Goals program did not create a set of alternative futures for the city. Instead, it worked from the presumption that conflicting community interests could be resolved and a common purpose found through the Goals process. However, this has not been the case. The first cycle of the Goals program neglected some of the city's most pressing social problems such as housing for the poor and integration of the city. While the second round has begun to remedy these specific deficiencies, the general problem remains. In striving to formulate a single set of goals from the very outset of the process, the aspirations of certain community groups were ignored and policy options were prematurely foreclosed. In neglecting the formulation of alternative futures, the

Goals process prematurely limited its ability to anticipate diverse needs and problems.

The Goals program never truly represented the pluralistic clash of diverse community interests. From the outset, Goals for Dallas was a project of the entrenched leadership and the product of the growing inability of that leadership to be effective. Its goals mirrored the implicit vision of the future held by the business leaders. The Goals process acted to consolidate elements of the community's leadership which had begun to diversify in the early 1960s. It also served as a forum in which a certain vision of the future—one already held by business leaders—might be legitimized through citizen participation.

The point is not that the Dallas Citizens Council or the Charter Citizens Association controlled the Goals process; they did not. At least, the control was not pervasive. Each goal or implementation tactic was not the conscious product of some preconceived plan. But the results of the process, the direction provided by the Goals projects, serve the established leadership (somewhat broadened as a result of the Goals process and other political changes) of the city. The Goals process neglected social issues in favor of capital-intensive projects and data gathering; it has served best those already best served by society.

How then is Goals for Dallas to be judged? It should be recognized as an effective leadership device, albeit one broadly framed. It has cataloged the aspirations and dreams of many within the Dallas community. Finally, it has helped arm the city for its rendezvous with the future by designing tools of anticipation and a structure that increases the leadership's sensitivity. But it is an imperfect instrument at best. As an experiment in anticipatory democracy it has helped to broaden the concern for the future among the citizenry, but it falls short on the range of the future it anticipated and the depth of democratic participation it encouraged.

CHAPTER FOUR

Alternatives for Washington

BY ROBERT L. STILGER

In 1974 Governor Evans initiated Alternatives for Washington with the statement that

> Our future need be imposed neither by the personal interests of an elite nor the impersonal force of history. It can be determined by all of the people of the state if they are willing to . . . devote the effort to the task. . . . I believe the citizens of this state can, in an orderly and rational manner, determine their future and assure such a privilege will also be available to generations yet to come.[1]

The Alternatives program, one of the most extensive of anticipatory democracy experiments, was designed to allow as many citizens as possible to examine the problems facing the state and to determine the preferred alternative futures state policy. It developed a unique combination of task forces: local meetings, random pollings, and media presentations. Under Governor Evans the program went through two phases: the first in 1974–75, which defined alternative futures and preferred policies within those futures, and the second in 1976, which examined the costs, benefits, and trade-offs among the policies chosen in the first phase. This article will review each of these stages and evaluate the success of the program.

PHASE I—1974: DEVELOPING THE ALTERNATIVES

The components of Phase I of the Alternatives program included:

1. The Statewide Task Force. The governor's office received more than four thousand names in response to a request for nominations to a statewide task force to oversee and develop the AFW program. A group of approximately one hundred fifty people was selected from this nomination list. Selection procedures paid attention to socio-economic status, geographic distribution, race, profession, and other criteria in an attempt (not completely successful) to form a "representative" task force. The task force met for four three-day seminars to examine the range of options for future growth and development in Washington State and to identify a range of desirable alternatives.

2. The Delphi Questionnaire. Nearly twenty-five hundred additional citizens were involved in a three-part mail questionnaire process. In the questionnaires, people were asked to consider trends within and outside of the state in terms of their past, present, and future effects on Washington. The statewide task force used information from this questionnaire process during its deliberations on the future.

The Delphi process arrived at a consensus conclusion that there would be "considerable population growth, deterioration in the quality of life, increased urban sprawl with loss of prime resource land, migration pressure, increase in national and world demands for Washington's food, power and forest products, and continuing trouble in the national economic system." Respondents identified Washington's primary problems as "tax base inequity, environmental deterioration, careless use of land, population influx, energy shortage, unemployment, inflation, poverty, crime, racial discrimination, and lack of government credibility."[2]

3. Area-Wide Conferences. In the summer of 1974 ten area-wide meetings were held throughout the state. Each meeting involved 150 to 200 participants who were specially invited by the governor. Their task was to examine the alternatives being developed by the state task force, to identify areas of agreement and disagreement, and to add local perspectives to statewide policy proposals.

4. Media Education. As the work of the task force progressed, a series of television programs was produced on the different alternatives being considered for Washington's future. Some of these programs featured a telephone "call-in" that allowed people throughout the state to call and give their ideas and opinions to television panelists. The final television program reviewed the state's growth and policy options covered in earlier programs and asked viewers to express their preferences on the statewide questionnaire.

5. *Statewide Questionnaire.* A lengthy questionnaire was published in most of the major newspapers in the state. The questionnaire asked for people's responses to a number of the ideas that the program developed, including their preferred future for the state as well as their preferences for specific policies. The task force had developed eleven futures, each with a dominant theme. Over twenty-six thousand preferences were tabulated from the newspaper survey.

Of these, 23 percent favored "Agricultural Washington," emphasizing increased agriculture, aquaculture and forest management. Twenty percent favored "Balanced Washington" combining agricultural expansion and international trade, 15 percent chose "Northwest Lifestyle" highlighting quality of life and environmental concepts. Least selected choices—getting 2 and 3 percent of the vote—were "Urban Washington" which placed priority on more liveable cities and "Post Industrial Washington," which pictured a technological world of service and communications industries. The remaining 28 percent of the choices were spread among six other suggested futures.[3]

6. *Survey Samples.* Finally, random sample telephone and mail surveys were conducted which asked for people's responses to many of the topics covered in the statewide questionnaire. Nearly four thousand people responded to these surveys from an initial survey group of six thousand.

Chart 1 graphically portrays the opportunities for direct citizen involvement and general public input. The responses of the participants using the different modes of involvement were remarkably similar despite the higher levels of education and income of task-force and area-wide conference participants. The composite picture of the Washington its citizens preferred include:

Moderate economic growth which places emphasis on expansion of agricultural, aquacultural and forest industries, while prompting new development of light manufacturing, science and technology, information and other service industries. Economic growth should not attract undue numbers of individuals from outside the state;

Careful attention to the size and distribution of the state's population, emphasizing population growth around smaller towns and cities and more even distributions of population throughout the state. Programs which stimulate economic growth in desired population growth areas and careful planning of public works projects;

Emphasis on people as Washington's most valuable resource. Human service programs, which provide access to employment opportunities, deter crime, foster adequate health care and housing, improve educational opportunities and finance schools adequately and equitably;

Streamlining operation of government at all levels so that it is more responsive to the public and more efficient;

Development of statewide plans for energy, land use, and transportation that complement growth and development goals—plans which emphasize coordination of state and local needs;

Protection of the natural resources which are not only the basis for the state's economy but for its quality of life as well. Use of renewable and nonrenewable resources must be managed. Sensitivity in use of resources—and recycling of used materials—is essential for the state's future.

These short summaries do not do justice to the depth of information that the state had gathered through the Alternatives for Washington program. For the first time in its history the state had a broad sense of public opinion regarding its future as well as a number of specific policy proposals. The program had legitimized the idea that the state had alternatives and that people ought to be active in charting its growth and development.

Governor Evans wanted to get some specific AFW proposals through the 1975 legislature, but he was unsuccessful. What proved more successful was a meeting of the AFW task force with key agency people. In fact, it was through this connection that AFW probably had its most direct impact on state government.

DIRECT CITIZEN PARTICIPATION
IN AFW PROGRAM—9,000 PEOPLE

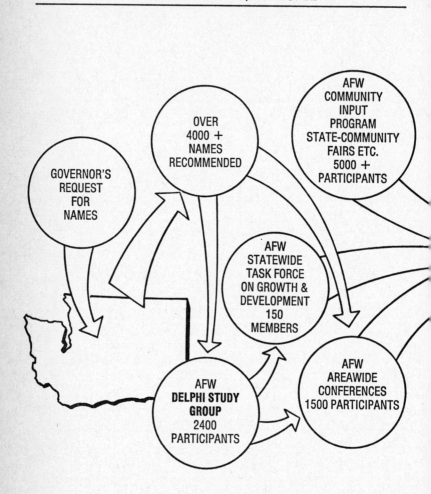

Source: "Alternatives for Washington—Survey Results and Policy Recommendations," January 1975, State Planning Division, Olympia, Washington

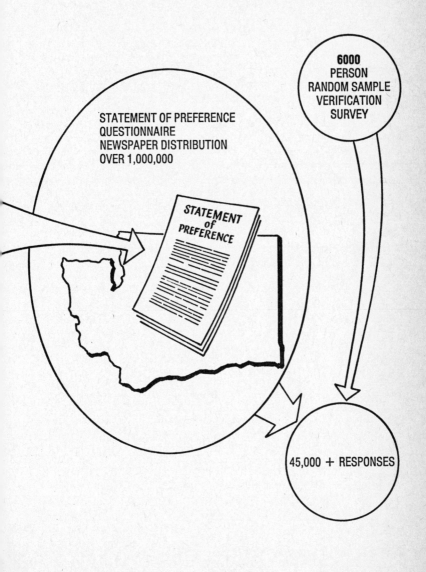

After the people expressed their opinions, Phase II of AFW tackled the more inherently difficult problem of implementation.

Governor Evans remarked about one major implementation difficulty, money: "It is very easy to select a rather utopian future, to list all the goals we would like to see achieved. It is quite another to recognize the costs of getting to those goals." He also realized that ". . . in the course of Phase Two we may find that there are some changing opinions of people, a recognition that if the cost is too high or the policy too difficult, they may choose to modify or change the ultimate goals they seek."[4]

The second phase also began to deal with the inherent contradictions between the different statewide goals that were expressed, the different choices for different geographical areas, and, again, the costs of achieving the goals.

Citizen choices called for moderate economic growth, environmental planning, and careful population distribution. Those goals were at odds with the desire to streamline and limit government since all three were perceived to require substantial government. Also, the desire to place strict controls on natural resource use and environmental pollution was, at times, at odds with the desire to stimulate growth of Washington's three main industries—agriculture, aerospace, and forestry. In addition, participants in the AFW program, on the whole, favored population increases around small towns and cities rather than in urban areas, although people living in those small towns weren't sure that was what they wanted. Finally, there was significant agreement on the need for a coordinated state land-use plan, but local areas weren't at all sure that they wanted the state interfering with their planning.

To begin the second phase, seven cost/benefit study teams were organized: 1) economic growth and population settlement, 2) environmental protection and land use, 3) natural resources and energy, 4) transportation and communications, 5) human development, 6) education and training, and 7) government. Teams included a cross section of technicians in the field, concerned citizens, members of the AFW statewide task force, and members of the legislature. Meeting regularly over several weeks, the economic growth teams developed policies based on the findings of Phase I. The other cost/benefit teams then used these policies as background information as they prepared their AFW-based policies and costs. The teams then worked to draft and redraft a report that summarized state goals within their study area, compared those goals to current developments in the state, formulated the objectives necessary to reach AFW goals, and indicated the social and dollar costs of implementing the proposed objectives.

There were still conflicts between the goals and objectives developed for different subject areas, but those conflicts were becoming more manageable; the state had begun to move toward concrete proposals formulated by citizens and based on citizen preferences. This work, which went on in the winter and spring of 1976, put the state in a position that allowed it to say to citizens, "This is what you said you wanted in 1974; here are some ways of meeting those goals; these are the costs involved."

Once the cost/benefit studies and proposals had been prepared, another round of citizen participation was launched in the summer and fall of 1976. The state produced audio-visual and printed materials summarizing the work of the cost/benefit study teams, and provided small grants to local communities for Town Hall Meetings on the AFW program. In September and October 1976 twenty-two Town Hall Meetings took place in different communities throughout the state. Participation in these meetings was open to the general public and more than 1500 people participated. Generally, the format of the meetings was one that encouraged people to compare goals and objectives developed by the cost/benefit study teams with local problems and to assess whether or not those statewide directions would help them resolve local problems.

A late 1976 publication, *An Agenda for the Future,* summarized the results of Phase II. This is the final report from the AFW program. In 1976 Governor Evans did not run for a fourth term as governor of Washington, and Dr. Dixie Lee Ray was elected. With different priorities on her agenda, she discontinued the program.

EVALUATION OF THE AFW PROGRAM

AFW created a vehicle for getting the whole state involved in planning a strategy for survival and, as such, was an *ipso facto* success.

Its limitations were both procedural and substantive.

Phase 1 of the process was structured in such a way that the choices presented to Washington residents by the statewide questionnaire were inconsistent and perhaps contradictory. Sorting out these inconsistencies into a realistic cost/benefit program that could be legislated into law was difficult indeed. Asking people to participate in a program that concludes without time schedules, clear objectives, and clear standards of accountability can leave them frustrated. This approach, however, was intended to give Washingtonians free reign in their first attempt at future planning. They were not, after all, experts with a honed sense of the practical and the precise.

Another problem that created tension throughout the program was the split between the governor and the legislature. The governor initiated the program, but the legislature practically killed it with indifference and even open hostility. The legislature refused to act on Evans's proposals that came out of the AFW in the first phase. It turned down, for example, a proposal for a Department of Transportation. The legislature felt an inherent hostility to an executive branch of government playing listening post to "grass-roots." After all, what is representation about? This breach between executive and legislative, exacerbated by peculiar tensions between this governor and this legislature in this time and place, does provoke larger questions on the relationship between existing political structures and this new wave of enthusiastic, but not permanently structured, participation.

Another problem was that the logistics in organizing such a major multilevel program were almost overwhelming. Activities had to be scheduled, meeting places arranged, printing deadlines met, television programs produced, reviewed, and broadcast. In addition, the staff was not only working with a program that was new to them, they were working with a program model or type that was new to the nation. Citizens, on the other hand, occasionally felt that the staff was providing too rigid a structure and that they, as citizens, ought to have been more integrally involved in the design and scheduling of activities. There was sometimes a feeling that the staff direction imposed a "hidden agenda" on the program and that the program was being steered in directions different than those that might be in the citizens' best interests.

When Phase II got off the ground in early 1976, it faced several important problems of its own. First, it was likely that Governor Evans would not run again for office; without the governor as its "mentor," the program needed to establish a new, wider credibility if it was to continue in the next administration. Also some of the program's momentum was lost because most people within the state had not heard anything about the AFW program in more than a year. This left the program with one year to complete its task of having citizens directly involved in formulating policy.

While the cost/benefit study teams worked reasonably well, the fall 1976 Town Hall Meetings program was a mixed success. The state had told organizations and groups in communities throughout the state that if they were interested in developing a local program that would help citizens in their area assess Alternatives for Washington, the state would cover their initial expenses. Twenty-two local planning groups came into existence—usually coalitions of organizations like the League of Women Voters, American Association of University Women, chambers of commerce—to plan, develop, and implement a program in their area. The state provided materials, technical assistance, and a communication/information link between separate programs. Newspapers and electronic media supported the program because releases were locally originated rather than coming from the capitol. People found out about the meetings and participated because local citizens knew how to get their friends and neighbors to participate. Meeting organizers were proud of their efforts because it was their program.

However, there were still problems. First, because funds terminated September 30, 1976, and because organizational work didn't begin until summer, most of the meeting had to be held in the month of September. Next, people continually wanted to know where their ideas were going, and they had to be told that the future of the program was entirely uncertain. Finally, the mini-grants primarily financed a single meeting and gave no funds for local follow-up work that could have led to the development of a community base for implementing the program's recommendations.

By the time Phase II was completed, the Evans Administration had learned a great deal about how to do effective citizen participation work on a statewide level. Had Phase II occurred near the beginning of Evans's term as governor rather than at its conclusion, and if it had won support from the legislature, the program might have produced the foundation for a viable, continuing program of communication between citizens and state government.

Although there has been no serious evaluation of AFW, some

lessons are written too large to avoid for any large political body interested in the same kind of anticipatory democracy program.

First, if a main goal of the program is to have a legislative impact, the legislature must be involved in formulating the program. Until legislators recognize the need for additional information on their constituents' needs and perceptions in relation to the future of the state, those legislators will not use information produced by the program. Citizen participation works best when citizens and government alike recognize the importance of closer and more effective communication.

Next, it seems that there may be more value in a program that focuses more directly on the interrelationship between local and state needs and problems. Many people find it easier to talk about the future of their neighborhood or community or county than they do to talk about the future of the state. Local experiences are more tangible and provide a better basis for assessment. In a profound sense, citizen participation is really a community-building process. It is difficult if not impossible to build a statewide community before local communities are able to function better. This is not to say that a statewide program is undesirable; citizens need a more effective voice in directing the future of their state also.

Any new program ought to cooperate with other similar efforts. In Washington, for example, the State Humanities Commission funds public dialogues on the future; many cities have citizen participation programs to help guide local policy-making; and numerous federal and state agencies conduct such programs for input to specialized areas. These different efforts need to be brought together if citizens are not to be overloaded with too many requests for their participation.

What, then, is the final score on AFW? What was its value? John Osman of the Brookings Institution, one of the principal architects of the AFW program as well as several other A/D programs in recent years, gave the following evaluation:

The participants were an extraordinary assembly of the citizens of Washington, committed and concerned about the future of their state. They did a remarkable job of dealing with Washington's problems and formulating the policies which would manage those problems. In all of the programs in the past half dozen years none has had the substance and significance of Alternatives for Washington. AFW demonstrates that the American people have the capacity to participate in the development of policy whether at the local, state or national level.[5]

Osman is positive that the results of the AFW program were better than those of any other project.

On the future of the AFW, Osman feels that

Too many people were deeply committed to let it drop. It would be a tragedy for any politician to take over the office of governor in the state of Washington and ignore the great effort on the part of a significant portion of the state's citizens to invent the state's future.[6]

II
Anticipatory Democracy and Legislatures

Legislatures are the branches of governments most directly accountable to the people. Yet their very nature resists long-range thinking. As Congressman Charlie Rose (D.-N.C.), a leader in the movement for greater foresight in Congress, points out in Chapter 5, "Members of Congress seek quick-fix solutions to problems because short-term results are more likely to keep us in office than the early and costly attempts to anticipate emerging problems." Congressman Rose goes on in his article to describe the futurist network—the Congressional Clearinghouse on the Future —that he and other members have developed to encourage more effective citizen input and foresight in Congress.

Congress in recent years has shown increasing interest in more systematic concern for the future. One indication of this is the provision of the House Rules that explicitly requires committees to exercise foresight responsibility. This foresight provision calls for committees to monitor trends and conditions and to do futures research and forecasting to determine the need for new legislation and the long-term impacts of legislation under consideration.

Congress poses interesting problems for citizen input on long-range policy formulation. In Chapter 6, William Renfro, a lawyer and futures-research expert formerly with the Futures Group, a leading futures think-tank, and I review the opportunities for more effective citizen input to the members of Congress, to committees as they develop legislation, and to the budget process or any national planning procedures developed to provide a more coordinated direction for the nation.

CHAPTER FIVE

Building a Futures Network in Congress

BY CHARLIE ROSE

"A sense of the future is behind all good politics. Unless we have it, we can give nothing—either wise or decent to the world."

C. P. SNOW

The people of the United States are rapidly losing faith in the institution of Congress and in their elected representatives. Many of our citizens do not believe Congress can solve the problems facing our nation, and most doubt that congressional leaders can set goals for the future. Harris, Gallup, Cadell, and almost all other pollsters find repeated evidence that Americans distrust government and give Congress low marks for its competence and efficiency.

Unfortunately, for the most part the people are right. Congress as a representative body doesn't act, it reacts. Members of Congress respond to their constituents' wishes and whims. We seek quick-fix solutions to problems because short-term results are more likely to keep us in office than the early and costly attempts to anticipate emerging problems. But our constituents are growing suspicious and demanding more from us. Sensing that the quick-fix patchwork syndrome provides only temporary relief, our citizens are forcing us to begin considering the future and alternative courses our country might take. It is a hopeful movement, but a hesitant one because most politicians are caught and paralyzed by their own brand of future shock. In spite of our generalist stance and our intuitive political sense, our personal visions of the future are cluttered by transient constituencies, communications campaigns, increased legislative demands, contracted time constraints, and special interest pressures. "How can I cope with tomorrow when I hardly have time to glance at today?" a harried member of Congress might utter in desperation and fatigue. Yet the inability to cope with tomorrow means that much of our work is irrelevant or redundant.

In this context I think it's important to review some of the efforts being made to get Congress and its members to look ahead more effectively, particularly through the work of the Congressional Clearinghouse on the Future.

In an effort to overcome some of its institutional problems, the House of Representatives during the 93rd Congress created the House Select Committee on Committees. Chaired by Representative Richard Bolling (D-Mo.), the Committee recommended in House Resolution 988 a number of procedural reforms and a clarification of committee jurisdictions. While some aspects of House Resolution 988 were not passed, those parts that were passed included the first explicit statement that House committees must examine the future systematically. Prompted by then Representative John Culver (D-Iowa), this "foresight" provision added to the House Rules the requirement that each committee (other than the Budget and Appropriations Committees):

. . . shall review and study any conditions or circumstances which may indicate the necessity or desirability of enacting new or additional legislation within the jurisdiction of that committee (whether or not any bill or resolution has been introduced with respect thereto), and shall on a continuing basis undertake futures research and forecasting on matters within the jurisdiction of that committee.

Committees and subcommittees regularly hold oversight hearings to look back at how legislation has been implemented. The foresight provision mandates that committees and subcommittees also look ahead, to explore emerging issues and alternative approaches to legislation. This approach does much to reduce the crisis orientation so prevalent in Congress.

Several committees have begun to implement their foresight responsibility by sponsoring hearings that explore emerging trends in their area. Others have had briefings by futurists for their staff and members, and have sought information on the long-range implications of legislation under consideration. And because of constituent pressure and the circumstances we see around us, interest in these future-accountability activities is increasing.

Citizen groups from outside Congress have come to our assistance. In September 1975 the Committee on Anticipatory Democracy, in support of the foresight provision, held an all-day seminar called "Outsmarting Crisis: Futures Thinking in Congress." Enthusiastic staff and members of Congress attended and heard co-sponsors Senator John Culver (D-Iowa), former Representative John Heinz, III (R-Pa.), and myself urge more congressional interest in looking ahead and increased involvement of citizens in the policy-making processes of government.

Alvin Toffler, author of *Future Shock,* Ted Gordon, president of the Futures Group, and Hazel Henderson, co-director of the Princeton Center for Alternative Futures, invited us to seek a futures perspective in legislation and policy analysis, and to rethink the function of Congress in the future. Response to the session was good, and Senator Culver, Representative Heinz and I were encouraged to bring futurists to the Hill.

In February 1976 Senator Culver and I co-sponsored a dinner for members of the House and Senate and invited Alvin Toffler and Ted Gordon to speak again. Toffler and Gordon urged Congress to become more active in planning for the future, lest the future be colonized by corporations and other special interests with the capability to do futures research and long-range planning. They reminded us that the foresight provision could be the tool to move Congress into the future and get a better hold on the long-range problems facing the nation and the world.

As a result of this February session, other representatives and I decided to establish the Congressional Clearinghouse on the Future. In April 1976, an advisory committee was formed consisting of Representatives Berkley Bedell (D-Iowa), James Blanchard (D-Mich.), Lindy Boggs (D-La.), John Breckinridge (D-Ky.), Millicent Fenwick (R-N.J.), Tim Hall (D-Ill.), Jack Hightower (D-Tex.), John Jenrette (D-S.C.), Henry Reuss (D-Wis.), Gladys Spellman (D-Md.), and myself.

Early planning for the Clearinghouse led to the following conception of its tasks and constituencies:

The primary function of the Clearinghouse was to be dissemination of information, focused on two areas: future-oriented citizen participation projects and legislative foresight. The goals we established for the Clearinghouse were:

1. To assist members of Congress and their staffs in their efforts to become aware of the ways in which the future is affected by today's decisions.
2. To help House committee members implement Rule X, Section 2(b)(1), which states that:

    . . . All committees and subcommittees (except Budget

and Appropriations) shall on a continuing basis undertake futures research and forecasting on matters under the jurisdiction of that committee.

And to help committees of the Senate initiate similar foresight activities.

3. To provide members of Congress with information about trends which may shape the future.
4. To identify citizens interested in the future and to assist members of Congress as they make contact with these individuals.

We have established the following ongoing activities to meet our goals:

1. The publication of a monthly newsletter;
2. The seminar series, "Dialogues on America's Future";
3. Formation of a congressional talent bank;
4. The development of a trend evaluation and monitoring (TEAM) program;
5. Identification of citizen participation projects around the country that are working on the future.

The first issue of *What's Next* was published in April 1976. It now includes information on citizen-participation projects, futures-research efforts, relevant reports and seminar presentations, a Futures Index of the *Congressional Record,* and a book forecast, which lists and abstracts about-to-be-published materials on the future.

The seminar series, "Dialogues on America's Future," is designed to bring together, for the purpose of dialogue, members of Congress and noteworthy individuals who are thinking provocatively about the future.

Such well-known personalities as Alvin Toffler, author of *Future Shock,* Dr. Margaret Mead, and Dr. E. F. Schumacher, author of *Small is Beautiful: Economics as if People Mattered,* have addressed my colleagues in the House and Senate.

Herman Kahn, director of the Hudson Institute, Professor Jay Forrester of MIT, and Ted Gordon of the Futures Group have spoken to us about growth issues and the economic stresses which result. Barbara Marx Hubbard, chairperson of the Committee for the Future, Arthur C. Clarke, author of *2001: A Space Odyssey,* and Isaac Asimov, science fiction writer, have shared their visions about the outer reaches of our society. Hazel and Carter Henderson, directors of the Princeton Center for Alternative Futures, and Elizabeth and David Dodson Gray, directors of the Bolton Institute, have spoken about trends in institutions and in individual lives which may have important implications for our future survival.

Willis Harman of Stanford Research Institute and Dr. Elise Boulding of the University of Boulder, Colo., have shared their feelings about the human value changes which are emerging in this transition time. And finally, Buckminster Fuller and John Kenneth Galbraith have simply inspired us to think—more creatively, more intuitively, more humanely—about the future.

Foresight skills—either forecasting and futures-research techniques or more general planning expertise—are not common in Congress. Each year thousands of bills are introduced and hundreds receive serious consideration. Yet these bills are seldom approached with foresight—in this sense a systematic concern for the trends that may affect the legislation and the side effects of the legislation itself.

In order to meet this need for foresight, the Clearinghouse has developed a flexible network called the Congressional Talent Bank, composed of individuals around the country who are experts in futures-research techniques and/or the future of substantive areas, such as energy or the environment. Congressional staff are now encouraged to use the Talent Bank to identify persons who could answer foresight questions. The number of individuals participating grows as the Clearinghouse staff identifies individuals who are working in areas with an emphasis on the future.

Congressional committees and subcommittees can use this new Talent Bank in several ways:

1. Witness lists can be provided with an indication of each individual's background and area of expertise.
2. Quick, easy-to-read responses to specific inquiries can be delivered to staffs within a week or two after the initial request. Background information will be made available when needed.
3. Informal meetings with Talent Bank participants can be arranged for members of Congress and their staffs. These ses-

sions may span whatever length of time is deemed necessary by those participating.
4. With the help of other support agencies on the Hill, foresight hearings to explore emerging issues and alternative policy options can be arranged with the Talent Bank participants and the Clearinghouse.

The Talent Bank allows new voices to be heard in congressional policy-making, by providing members of Congress and committees with additional expertise on future impacts and alternatives to bills.

The Clearinghouse is also developing a trend evaluation and monitoring (TEAM) program. Congressional staff people who are directly involved in the TEAM project monitor over seventy periodicals and regularly analyze abstracts in these four categories: science and technology, social sciences, business and economics, and politics and government.

Quarterly briefings for members of Congress will alert us to those issues most likely to be in the headlines several years from now.

Emphasis on citizen participation has been strong. Members of Congress are interested in finding better ways to respond to their constituents' interest in policy and in finding methods to enable them to participate more fully in government.

Our efforts in this area have included the following:

1. Robert Theobald, author of *Beyond Despair,* met with members of Congress and staff to discuss ways citizens might be questioned about their wants for the future. He developed a questionnaire for constituents, which I used in my district. I introduced my constituents to the questionnaire by saying, "The solutions to the problems that face our country are not simple. Members of Congress can no longer pretend to act alone. I need your help."

And help they did. Over four thousand citizens from eastern North Carolina wrote extensive responses, explaining what they were doing or would like to do to improve the quality of life in their communities. By sketching their hopes and dreams, these citizens helped me know how I could help them realize their aspirations. And I also gained better understanding of the areas where they needed more information and education so that their input to me and my staff would be more useful and realistic.

2. Continuing our emphasis on dialogue between citizens and Representatives and our focus on citizen-participation projects, we invited Dr. Edward Lindaman, president of Whitworth College in Spokane, and John Osman of the Brookings Institute to lead a seminar on the Alternatives for Washington Program in Washington State.*

Dr. Lindaman chaired the program and Mr. Osman designed the process involving over sixty-five thousand citizens in Washington. They noted the importance of state planners of citizens' definitions of the future. Control of the program was not exclusively in the hands of citizens or government. Rather, the two worked in conjunction with each other. We heard about the pitfalls and the successes of this innovative program in anticipatory democracy. There were two especially important aspects of the program. First, the process was open-ended and the leaders were not to tell the people what to think or say. Second, experts were used to clarify citizen preferences after citizens had said what they wanted for the state.

3. A politician's sense of the future is often a reflection of what is important to constituents, and we have sought to inform members about citizen activities—particularly the goals, futures or tomorrow projects—in their own states. For example, the Clearinghouse developed a comprehensive list of persons and projects in North Carolina that focus in some way on the future and gave it to the North Carolina congressional delegation. We have furnished other congressional delegations with similar information so that they will have a better perspective of such activity statewide.

The Clearinghouse has also made use of congressional support services. The Futures Research Group of the Congressional Research Service at the Library of Congress has compiled a report for the Clearinghouse entitled "Citizen Futures Organizations: Group Profiles," which describes anticipatory democracy projects around the country. This report has enlarged our understanding of all of these projects and provides us with various methods and experiments involving citizens in thinking about the future.

Besides our focus on citizen-participation projects, we have sought ways to help committee staffs implement the foresight provision. Dennis Little, director of the Futures Research Group, and

---

* Editor's note: Chapter 4 describes the Alternatives for Washington program.

his staff spent two days with committee and congressional office personnel in October 1976, explaining the various methods of futures research; and Joseph Coates, assistant to the director of the Office of Technology Assessment (OTA), has explained the functions of technology assessment and the relevance of OTA for committee foresight work.

In general, our activities, directed by Clearinghouse director Anne Cheatham, have been well received. Nearly 500 out of a total of 535 congressional offices have asked to receive regular information from the Clearinghouse. Several committees have sought assistance in preparing foresight hearings and in developing other means to meet their foresight responsibility. Almost two hundred members of Congress have attended at least one of our "Dialogues" dinners, and our original Advisory Committee has swelled to twenty-three members of the House and four senators.

The relevance of the Clearinghouse for anticipatory democracy is clear. The Clearinghouse is working to encourage citizen participation, but its major focus is encouraging more foresight in Congress. But even in this, citizen participation has a fundamental role. Members of Congress listen to their constituents. If voices for increased foresight and long-range planning are raised across the land, congressional foresight activities will accelerate. The Clearinghouse has the capacity to circulate information, raise consciousness and introduce new questions into the legislative process. But because citizens can vote us in or out, they have the power to encourage a more forward-looking approach in Congress.

In a sense the Congressional Clearinghouse on the Future is breaking new ground and tilling the soil. The citizens of America will have to plant the seeds. Representatives and senators are frustrated and frightened by our seeming lack of control. Difficult questions confront us, forcing us to make increasingly difficult decisions. While we are urged to think about future implications of our actions, we often simply do not have the time. Yet if we get enough prodding from our constituents we will have to make the time.

The growing season may be longer and more painful than some would wish, but if these efforts are in any way successful, the Congress and the American people will enjoy a good harvest. And whatever we harvest, we harvest together.

CHAPTER SIX

Citizens and Legislatives Foresight

BY CLEMENT BEZOLD AND WILLIAM L. RENFRO

What does anticipatory democracy mean for the workings of legislative bodies? How can the problems of lack of future consciousness and lack of participation at least be ameliorated (if not overcome) in the workings of legislative bodies such as the U.S. Congress?

The legislature provides a unique focus for citizen involvement in that citizens elect its members, who are periodically accountable to their constituents. The votes cast by individual citizens, however, seldom provide accurate guides for the multitude of specific decisions facing a member of Congress once he or she attains office.

This article explores the legislative context within which decisions are made by focusing on the U.S. Congress (although the principles are the same for any state or local legislative body) and shows why normal legislative procedures militate against more systematic consideration of the future. After defining legislative foresight—the systematic consideration of the future within the legislative setting—a variety of methods for providing citizen input into the legislative foresight process are discussed. These include input provided directly to the individual member, input into the committee process of the legislature, and input into the national budgetary process.

WHY IS IT DIFFICULT FOR CONGRESS TO ANTICIPATE EMERGING PROBLEMS?

A legislature by definition provides each of its members an equal vote in passing legislation. Members each have their own goals and it is from this pluralism of goals and the ensuing conflicts that policy emerges. The long-range thinking, planning, and decision-making that characterize hierarchical organizations, such as corporations, are not part of the legislative process.

Legislative, especially congressional, policy-making often lacks focus. This results not only from the plurality of goals expressed by the 535 individual members of Congress, but also from that body's tendency to address issues of concern to organized interests, a lack of effective policy leadership, and the decentralization resulting from the division of work among the various committees and subcommittees.

Committees and subcommittees rarely consult among themselves on matters of mutual concern. Thus there is rarely an opportunity to examine comprehensive approaches to national problems, much less the cumulative effects of piecemeal approaches.[1]

Because the agenda of Congress is so crowded, its policy-making is frequently harried. The agenda is predominantly set by current and past issues embodied in existing legislation. Putting new issues on the agenda requires effort on the part of legislative "champions" of the issue. Such champions come more readily to the fore where an issue has widespread popular attention, which generally occurs only in periods of crisis.

A popular perception among many elected officials appears to be that the self-centered and individualistic nature of liberal democracy has a direct effect on the ability of elected representatives to anticipate emerging problems and to direct the allocation of resources to combat them. As one member of Congress put it, "Forcing the country to meet problems before they reach a crisis state necessitates foregoing current expenditures and satisfactions. This requires a discipline that isn't in the personal or political lives of the people."[2]

Another member of Congress stated:

There is a problem with legislating in advance; programs cost money . . . The public does not want something they don't think they need and they don't see the current need for dealing with anticipated problems. . . . Congress has a representative function. The public which is represented is not interested in the future in any specific terms. In effect, a member has to become a salesman for the problem; a crisis helps sell the urgency of the need to deal with the problem.[3]

Some recent polls, however, suggest that there is often public support for changes before a crisis makes them visibly necessary.[4] And many elected officials hold to the philosophy that their task as representatives of the people includes introducing issues and educating citizens—in essence, providing leadership. In recent years in particular, there has been a growing interest by many members of Congress in more systematic consideration of the future—in congressional foresight.

Oversight by legislative bodies entails looking backward to see how well the executive branch is implementing programs. While this is a regular part of the work of Congress, *foresight*—a systematic looking ahead—is a concept that is only emerging. The cause of foresight has been aided by several recent developments, including the establishment of the Congressional Budget Office and of the Office of Technology Assessment. The first use of the term "foresight" within Congress came in 1974 when Senator John Culver, then a member of the House, was responsible for the inclusion of a "foresight provision" in the House reforms of that year which required committees to do futures research and forecasting.[5] Foresight activity within Congress is being encouraged further by the Congressional Clearinghouse for the Future, the network of members of Congress and staff that is spreading information on futures research, aiding committees with foresight suggestions, and providing futures-research experts to testify.*

Legislative foresight provisions require Congress to take a longer and broader look at its policy-making. Foresight activities

* Editor's note: See Chapter 5 for more information on the Clearinghouse.

contribute to the legislative process in four major ways: 1) by providing early warning—identifying emerging issues that may require prompt attention; 2) by forecasting the long-term impacts of, and alternatives to, proposed legislation; 3) by setting directions and priorities and clarifying the cross impacts and trade-offs among different policies and programs; and 4) by adding a further dimension to the oversight responsibility of the legislature by clarifying the expected future effects of the legislation.

In the legislative setting, time is often at a premium and political information (who is for or against a bill) is more easily understood and identified than information on the long-term impact of a bill. Yet recognition of the need for futures information is growing. Several House committees have had foresight hearings. Information on the side effects of legislation—in the form of impact statements on the family, inflation, free enterprise, arms control, and the court system—has been called for.[6] While the House established its foresight responsibility in 1974, the Senate, in its reviews of its operations and committee structure in 1976 and 1977, further stimulated development of foresight activity in that body. The Commission on the Operation of the Senate recommended that the Senate:

Establish in or through the majority and minority policy committees responsibility for foresight—early identification and analysis of major policy problems. These committees should:

- Stimulate inquiry by appropriate standing committees of emerging problems before they become matters of public concern and hasty legislative action.
- Insure that legislation coming to the floor is accompanied by sufficient analysis to illuminate all relevant considerations.[7]

The Senate's Select Committee on the Study of the Senate Committee System felt that foresight was an "area of great importance for the operation of an efficient and effective committee system" and provided the Senate with more information on its foresight options.[8]

These and other indications of the growing interest in recent years in foresight are shown in Figure 1.

FIGURE 1.

Select Committee on the Study of the Senate
Committee System develops foresight option

Senate requires regulatory impact statements

Full Employment and National Growth
Act reintroduced by Humphrey-Hawkins

Commission on the Operation of Senate recommends foresight

Advisory Committee on National Growth recommends more foresight

Congressional Clearinghouse on the Future formed

Full Employment and Balanced Growth
Act introduced by Humphrey-Hawkins

Foreign Relations Authorization Act requires arms control impact statements

Balanced Economic Growth Act introduced by Bolling

Balanced Growth and Economic Planning Act introduced by Humphrey

CRS forms Futures Research Group

House adopts foresight provision; requires inflation impact statements

Congressional Budget Office established

Balanced National Growth and Development Act introduced by Humphrey

National Growth Policy Planning Act introduced by Hartke

Mondale reintroduces Goals and Priorities Act

Technology Assessment Act of 1972 establishes OTA

Full Opportunity and National Goals and Priorities Act introduced by Mondale

Legislative Reorganization Act of 1970, Congressional Research Service established

| 1970 | 1971 | 1972 | 1973 | 1974 | 1975 | 1976 | 1977 |

Adapted from: Forecasting and Futures Research in Congress: Background and Prospects, William L. Renfro, Congressional Research Service, Library of Congress, Multilith #77-169SP.

CITIZEN INPUT TO CONGRESS

One of the strengths of Congress is its openness to diverse inputs; the opportunities for citizens to affect congressional decision-making abound. Yet the cost in terms of time, money, and organizational skills necessary for effective input and most people's lack of awareness of congressional operations mean that the bulk of input Congress receives as it moves toward policy-making is from well-organized special interests. It is these groups that can identify where within Congress the relevant work is being done on any particular issue; they also are able to supply some of the best forecasts of the impact of pending legislation.

The interest-group nature of much of current input into the legislative process has some special results for the foresight concerns of identifying emerging issues, forecasting the impacts of legislation, and setting priorities.

In addition, members of Congress receive a constant stream of information from their constituents, but this usually does not deal with emerging issues, except when they approach a crisis state. The information is seldom related to the potential impact of legislation in a way that is useful to the committee working on it. Similarly, citizens seldom are able to contribute to the choice of national priorities or major directions.

THE MEMBER OF CONGRESS

When the first Congress convened, each member represented an average constituency of about thirty thousand residents. But since it was not possible to communicate frequently over long distances, even this relatively small group must have been difficult to represent in full. With the evolution from a small agrarian society with a part-time Congress, first to an industrial society and then to a postindustrial society, the number of constituents per member has grown to almost five hundred thousand. With the advent of faster and cheaper communications, it is possible for a member to communicate through the media to all or most of his or her constituents. This tremendous communications capability has, however, led many citizens to see communication with elected officials as a one-way street: the ease with which members can communicate with their constituents aggravates the frustration of the constituent in communicating *to* the member.

The campaign process—while providing more intense communication than usual—does little to alleviate this sense of frustration. During campaigns, candidates get input from constituents on many issues, yet they seldom get an overall sense of how constituents feel on the range of issues that will confront them. Citizens in turn may be bewildered by the variety of issues, and campaigns do little to raise the level of public understanding.

The growth in recent years of the federal government is an additional factor affecting the type of communications members of Congress receive from their constituents. Concomitant with the development of the industrial and postindustrial societies, the role and nature of government have changed. Today the federal government supplies a whole host of goods and services: it administers income-transfer programs, attempts to protect the environment, determines the rights and responsibilities of employers and employees, licenses and oversees hundreds of activities in the private sector, directs the resolution of social conflicts on many dimensions, and accounts for almost one third of the total economic activity in the country. This broad and ever-growing range of government activities has given members of Congress both individually and collectively ever-greater oversight responsibility. And as government affects more aspects of our everyday life, there are increasing opportunities for mistakes by government agencies; thus constituent contact with members of Congress has increasingly focused on problems in existing programs. Members of Congress and their staffs spend much time and effort acting as ombudsmen for constituents. While this is an important service and could, if analyzed properly, point out problems in current programs or agencies, it can—and often does—lead to a short-sightedness that ignores the need for citizen input on future programs as well as on operational problems with current programs.

How can citizens communicate more directly and more effectively with their representatives to aid in congressional foresight? One possibility is to replicate the process in programs such as Goals for Dallas or Alternatives for Washington through American Futures Committees in the congressional district or in the state.

American Futures Committees in Congressional Districts.   The concept of district advisory groups is not new; members of Congress often have formal or informal advisory committees composed of close associates, former campaign workers, and leading citizens. The idea of building a citizen-participation project open to all citizens and focused on defining alternative futures and on expressing and articulating goals is now only in its experimental stage. Congressman Wyche Fowler (D-Ga.) is designing such a citizen goals project in Atlanta. As one of the founders of the Atlanta citizen goals project, Atlanta 2000, Congressman Fowler was experienced in the concepts of anticipatory democracy, recognized its value, and now wants to apply it to national decision-making.

Some aspects of the American Futures Committees would differ from the state and local projects described in the first four chapters of this book. Their purpose would be to give congressional representatives some sense of his or her constituents' visions of the nation's future. While some attention should be given to the future of the district, the member usually has a fairly clear sense of the federal issues that most directly affect the district. Also, most of the decisions that directly and specifically shape a district's future are made in city halls, county councils, and state legislatures, rather than in Congress. Thus the congressional district American Futures Committee should be used both to inform citizens of the range of futures for the nation and to allow them to design and evaluate preferable futures, policy alternatives, and goals that the member can then use as he or she votes on *national* policy. Public opinion surveys have shown that most constituents are not well-informed about national issues in general and are even less informed about legislation still pending. Such district exercises could give citizens the opportunity for more informed input to their representative on the directions of American society and could help to overcome the reluctance some members feel exists in their constituencies to anticipating emerging problems.

Constituent Polls and Surveys.   Members of Congress frequently seek citizen input by surveying their constituents, often by polling every "postal patron" in the district or those who normally receive the member's newsletter. Such survey information can be used to aid in foresight by adding questions on constituents' preferred alternative futures and on alternative policies and goals.

Congressman Charlie Rose (D-N.C.) has polled his constituents in this manner, raising questions of the type conceived by Robert Theobald on quality of life and on federal-spending priorities. Such polls could be used to raise new possibilities and to encourage imagination on the part of constituents. While polls do not encourage the kind of assertiveness that is the ideal form of citizen participation, they can serve to educate the public on the range of choices facing the member and can contribute to building a constituency for anticipating problems.

Because those who feel most strongly on particular issues and those with somewhat more education and higher incomes are most likely to respond to questionnaires, this type of mass-mailing poll may give an inaccurate picture of the views of the entire constituency. One way to remedy this situation is to supplement the postal-patron poll by polling a statistically balanced sample over the telephone or in person. This provides a more accurate picture of opinions in the various sectors of the district. Combining both approaches—one that allows constituents to self-select and a selected sample for verifying the first set of results—has been used in such A/D exercises as Goals for Georgia and Alternatives for Washington. Through polling techniques, constituents could become involved in foresight activities by responding to questions about emerging issues, their feelings on the long-term impacts of specific legislation, and their preference for allocating the federal budget.

FORESIGHT IN CONGRESSIONAL COMMITTEES

The major legislative work of the Congress is done in committees and subcommittees. In introducing foresight into House procedures, therefore, the House assigned the major responsibility for legislative foresight to its committees. The House Select Committee on Committees, often referred to as the Bolling Committee after its chairman, Richard Bolling (D-Mo.), produced the committee reform amendments of 1974. The Bolling Committee was prompted by then Congressman (now Senator) John Culver to invite leading futurists to testify about the need for Congress to look ahead. Ideas developed in these and other Bolling Committee hearings, coupled with Culver's persistence, led to the requirement that the standing committees of the House give more systematic attention to the future. The 1974 Committee Reform Amendments that added the foresight provision to the procedural rules of the House required that:

. . . each [standing committee other than Budget and Appropriations] shall review and study any conditions or circumstances which may indicate the necessity or desirability of enacting new or additional legislation within the jurisdiction of that committee (whether or not any bill or resolution has been introduced with respect thereto) . . .

. . . and shall on a continuing basis undertake futures research and forecasting on matters within the jurisdiction of that committee.[9]

In addition to these general responsibilities in the foresight provision, specific foresight responsibilities with regard to the impact of tax policies and inflationary impacts of legislation were added as well:

Each standing committee of the House shall have the function of reviewing and studying on a continuing basis the impact or probable impact of tax policies affecting subjects within its jurisdiction . . .[10]

Congress has often required committees to include in their reports on legislation statements on the impact of the legislation on current laws and the budget. The Committee Reform Amendments, as adopted, added the requirement for an inflation impact statement.[11]

In its report on the Reform Amendments, the Bolling Committee outlined the intent of the foresight provision:

The recommendation of the select committee also includes a "foresight" responsibility for each standing committee. That is, these legislative units would have the additional responsibility of identifying and assessing conditions and trends that might require future legislative action. More specifically, this would provide a locus for the systematic, long-range, and integrated study of our principal future national problems. . . . In addition, by means of futures research . . . the costs, benefits, and effects of the various options, including present programs, could be assessed and compared.

In this way, it is hoped, the House may become more responsive to national needs, anticipating problems before they become crises.

The proposed "foresight" function should provide a better basis for substantive legislation as well as oversight. It should also assist in setting national priorities and making budget allocations.[12]

In the Senate, the Commission on the Operation of the Senate and the Select Committee on the Study of the Senate Committee System have made recommendations and provided information on conducting foresight.[13]

As noted above, foresight has four major roles in the legislative process:

1. to improve early warning of issues, problems and opportunities that might become the subject of legislation;
2. to develop a greater awareness of the future in drafting and preparing legislation, including the preparation of forecasts of the primary or intended as well as the secondary or side impacts of legislation. These are known as impact forecasts;
3. to encourage the conscious coordination of policies across committees by identifying the cross impacts of legislation and setting priorities through the budget process and other mechanisms for establishing coordinated national policy;
4. to support subsequent oversight activities of Congress and committees.

Citizen involvement in each of these categories of foresight activity includes both direct participation by citizens or citizen groups and efforts by the committee to poll or otherwise get a better idea of citizens' preferences.

Early Warning.   Often it is possible to develop "early warnings" of likely problems and emerging issues by using such methods of forecasting and futures research as trend extrapolation, cross-impact analysis, and simulation models.[14] The energy crisis, for example, was forecast in various places prior to 1973 when the Arab oil boycott made it a matter of fact.[15] That Congress has recognized the value of these early warnings is indicated by the use it has made of the Congressional Research Service (CRS) and the Office of Technology Assessment (OTA). While the principal responsibility of CRS is to help committees in analyzing, assessing, forecasting impacts, and otherwise evaluating legislative proposals, it also has a responsibility to prepare a list of emerging issues for the committees of each new Congress.[16] Congress further expanded its resources for early warning in 1972 with the formation of the Office of Technology Assessment. OTA is assigned the "basic function" of providing "early indications of the probable beneficial and adverse impacts of the applications of technology . . ."[17]

Although these early warning resources can play an important role in the Congress, an essential element necessary for the effective use of early warning information is missing: without public awareness and public support for needed measures, Congress often has been unable to act. Citizen participation is essential if the early warning systems are to be effective.

The energy crisis again provides an excellent example. In spite of the many early warnings, the public remained largely oblivious to the emerging problem. Without needed public support, ideas and legislative proposals that would have addressed the problem were either not developed or allowed to die. Public support and recognition of the need for sacrifices are critical if solutions that entail some hardship are called for.

Committee foresight hearings facilitate the early warning process. Several committees have held foresight hearings to explore emerging issues and to develop a better understanding of the future. These foresight hearings generally enlist expert testimony to identify trends and emerging issues. To broaden the input into such hearings and as a way of structuring them, committees could also develop their own lists of emerging technological, social, and political issues. These could be gathered from a variety of sources, including the Congressional Research Service, the Office of Technology Assessment, groups working on alternative policies or life styles such as those listed in Appendix 4 of this book, programs designed to monitor trends on an ongoing basis[18], the district level American Futures Committees referred to above, and citizen groups that have systematically considered the future (such as those described in Chapters 1 through 4 and listed in Appendix 2). Citizens and citizen groups then could be polled to provide further input into the process.

Foresight hearings could involve committee members and others in developing alternative futures for the issues that concern them. By involving committee members, those groups that normally lobby or work with the committee, and a wider range of citizens and citizen groups, foresight hearings and other early-warning activities could work both to pinpoint areas of agreement and disagreement and to better inform the participants. Such a heightened level of information about potential problems is likely to bring about an increased willingness to make the sacrifices that may be needed.

Developing Legislative Proposals and Impact Forecasts. Developing legislation involves political, legislative, and analytical functions. The foresight component in developing legislation is largely analytic, although it frequently affects the political aspect of drafting legislation as well. For discussion purposes, foresight is here explored in the context of its primary role in the development of legislation—supporting legislative analysis, evaluation, and assessment.

All legislation involves some assumptions about the future, however simplistic. The role of foresight in the legislative process for issues already identified should begin with these assumptions and then go on to assess their validity in a process that might include the following steps:[19]

1. Making explicit the assumptions about the future underlying or motivating proposed legislation;
2. Determining the objective indicators of performance that could be used to quantify these assumptions. For example, a bill might involve assumptions about birth rate, consumer price index, gross national product, steel production, housing starts, disposable personal income, computer sales, oil imports, etc.;
3. Compiling forecasts of these indicators from sources in government, industry trade associations, unions, think tanks, public literature, etc.;
4. Analyzing how differing forecasts affect the proposed bill and determining alternative futures that might result from the differing assumptions;
5. Selecting forecasts of social conditions to be used in the bill and calculating the magnitude of the various forecasts in the related sections and titles of the bill;
6. Developing forecasts of the expected primary impact on the objective indicators of performance;
7. Identifying potential secondary effects of the legislation and developing forecasts for these.

The results of such a process could be included in the report on the bill that must accompany it when it is reported from committee to the floor of the House or Senate. This notion received support from the Commission on the Operation of the Senate as well as from the Advisory Committee on National Growth Policy Processes. The Advisory Committee recommended that:

The congressional committee report accompanying each bill (reported to the floor of the House or Senate) include an outline of the bill's foreseeable indirect and middle to long-range effects, as well as a concise statement of the general goals and specific objectives to which the bill is directed.[20]

Currently, the House requires impact statements on how proposed legislation would affect federal law, the budget, and inflation. The Senate requires impact statements for federal law, the budget, and regulatory agencies. In the past few years, there have been numerous proposals for specific impact statements on the likely effect of legislation on such things as the court system, the family, arms control, and regulation.

A more effective approach would be to require a generalized impact statement that forces the committees to seek out primary and secondary impacts, rather than assuming that a bill will affect all predetermined categories equally. The principal advantage of this type of impact forecast is the ability of the committee to focus on those areas where the impact of the bill would be most important. Virtually all bills affect the status of federal law and most bills have some effect on the federal budget. But fewer bills affect either inflation or regulatory agencies. The use of generalized impact forecasts would allow a member of Congress to ask the committee handling a bill to summarize the bill's potential impact on the areas of greatest concern to that member—something the present arrangement does not permit.[21]

The Senate Select Committee on the Study of the Senate Committee System provided the Senate with a description of how to develop impact forecasts.[22] Based on this work, Senator Gary Hart requested from the Congressional Research Service the first impact forecast of expected consequence for the National Waste Heat Recovery Act (S.1363), a bill designed to encourage industrial use of the energy generated in conjunction with production. In the graph that follows, the shaded area shows what would happen if the bill were enacted—the percentage of electricity generated from steam used in industrial plants could be doubled in the next twenty-five years.[23]

The impact forecast just illustrated focuses on the primary or intended impacts of a bill. There are, of course, always second- and third-order effects that may not be immediately apparent, but which in the long run may be the most important effects of legislation.[24] Undesirable secondary effects are generally raised by opponents of a bill. The advocacy nature of the legislative process, however, leads proponents to avoid any systematic treatment of the negative side effects. Foresight, in this sense, involves a higher standard of advocacy—one in which positive and negative consequences receive adequate attention by proponents and by committees handling legislation.

Organized interest groups generally have sufficient information, organizational skill, and analytical resources to raise questions about those secondary impacts that are most important to them or that support their positions on the legislation. Yet the poor and unorganized—on whom negative side effects of even well-intentioned legislation most often fall—seldom are knowledgeable about pending legislation or its likely impact. Even the citizens' groups that represent them seldom have the resources for this type of analysis. In the area of federal housing policies, for example, a report for a House committee found significant secondary effects that had not been forecast:

It seems anomalous on hindsight that at the same time that suburbanization was subsidized for the middle- and upper-income groups, public housing and low- and moderate-income housing programs were concentrated in central city locations. Although the volume of housing built with federal assistance for this purpose has not been significant in recent years, the overall effect of federal housing policy appears to have been to reinforce metropolitan dispersion of middle-income families while tending to reinforce the concentration of lower-income families in the central city areas.[25]

Committees, therefore, should encourage citizens' groups to comment on the likely impact of legislation and should seek out those groups that have been most affected, particularly by the unintended consequences of previous legislation recommended by the committee and passed by the Congress. As A/D exercises

Percentage of Electricity from Co-Generation

PERCENT

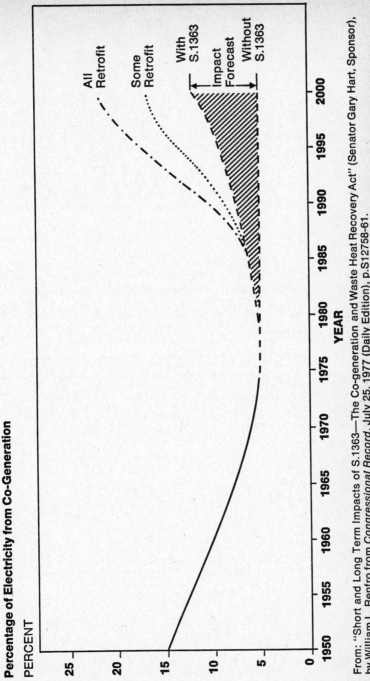

From: "Short and Long Term Impacts of S.1363—The Co-generation and Waste Heat Recovery Act" (Senator Gary Hart, Sponsor), by William L. Renfro from *Congressional Record*, July 25, 1977 (Daily Edition), p.S12758-61.

(such as Alternatives for Washington) that involve more people in examining the long-term impacts of policies grow, they can be used for citizen input into pending legislation.

Another role for citizens to undertake in this area is to call for more balanced treatment of the pros and cons of proposals. It is important that citizens call for this higher standard of advocacy and that they applaud the efforts of their representatives when they move toward a more frank discussion of the full range of positive and negative consequences.

Oversight. Foresight can support the oversight function of specific committees by clarifying what the legislation is intended to do and providing forecasts of its intended effects—that is, of its objectives—which can then be evaluated. For example, committees can use data about constituent complaints to members of Congress to analyze whether predicted primary or secondary effects of particular pieces of legislation manifested themselves.

CONSIDERATION OF THE CROSS-IMPACTS OF LEGISLATION

The budget is an important tool for considering the cross-impacts of various pieces of legislation. In the absence of other effective mechanisms for coordinating national policy, the federal budget has long been recognized as a major instrument for shaping it. In the budget, all policies are related to each other in terms of their dollar costs. Despite the fact that these relative monetary comparisons often fail to consider the real cross-impacts of different programs and policies, their duplication, or their long-range impacts, the budget still provides the major mechanism in this country for setting national priorities. In 1921 Congress gave the President the power to formulate the budget to prevent the chaos that resulted when executive agencies made direct budget requests to the relevant congressional committees. This represented a significant increase in presidential power.

In the early 1970s President Nixon infuriated Congress by impounding legally appropriated funds. (The Supreme Court later ruled this challenge to the congressional "power of the purse" unconstitutional.) In response to the Nixon impoundments and because of growing interest in Congress (particularly in the Senate) for a more assertive role in setting national priorities, Congress established its own budget process and the Congressional Budget Office.

How can citizens become involved in the budget process? How can members of Congress get a better sense of how the nation as a whole and their particular constituencies prefer federal funds to be spent? There are at least three possible ways that citizens could identify their spending priorities for policy-makers: 1) polls; 2) comment on the income tax return form; and 3) participation in a national A/D process.

The Congressional Budget Office (or the Office of Management and Budget or another entity) could poll citizens on their preferences. Because of the complexity of the federal budget, it would be necessary to provide citizens with some educational materials on the trends and significance of spending in the various budget categories before polling them. It would be important to involve a large enough sample to identify preferences among various income levels and social groups. Such polls could include questions not only on the coming fiscal year but also on alternative budgets five and more years into the future.

The Congressional Budget Office already has had some experience preparing alternative future budgets that show the variation in expenditures over a five-year period based on differing assumptions. For example, one of CBO's first reports in 1976 examined the shape of the federal budget in light of three different assumptions: a) increased national security; b) federal resources concentrated on social programs; and c) control in many spending areas returned to state and local governments.[26]

The federal income tax form provides a very sensible way for the government to ask citizens to advise it on how much and for what purposes their money should be spent. While such information would be helpful for the coming fiscal year, it would be even more useful to have citizens indicate what government spending should be in five to ten years. Educational materials would be necessary to inform citizens of the meaning of the choices and to suggest some major alternative future budgets. Additionally, it would perhaps be necessary to remind citizens of the benefits of government expenditure since they would be making their suggestions at a time when they are most aware of the costs.[27]

A national A/D process would provide a third way for citizens to make choices about coordinated federal policy. Other chapters in this book suggest a number of possible A/D approaches:

- development of holistic scenarios for the future of the country along with the policy implications of these various scenarios as was done in Alternatives for Washington (see Chapter 4);

- identification of major trends and their implications for the issues facing the Congress, similar to what was done for the Minnesota legislature (see Chapter 1);

- participation by key members of Congress in an ad hoc Growth Policy Committee, similar to the Minnesota experience;

- an A/D referendum that would periodically provide an opportunity for citizens to express their long-range goals and priorities;

- a survey of the population on its preferences for the future of the nation and specific regions, including policies and priorities (see Chapter 1).

While some of these notions may seem unprecedented or unworkable, they have been suggested as part of the constitutional revision processes in Florida and Hawaii in order to give citizens more direct access to the policy process. The goal is to give them a chance to pass judgment on alternative futures and policies rather than simply on candidates.[28]

Citizen input in congressional foresight via the budget process or other planning mechanisms may be operated by an independent Commission on America's Future as suggested by Senator Hubert Humphrey[29] or a Commission on National Growth Policy as recommended by the Advisory Committee on National Growth Policy Processes.[30] Or Congress could choose to have one of its committees or support organizations perform that function.

A process of developing alternative futures for growth policy options would move beyond the budget process, would gain publicity for the key choices and would give elected officials a better sense of what the preferences of citizens are for the major directions of the nation.

CONCLUSION

In an environment characterized by a harried pace, fragmentation of policies, and reverence for the time frame of election cycles, the call for a longer and broader view of policy-making through foresight is not readily or loudly made.

Despite this handicap, legislative foresight has grown in recent years as a result of the leadership and political will of a few key members of Congress, the growth of techniques for exploring the certainties and uncertainties of the future, and most importantly, a growing recognition on the part of the public that the crisis decision-making of recent years and the greater uncertainty of the future require new and more forward-looking ways of doing things.

A fundamental task of anticipatory democracy then is to encourage the growth of legislative foresight while ensuring that citizens are given a role to play in it. As noted above, this can be done by adjustments to what are currently the most common forms of citizen input—through constituent contacts with their members; by more aggressive work on the part of committees to seek out citizen attitudes on emerging issues and directions; and by the development of methods in and beyond the budget process that put current decisions on national priorities in the context of the longer-range preferences of American citizens.

III

Anticipatory Democracy in Policies and Programs

While legislatures are the part of government most directly accountable to the people, important decisions are increasingly being made in the executive branch of government, in federal programs, and in connection with federal programs.

In Chapter 7, Nelson Rosénbaum, an expert on citizen participation at the Urban Institute, describes the growth of citizen involvement in federal programs. He notes that the type and level of citizen participation have changed as the locus of decision-making has changed. The possibilities for active citizen involvement in the decision-making process have steadily increased with the broadening of the power of the electorate through referendum, initiative, and recall; with the introduction of accountable administrative procedures; and with the advent of current programs mandating active citizen participation in the formulation of agency plans and programs.

Health care is essential to our lives, yet most citizens have little or no control over the medical complex that "cradles and graves" us all, and that encourages treatment more than prevention as a health strategy. In Chapter 8, Rosemary Bruner, a citizen activist and health planner, describes the issues involved in citizen activism on health issues, particularly what is necessary to shift the emphasis from treatment to a greater awareness of the merits of prevention.

She reviews the range of opportunities, including specific federal programs, through which citizens can play an active part in affecting local health policy.

As the chapters on the various A/D projects in cities and states show, A/D programs—as most citizen-participation programs—can suffer from a lack of genuine minority involvement. In Chapter 9, Lawrence Auls, a community organizer and black business developer, reviews a Year 2000 project in Columbus, Ohio, in which the citizens of a predominantly black area speculated about their long-range future. The results of this process were used to guide other decisions by the local Model Cities Program, under whose auspices the Year 2000 project was conducted.

The present complexity of society results in part from the increasing diversity and sophistication of our technology. As Marshall McLuhan notes, "We shape our tools and thereafter our tools shape us." Yet the secondary effects—the ways in which tools shape us—have seldom been seriously considered. The movement toward technology assessment seeks to reverse this process and to consider systematically the impacts a range of technologies potentially may have on us prior to making decisions.

The federal government has made a major commitment to this process by establishing the Office of Technology Assessment. In Chapter 10, Byron Kennard of the National Council for the Public Assessment of Technology describes the ways in which citizens can insure that an adequate assessment considers all the possible side effects, including the social impacts that are often overlooked.

CHAPTER SEVEN

The Origins of Citizen Involvement in Federal Programs

BY NELSON M. ROSENBAUM

American democracy was founded on principles of limited governmental authority and formal public accountability. These principles, so deeply embedded in American political culture, also furnish the intellectual roots of the contemporary movement for greater citizen involvement in governmental decision-making. The demand for expanded citizen involvement represents the latest chapter in the continuing evolution of popular control over government in the United States. For more than two centuries, the fundamental objectives of democratic practice have remained constant: to insure that public policies correspond closely with the needs and preferences of affected citizens, and to prevent government from overstepping the bounds of its limited authority.

Responsiveness to citizen desires and respect for citizen rights constitute the essential underpinning of consensual democracy. If public policy consistently diverges from the direction of public preferences, or if government persistently impinges upon basic rights and liberties, the motivation for voluntary allegiance and compliance is eroded. Coercion must then be substituted for voli-

Grateful acknowledgment to the Urban Institute for these excerpts from *Citizen Involvement in Land Use Governance: Issues and Methods* by Nelson M. Rosenbaum (Washington, D.C.: The Urban Institute). Copyright © 1976 by The Urban Institute. Reprinted by permission.

tion, and the democratic system degenerates into authoritarian rule.

The historical background and philosophical significance of contemporary demands for citizen involvement in governmental decision-making often have been ignored or forgotten. Citizen involvement is addressed, both in the literature and in practice, on a cynical, expedient, and self-serving level. Given the lack of positive legislative direction, bureaucrats and administrators often define citizen-involvement objectives in terms of their own priorities and functions; these may include such goals as "enlarging public support for the agency," "mobilizing a constituency to implement the plan," or "improving the efficiency of information-gathering."

None of these goals is necessarily an undesirable consequence of citizen involvement, but they are all secondary. Such objectives fail to acknowledge and respect the primary purpose of citizen participation: to increase the responsiveness and accountability of government to the citizens affected by public decisions.

Bureaucratic and administrative power has grown alarmingly in both its reach and the scope of its discretion. The expansion of opportunities for direct citizen involvement is a necessary antidote, an appropriate adaptation of democratic practice to modern conditions.

This challenge requires more than the routine inclusion of mandates for "widespread," "effective," or "meaningful" citizen involvement in statutes and ordinances. As Congress belatedly recognized in its experience with the citizen-involvement provisions of the Community Action and Model Cities Programs, decisions on basic and sensitive issues of program authority and responsibility cannot be left to planners and administrators. Rather, it is essential that legislators and elected executives show a more critical and sustained interest in the objectives and organizational structure of citizen involvement programs. Officials can achieve that aim by defining more specific statutory mandates and by exercising more intensive oversight of implementation efforts.

ORIGINS AND OBJECTIVES OF
CITIZEN INVOLVEMENT

The struggle for greater popular control over government in the United States is characterized by two complementary themes.

First, reform groups have traditionally made great efforts to expand the scope and significance of voting participation in the American political system. The main effort has focused upon the extension of voting rights to new segments of the population, thus expanding the opportunity to gain recognition of their needs and preferences of these groups. A parallel effort has been devoted to making greater numbers of government officials subject to elections.

The second theme is the effort to supplement voting rights with opportunities for direct citizen intervention and influence in decision-making processes. The United States enjoys a more deep-rooted tradition of direct citizen involvement in government than most other democracies (e.g., the New England town meeting model), but only in the twentieth century has this tradition risen to prominence in other settings and areas. Election of governmental officials, after all, provides only an indirect and imprecise means for affecting policy. As government has grown larger and more complex, and broader discretion has been accorded to nonelected officials and administrators, the expansion of opportunities for direct intervention has become a major reform objective.

ROLE OF VOTING PARTICIPATION

Borrowing heavily from Montesquieu, the federal constitution of 1789 and the initial state constitutions of the Revolutionary era relied primarily on the balancing of powers among the three branches of government to protect against arbitrary or capricious action by any particular official or institution. The concept of democracy embodied in the founding documents certainly did not envision the enforcement of responsiveness through accountability of public officials to a mass electorate.

The constitutions of the thirteen original states all incorporated either a property-holding or tax-paying qualification for exercise of the franchise. In addition, only a few offices were subject to popular election: president and members of Congress on the federal level, representatives on the state level, council members on the local level. Indeed, the extent to which popular control over government was limited in the Revolutionary era may be gauged by the fact that, with the exception of the Massachusetts constitution of 1789, none of the state constitutions were submitted to the enfranchised voters for ratification.

The movement for change in this highly restricted conception of democratic practice began almost immediately after the founding of the nation. In the period between the 1790s and the 1830s, the first great struggle for increased popular control was waged by citizen activists who hoped to extend the suffrage to all white males. The impetus for change came primarily from frontiersmen, nonlanded farmers, and the growing numbers of urban laborers and artisans who were effectively disenfranchised and politically powerless under the early constitutional acts.

The concept of broader and more intensive popular control over government first found favor, as might be expected, in the "frontier" states of Vermont, Kentucky, and New Hampshire. However, there followed a long and difficult struggle to extend the practice to the rest of the nation. In large, dominant states, such as New York and Virginia, white male suffrage was bitterly resisted by established landowning elites. Following the aristocratic conceptions of parliamentary democracy found in the writings of Locke and Burke, the landowners found the prospect of accounting to the "vulgar masses" unsettling. Nevertheless, by the 1830s most states had adopted universal white male suffrage.

In successive periods of American political development, extending to the contemporary era, the franchise has been gradually extended to other major groups and segments of the population, including women, blacks, and youths. Each advance, accepted today as an incontrovertible aspect of normal democratic politics, was vigorously resisted by established political elites of earlier periods as a radical and dangerous innovation. Opposition was based on many of the same arguments heard in today's debates over direct citizen involvement in decision-making: extending participation rights would be too costly or disruptive to government efficiency and stability; the disenfranchised group is too ignorant, uninterested, and unreliable to be entrusted with participation rights; government must be insulated from the passions of the mob.

In each case, an overriding positive principle triumphed: that government exists to serve all the people and must therefore take cognizance of their varying needs and preferences. Our basic historical impulse has been to take the risks and bear the costs associated with a broad-based, egalitarian conception of democracy.

Paralleling the struggle for liberalizing voting rights, reformers also attempted to extend the impact of the vote. During the mid-1800s a number of states first authorized direct popular election of mayors and other local administrative officials. In the same period, many state officials—including the governors, lieutenant governors, attorneys general, and some administrative officials—were also subjected to electoral tests.

This "long ballot" movement, which lay at the heart of the Jacksonian conception of democracy, was based on many of the same themes and propositions that animate the citizen-involvement movement today—the desire to insure a representative bureaucracy, the governing class, the emphasis on political accountability.

By the early 1900s ballots reached extraordinary lengths, as every official from water commissioner to dogcatcher was included in local elections. On the state level most of the new regulatory commissions of the 1880s and 1890s (e.g., railroad and public-utility commissions) were made elective. After a long struggle, U.S. senators were finally subjected to popular vote.

As ballot length grew, a certain amount of disillusionment set in with sole reliance on the vote as a means of popular control over government. This disillusionment was crucial in the overall evolution of American democratic practice, since it gradually deflected much interest and attention away from voting participation toward more direct mechanisms of citizen intervention and influence in decision-making.

Proponents of the "short ballot" and advocates of "direct democracy" raised a number of arguments against sole reliance on the vote: 1) most voters were unable to assemble adequate information to make intelligent choices on long lists of governmental officials; 2) municipal- and state-level political machines exploited the long ballot by sweeping in slates of incompetent wardheelers; 3) the proliferation of elected officials made it difficult to coordinate governmental policy and to focus responsibility for success or failure; and, 4) perhaps most importantly, the periodic election of government officials provided only a very uncertain and infrequent mode of enforcing limits upon governmental discretion.

These arguments continue to have much force today. Certainly the vote remains the basic, most powerful technique of popular control over government. Reformers continue to struggle over extension of the franchise and the appropriate scope of elections. However, there is widespread recognition that the vote alone cannot "fine-tune" the operation of our democracy. Important policy issues are too numerous and complex to be dealt with meaningfully in election campaigns, elections are too infrequent to have a substantial impact in enforcing responsiveness and accountability, and too much authority has been delegated to administrative officials and bureaucrats. Thus, the preeminence of the vote in American democratic practice has been increasingly challenged during the twentieth century by the rediscovery of the neglected tradition of direct public involvement in decision-making. The challenge has been to adapt this tradition to modern conditions and needs.

EVOLUTION OF CITIZEN INVOLVEMENT— INITIATIVE, REFERENDUM, AND RECALL

The initial focus of the movement for direct citizen involvement in governmental decision-making was the expansion of popular control over legislative action. This is understandable, since legislatures still dominated governmental decision-making in the early 1900s.

The movement for direct citizen involvement arose primarily as a result of discontent with the arrogant and corrupt actions of state and city legislators. Given the iron grip of big-city machines on traditional partisan elections, reformers searched for some other means of insuring responsiveness to popular needs and desires and preventing arbitrary and capricious governmental actions. The approach progressives and populists of the early 1900s supported was a combination of closely related procedural innovations: initiative, referendum, and recall.

Initiative allows citizens to propose legislation by petition. Referendum provides veto power over particularly sensitive and important legislative acts. Following the tradition of innovation in democratic practice by frontier areas, South Dakota was the first state to authorize statutory initiatives and referenda in 1898, and San Francisco was the first municipality to provide for statutory referenda. From 1900 to 1920, the years of greatest "progressive" influence, twenty additional states, most in the West and Midwest, adopted the initiative and referendum in some form. Initiative and referendum also spread rapidly on the municipal level under constitutional enabling provisions in thirty-three states.

The recall provides an opportunity for citizens to specify a particular set of grievances against a legislator or other elected official and to require a special election by petition. In 1903 Los Angeles was the first municipality to adopt the recall; in 1908 Oregon was the first state. In subsequent years the recall was authorized for removal of state-level officials by fourteen states; the process was authorized at the municipal level through state-enabling legislation in thirty-nine states.

There is little research on the policy impacts of initiatives, referenda, and recall actions, but these have generally been in reaction to a crisis or scandal, or they have been narrowly drawn. Thus while useful for specific policies, they have not yet developed into techniques for broader statements of citizens' goals for the city or state.

POPULAR CONTROL OVER
THE ADMINISTRATION

During the period from 1900 to 1930, when the movement for direct involvement was focused on initiative, referendum, and recall, there was not yet much concern about popular control over the authority exercised by administrative officials—i.e., staff members of bureaucratic agencies, citizen members of regulatory commissions, appointed officials of government departments. Historically, the amount of authority allocated to appointed officials and administrators was small. As Lord Bryce noted about the American version of democracy during the 1880s:

It is a great merit of American government that it relies very little on officials (i.e., administrators) and arms them with little power of arbitrary interference. The reader who has followed the description of federal authorities, state authorities, county and city or township authorities, may think there is a great deal of administration; but the reason why their descriptions are necessarily so minute is because the powers of each authority are so carefully and closely restricted.[1]

EXPANSION OF ADMINISTRATIVE POWER

The beginnings of change in this pattern of strong legislatures and weak bureaucracies are found in the early 1900s. As part of the overall "progressive" effort to contain the power of corrupt legislatures, reformers fought to insulate the bureaucracy from gross political pressure through the introduction of professional civil-service systems based on the merit principle. Efforts also were made to strengthen the independence of citizen regulatory commissions, such as the Interstate Commerce Commission on the federal level and public utility commissions on the state level. On the local level, reformers emphasized new forms of organization, such as the council-manager system, which broadened administrative prerogatives.

The center of progressive influence in expanding administrative autonomy and discretion—both within its own agencies and commissions and, by example and encouragement, at state and local levels—was the federal government.

In the early 1920s, to take a crucial example, the Commerce Department, under Secretary Herbert Hoover, prepared, publicized, and proselytized the Standard State Zoning Enabling Act and the Standard City Planning Enabling Act. Upon enactment by state legislatures, these laws allowed local governments to set up planning and zoning commissions. These independent bodies, in conjunction with their professional administrative staffs, were vested with extremely wide discretion (e.g., "promoting the health, safety, morals, or the general welfare of the community"), and their decisions were subject only to often cursory review by local legislative bodies and potential appeal to the courts.

The pressure of abrupt economic collapse in the 1930s resulted in a rapid acceleration of this trend toward expansion of administrative power. Many specialized administrative bureaucracies and new regulatory agencies were established and provided with extremely broad discretionary powers. As James Landis noted in his classic essay, the delegation of broad powers to agencies resulted from a profound feeling of helplessness on the part of the traditional branches of government: "The administrative process is, in essence, our generation's answer to the inadequacy of the judicial and legislative processes."[2]

The new federal programs of the 1930s and 1940s also spawned large bureaucracies at the state and local levels, particularly in the social services. The reliance of these bureaucracies on federal funding provided an extra layer of insulation from "parochial" political pressure and control.

During this period of enormous expansion of discretionary authority in administrative agencies, there was still great faith that the "neutral competence" and "professionalism" of the newly expanded bureaucracies and commissions would lead to accurate, rational determination of the broad public interest and to efficient management of the government. Of course, there were some vocal opponents of the departure from carefully specified mandates and limited authority, but these critics came primarily from the ranks of the "vested interests" whose actions were subject to governmental regulation and scrutiny. Since most of the protest came from those whose activity was deemed to be contrary to the broad "public interest," the criticism merely reinforced confidence in the objectivity and responsiveness of administrative agencies. Only a few prescient independent observers in law and political science perceived the great danger to democratic practice in the delegation of such broad discretion to administrative bureaucracies and independent commissions.[3]

It was not until after World War II that public concern about the control of administrative discretion began to develop into a major force. This concern was stimulated by a number of factors, including pervasive discontent with oppressive wartime administrative controls and growing unhappiness among minority and low-income groups over arbitrary and arrogant bureaucratic decision-making in the development of new social programs.

Perhaps the single most important factor in the genesis of the movement to bring the bureaucracies under greater public control was the recognition that the aggressive, adversary relationship between regulatory agencies and regulated parties that prevailed during the New Deal era had been transformed into a more comfortable cooperative posture. As numerous critics and observers discovered, regulators and regulated parties formed powerful, autonomous "subgovernments," within which bargaining and back scratching were the prevailing norms.[4]

This cooptation or "capture" of the bureaucracies and commissions, particularly at the federal level, was widespread enough to cause severe disillusionment with the doctrines of "neutral competence" and "professional objectivity." This disillusionment led to a return of the traditional emphasis on strong popular control over government.

APPROACHES TO POPULAR CONTROL

Over the last thirty years two broad schools of thought have competed on the issue of how administrative decision-making can best be brought under firm popular guidance and control. One school emphasizes the need to assert popular control through the elected branches of government, with the public playing an *indirect* role through the vote. The other school of thought, which is of immediate interest in this study, stresses the need for *direct* citizen intervention in administrative action.

Within the first school of thought, most observers have focused their criticism on the legislatures for their failure to specify precise standards and rules in legislative mandates to administrative agencies.[5] The delegation of broad discretionary policy-making authority, it is charged, stems more from laziness, habit, and political cowardice than from necessity. In this view, legislatures should also exercise vigorous and continuous oversight over the actions of administrative agencies, thereby stimulating responsiveness and enforcing accountability.

These arguments have had some impact on legislative behavior. On the federal level, for example, Congress has established specific standards for the guidance of administrative decision-making in the areas of air- and water-quality control. Such standards were unheard of in previous regulatory statutes. During the past decade there has also been a dramatic upsurge in the amount of oversight activity in Congress.

State and local legislatures have also been more vigorous in guiding the exercise of administrative discretion. In the area of land use, for example, the Florida Environmental Land and Water Management Act of 1972 was severely criticized as establishing a "process without a policy"—i.e., conferring an enormous amount of administrative discretion on a planning and regulatory agency without any substantive guidance and controls. The Florida legislature responded to this criticism in two ways: first, by establishing in 1973 a special oversight process for the review and approval of growth management rules; and second, by enacting in 1974 a statement of growth management goals for the guidance of administrative agencies. A similar legislative contraction of administrative discretion took place during 1975 in Hawaii when the legislature adopted a set of land-use goals and guidelines to bring the previously unfettered State Land Use Commission under stronger popular control.

These examples are, however, relatively isolated. Even with the benefit of enormous staff resources, the legislative norm in Congress remains the broad delegation of discretionary authority. Oversight is spotty, depending on the personal interest and ideology of the relevant committee chairperson. At state and local levels, the ability of legislatures to supervise administrative action is limited further by the part-time character of legislative work. Thus, while some legislatures have demonstrated that they can exercise close supervision of administrative action, the promise of active control remains largely unfulfilled.

A second theme in this school of thought is the effort to increase the capacity for coordination and control of administrative agencies by elected executives. Many critics and observers maintain that chief executives must concentrate power in their offices so as to bend the bureaucracy to the will of the people, as expressed in their electoral mandate.[6] This doctrine of strong executive leadership has been embraced by many presidents, governors, and mayors in the postwar era.

In many cases, governments have been reorganized with this doctrine in mind, but the results have not been highly encouraging in terms of reasserting popular control. First, there is an inherent danger of excessive concentration of authority and abuse of discretion by the chief executive—a problem especially apparent at the federal level. Second, this approach places extraordinary and unrealistic burdens on the electoral process as a means of conveying public opinion on a wide range of activities and agencies. Given the typical nature of election campaigns for top executive offices, it is rare that sufficient information is exchanged to fulfill these functions. Finally, the ability of strong executive leaders to control administrative discretion and insure responsiveness to public preferences is limited by such personal factors as lack of time, lack of interest, and poor legislative-executive relations.

As an alternative to increased legislative and/or executive direction over administrative decision-making, the re-emerging tradition of direct citizen involvement in government has made itself felt with great force in the postwar era. The major impetus for expansion of direct participation rights and opportunities has come from three groups.[7]

First, many social scientists and policy analysts have stressed the need for direct public involvement because of disillusionment with the ability of legislatures and executives to improve responsiveness and accountability. These advocates have also emphasized that direct participation in decision-making is valuable in itself as a means of building a sense of responsibility and self-confidence on the part of alienated and disadvantaged members of society.

Second, the direct involvement approach has been pushed strongly by many traditional middle-class supporters of "good government"—e.g., neighborhood associations, environmental organizations, and consumer groups. From the perspective of these citizens, direct participation is valued as a means of counteracting and overcoming the privileged relationship between administrative agencies and the vested interests they are supposed to regulate.

Finally, direct citizen involvement has been emphasized and supported by blacks, poor people, youth, and other disadvantaged groups who view participation rights as a means of obtaining more responsiveness from social service and community development bureaucracies.

Legislative and executive response to advocacy of direct citizen involvement in administrative decision-making has taken two courses: 1) passage of general procedural acts and ordinances facilitating access and accountability, and 2) inclusion of legislative mandates in statutes and ordinances requiring administrative agencies to establish systematic citizen-involvement programs.

ESTABLISHMENT OF PARTICIPATION RIGHTS

The landmark Federal Administrative Procedure Act of 1946 was the opening round in the expansion of the general participation rights and opportunities of the public.[8] By requiring agencies to meet certain minimum standards of fairness and openness in their decision-making procedures, and by giving citizens the right to judicial relief in case of agency failure to comply, the Administrative Procedure Act broke new ground in enforcing public access and bureaucratic accountability. Some public involvement, such as mandatory public hearings or review and comment on proposed regulation in the *Federal Register,* were first authorized by the Administrative Procedure Act and its subsequent amendments. Most states and localities adopted administrative procedure acts of their own during the 1950s and 1960s.

In the 1960s, as federal programs again expanded rapidly and several new popular movements developed (e.g., civil rights, consumer, and environmental movements), attention again turned to the expansion and protection of general public-participation rights in administrative decision-making. The most significant acts on the federal level were the Freedom of Information Act (1966) and the National Environmental Policy Act (1970), both of which created broad new information and accountability obligations for administrative agencies and made these rights judicially enforceable by the individual citizen. In the past few years, these acts have also spread rapidly at the state level and, to a lesser degree, at the local level.

The states have also pioneered in the expansion of general participation rights and opportunities. Most prominently, it is at the state level that "sunshine laws" or open-meetings acts originated. Most states now have laws requiring all meetings of administrative agencies to be open to the public. Even more significantly, some states have pioneered in codifying explicit sets of participation standards to which all administrative agencies must adhere. For example, Montana's 1972 constitution requires citizen participation in the operations of all government agencies, and a recent statute in that state provides a comprehensive set of procedural minimums with which agencies must comply.

While general acts and orders of the type discussed above establish a framework of accessibility and accountability that is the necessary core of citizen involvement in administrative decision-making, they are not sufficient to insure that an agency will become more responsive to popular preferences. In the timeless ways of the bureaucracy, minima have a tendency to become maxima. Open meetings, notification procedures, public hearings, and other formal rights in and of themselves do not necessarily produce greater popular guidance and control. These procedural norms are passive; they may or may not be used positively to bring about a change in decision-making patterns. Recognizing these limitations, many groups have demanded more specific legislative mandates for citizen involvement which would place an affirmative obligation on administrative agencies to solicit participation in particular policy decisions.

AUTHORIZATION OF SYSTEMATIC INVOLVEMENT PROGRAMS

The Federal Housing Act of 1954 was the first major statute to incorporate a specific mandate for citizen participation. After five years of contentious and frustrating experience with federally financed urban redevelopment under the Housing Act of 1949, the revised statute sought to make administrative decision-making more responsive to popular needs and desires by requiring a *program* of citizen participation in the planning and execution of projects. The new concept was incorporated in the statute as a response to critics who claimed that the urban redevelopment had resulted in a brutal, inhumane approach to social problems.[9]

The program established Project Area Committees of local residents to review urban-renewal plans. These committees had no formal veto but their opinion was considered by relevant governments. The time horizon for these committees was often only two or three years and was in response to specific project proposals or urban-redevelopment plans. Thus they represented a step forward for participation but did not empower citizens to formulate their own long-range plans.

As in the area of general participation rights, congressional attention to the need for specific citizen-involvement programs accelerated greatly in the 1960s, as vast new social programs were authorized and citizen discontent and militance increased. The well-known mandate for "maximum feasible participation of the residents of the area and members of the group served" was incorporated in the Community Action Program legislation of 1964 as a significant expression of this concern. The desire to keep administrative discretion under control was also evident in the mandate for "widespread participation" of affected citizens in the planning and execution of the Model Cities program (1966).[10]

Despite the critical nature of much of this commentary, it was these two federal statutes, more than any other sources, that popularized and legitimized the concept of systematic citizen involvement programs, a concept subsequently incorporated in many other pieces of legislation at all levels of government. Indeed, the need for positive programs of citizen involvement in administrative decision-making seems to have become a new norm—although, as previously stressed, much confusion and uncertainty remains among legislators and elected executives about the meaning of the terms "widespread," "effective," or "meaningful" citizen involvement.

CITIZEN PARTICIPATION IN LEGISLATIVE DECISION-MAKING

With administrative agencies increasingly required to operate under more rigorous requirements for citizen access and involvement, reform efforts have recently turned toward establishing similar opportunities for popular participation in legislative decision-making. Referendum and initiative remain the most powerful and direct means of citizen intervention in legislative action, but these methods are quite clumsy and ponderous. They provide only a simple yes-no approach to public influence in the development of legislation.

Fueled by discontent with the political corruption of some legislators and distrust of the lobbying power exercised by specialized interest groups, several changes in legislative practice have been implemented in the past few years. One of the most prominent reforms promoting access and accountability is the application of open-meeting requirements to legislative deliberations. This reform is most common at the state level, but Congress is currently implementing legislative openness requirements and many local legislatures also operate under such self-imposed rules. The crucial function of these sunshine laws is to open the meetings of legislative committees so that citizens can be made aware of the crucial trade-offs and compromises that take place off the floor of the legislature.

A more advanced form of participation in legislative policy-making is the type of activity mentioned earlier in Alternatives for Washington, Goals for Dallas, Hawaii 2000. One function of these programs is to attempt to clarify citizen priorities and preferences prior to budgetary or other basic decisions by the legislature.

SUMMARY

Today we are in the midst of profound changes in American democratic practice. These changes are deeply rooted in the historic tradition of close popular control over government, but they also represent new departures in the relationship between citizens and decision-makers. Most importantly, there is no longer exclusive reliance on elections as the major means of influencing governmental decision-making. Starting with the referendum and initiative in the early 1900s, reformers have increasingly emphasized the need to enforce responsiveness and accountability through direct citizen intervention and involvement in decision-making (see Figure 1).

In the postwar era, from the early administrative procedure acts through the citizen-involvement mandates of the present, the focus of reform efforts has been on improving the process of administrative decision-making. As bureaucracies and agencies have grown dramatically in power and size, citizens have demanded and received more rigorous safeguards of access, openness, fair-

FIGURE 1. **Formal Opportunities for Citizen Involvement in Governmental Decision-Making**

		INDIRECT INVOLVEMENT	DIRECT INVOLVEMENT
A.	Legislative decision-making	Partisan or nonpartisan election of legislators and chief executives	Initiative and referendum
		Recall of legislators and chief executives	Goals programs and citizen participation on legislative committees
B.	Administrative decision-making	Partisan or nonpartisan election of selected administrative officials	Participation opportunities under administrative procedure acts, freedom of information acts, and related statutes
		Legislative and/or executive oversight of administrative decisions	Mandated citizen-involvement programs

ness, and redress. The objectives of this reform effort are quite simple and straightforward: to insure a reasonable correspondence between public policy and public preferences, and to prevent arbitrary and capricious transgression by government upon fundamental individual rights. The demand for increased participation rights and opportunities has also spilled over into the legislative arena, particularly in such basic and highly sensitive areas as the formulation of growth policy.

CHAPTER EIGHT

Consumer Activism in the Future of Health Care

BY ROSEMARY H. BRUNER

It is the consumer of health services who will determine the future of health and medical services in this country. Until now, because the medical establishment has controlled health policy, most policy decisions were motivated not by health needs but by money. We all know horror stories about the cost of medical care, doctors' indifference to patients, rip-offs of the public purse by practitioners and nursing homes.

Recently, however, the government and the consumer have begun to fight to gain improved services and control over costs. The medical establishment is fighting just as hard to keep control over health policy. While the outcome of that conflict has not yet been resolved, I predict that the consumer will win. Costs will be contained and services will be improved as soon as the consumer and consumer-advocate groups are able to gain access to the decision-making process.

The traditional medical establishment has come slowly and painfully to recognize that the consumer is beginning to demand some voice in health decisions. Many government officials recognize and support this trend. As one congressman commented, "There are only 380,000 doctors in this country; my constituency is larger than that. It's time I started to consider the needs of my own people instead of trying to please doctors."

However, because of the power of health providers, the complexity of the present system, and the mythology surrounding both health and medicine, consumers individually or as groups find it extremely difficult to sort out and identify the entry points to decision-making. Anticipatory democracy is the perfect vehicle for citizens concerned with health needs and with exercising control over the delivery of health care. Enough is known about the causes of disease and disability that it is possible to anticipate health-delivery needs and to prevent predictions of ever-rising health costs from becoming a self-fulfilling prophecy.

MYTHOLOGY OF MEDICINE

The mythology of medicine implies that the use of medical services can have a dramatic effect on health. Our belief in this mythology has led us to assume that doctors, hospitals, and medical research and technology will protect us from disease, disability, discomfort, and ultimately, from death.

Before our understanding of the human body and of the workings of disease had progressed sufficiently to distinguish among disease categories, health and life span were seen as controlled by forces beyond human comprehension. Better nutrition was the first factor to change in what appeared to be the capriciousness of fate. As improved agricultural practices produced more and better food during the second half of the eighteenth century, the individual's resistance to disease improved. Longer and healthier lives reduced society's need for work-force replacement and the individual's need for personal security through a large family. The result was a decline in the birth rate (indicating that when individuals no longer feel the need for large families, they voluntarily practice birth control, some form of which has been known in all societies). With a lower birth rate, deaths associated with childbirth were reduced. With fewer, stronger babies, infant mortality fell. This link between nutrition, increased resistance to disease, longer life span, lower birth rate, lower infant and maternal mortality can still be observed today in underdeveloped countries.

The second major change came with improved sanitation. Although hospital deaths declined dramatically as a result of Joseph Lister's campaign in the 1860s for sanitary surgical procedures and Florence Nightingale's efforts for hospital sanitation, the real changes first took place in the community and the home. The recognition in the mid-1850s of the importance of clean water and sewage disposal to control the spread and transmission of disease caused another major drop in mortality rates.

The survivors of each of these major eras of change were probably those with the strongest gene strains. Each time survivors mated with survivors, the gene base was strengthened. The elderly of the present population—most of whom survived a childhood of little or no artificial immunization, hazardous childbirth conditions, and the major flu epidemic of 1918—indicate the strength of the gene base as it developed as a result of improved nutrition and environmental conditions. In spite of the historical evidence of long-term increases in life expectancy and decreases in birth and mortality rates, today's medical mythology credits the development of immunization and the introduction of antibiotics with the advances in life span made in this century. Only recently has this mythology come to be questioned. For while immunization and antibiotics conquered the contagious diseases, particularly smallpox and diphtheria, major advances in the lowering of mortality rates and in increasing life expectancy had already been made through better nutrition, improved sanitation, and a stronger gene bank. But the importance of improved nutrition and public sanitation were not popularly associated with better health and increased life span and were long unrecognized.

The medical community was quick to accept the mantle of the medicine man/witch doctor and take credit for the advances. People have always feared the unknown. Fatal diseases, which struck seemingly at random and from an unknown source, made frightened people willing to abandon their souls to the church and their bodies to doctors. In both cases, the mysteries of practitioner expertise seemed beyond the comprehension of the untrained. Only recently has the public demanded a demystification of medical ritual. It is interesting that this demand coincides with one of the current trends in religion, namely an increasing demand for a rationalization of and participation in religious ritual.

HEALTH CARE VS. MEDICAL CARE

While many aspects of health and medical care may remain beyond our control, it is important to understand and to differentiate between those factors we can control and those we cannot. An important first step in this process is to recognize that there is more than a semantic distinction among the terms "health," "health care," and "medical care."

> *Health* can be defined as a state of well-being with the absence of disease or disorder.
>
> *Health care* is the prevention, control, and treatment of non-traumatic illnesses. It may require medical supervision and/or assistance. Health care is, in part, what is commonly referred to as "preventive medicine," which involves everything from weight control to holistic medicine.*
>
> *Medical care* is the treatment of those breakdowns of the health state which necessitate the interference of highly trained and skilled technologists and institutions, i.e., doctors and hospitals.

Health is not the same for each individual. As in most states of nature, there is a scale from good to bad. An individual's location on that scale depends on his/her personal history, particularly the interplay of three primary variables: nutrition, environmental influences, and his/her unique gene structure.

The distinction between health care and medical care is an important one that should be well understood. With the exception of accidents, suicide, homicide, and other forms of deliberate violence, illness or "being sick" is most common among children and

---

* Holistic medicine is the treatment of the whole human organism. It combines self care with the scope of general practitioner and the methods of various traditional or folk practices. Since the decline of the general practitioner, the pediatrician's treatment of all aspects of a child's health is the largest major example of holistic medicine in this country.

the elderly. The prevention, control, and treatment of many non-traumatic illnesses (for example, the common cold, flu, or insomnia) is best performed by the health-care establishment. While treatment may take place under medical supervision, because the diseases or disorders are either chronic or self-limiting, the problem demands a *health care,* not a *medical care* solution.

At the clinical level, disease and disorders fall into four levels: 1) those that can merely be diagnosed; 2) those that can be treated; 3) those that can be cured; and 4) those that can be prevented with routine care. However, the preventable (or prevented) rarely find their way to Marcus Welby. They are the routine, predictable, and unglamorous conditions of life.

The diseases of children, many of which are now preventable through immunization, are for the most part self-limiting; that is, the disease lasts a predictable period of time and then disappears. While the acute episode may be frightening to parents, most such episodes pass and need only minor medical and custodial care. For proof, one need only look at the income of pediatricians (lowest of all specialists), their long hours (caused by the demands of frantic parents), and the small size of the pediatric wards of most general hospitals. In addition, good prenatal care would prevent or modify the effects of many serious childhood conditions. Prenatal care is primarily a monitoring process. In this field as well, there is little glamour and the financial rewards for the doctor are not great. In both prenatal care and pediatrics, medically supervised paraprofessional personnel could be used far more extensively. A large body of literature suggests that both the provider and the patient find this mode of delivery satisfactory to excellent. More extensive use of paraprofessionals would mean that at a relatively low cost, high benefits would result for both the patient and society.

The segments of the population in greatest need of these services are the rural poor and the inner-city poor: those known to be financially unable to pay for such services. Thus there is little incentive for the medical establishment to seek out those in need. The middle-aged, middle-class heart-attack victim rushed to the hospital's coronary intensive-care unit and saved from death by the skilled cardiac specialist and high-technology instruments, while dramatic, is not the average health need.

Circulatory problems (which result in strokes and heart attacks) and most cancers are the diseases of degeneration, of aging. While perceived as desirable, long life, for both humans and machines, does have drawbacks: mechanisms wear out, some more slowly and gracefully than others. Some need less care and repair than others, but an end is inevitable. The needs of the elderly are also considered unglamorous. However, their disease states, unlike those of their children, are not self-limiting. The diseases that afflict the elderly may be long, painful, and humiliating to both the patient and the provider of care because of their inability to control a process that may be costly and require long-term custodial care. While this process of disintegration faces all income groups, those most in need are, again, primarily the poor.

The diseases of those who are neither children nor old also need to be examined. In most cases the causes of disease for this middle-aged group are primarily of an environmental nature: they may be self-induced through smoking, obesity, or addiction, or they may be caused by environmental hazards such as industrial or automotive pollutants. Once they have developed, these diseases require remedial treatment by the medical establishment.

This kind of categorizing of major disease groupings indicates that many health problems need either no care or health care, but little medical care. However, because of the mythology and the economic structure that has developed around the medical establishment, we have opened a Pandora's box whose evils can easily defy our control. Ivan Illich calls it "the political uses of natural death."

EXPENDITURES FOR MEDICAL CARE

Medical care (whether limited to its proper meaning or not) is the part of the system that we hear the most about because it absorbs the most money. We have become numbed by hearing that "health care" expenditures are somewhere between 8.5 and 10 percent of the gross national product. If we examine where that money actually goes, we learn that most of it is paid by the consumer in the form of either direct payment to providers, payment of insurance premiums, or the 30 or more percent of all taxes (state, local, and federal) that finds its way to the health providers through a wide variety of government-financed health services. A smaller portion is paid out by employers either for employee benefits or in taxes.

If all these expenditures resulted in a healthier population, there would be no cause for criticism. Yet because the medical establishment has never devised an acceptable set of indicators for measuring health, except the obvious one that the patient is still alive, we really do not know how our enormous national "health" expenditures actually affect health.

Two outcome measurements do exist by default. Both indicate that we are getting very little for our money. These are the statistics that compare us with other developed, western industrial countries in terms of male life expectancy and infant mortality. They tell us that our male population dies younger and more of our babies die in the first year of life than in the other countries most like our own. Yet we supposedly have the best-trained doctors and the best-equipped hospitals in the world.

But this has nothing to do with health. This statement is the key for any consumer who wishes to get involved in attempting to influence health decisions. Our allocation of resources, both public and private, places such emphasis on medical care that we lose sight of the real issue—health. Yet the predictable results of good health care suggest that the development of a good system of health-care delivery should be the dominant contender for funds and expansion.

The inability of the health-care sector to function at peak efficiency because of the lack of funds and personnel provides the patients for the medical-care sector. *If* we provided better nutrition, *if* we provided a better environment for our citizens, *if* we provided better primary care to pregnant women (especially teen-agers) and children, *if* we provided better home care for the elderly, *if* we provided an adequately trained and compensated health corps, we would be able to ensure better health for all citizens who wish it. Yet rather than move in this direction, we have created—and continue to feed—a money-eating monster that gives us little in terms of better health and over which we seem to have little control.

Let us now look at the ways in which health advocates may effectively try to influence and change the health system so that it benefits the total population. We are not ignorant of the present health and the predictable health needs of people. There are many indicators available that tell us much about the health of the American population. We know approximately how many babies are born each year and how many survive the first year of life. We know by geographic region and by rural, suburban, and city locations where those babies are born. We know the age and race of the mother. In some states, we know if and when she received prenatal care. We know the length of pregnancy relative to full-term and the birth weight of the baby. We know still other things about each baby, and we know an equal number of health facts about many other groups in the populations. This kind of information is important to developing the kind of system that will contribute to the *prevention* of disease and health breakdown.

Important inroads have already been made toward demystifying the doctor's special ability. The increase in the numbers of malpractice suits is a product of this demystification. While malpractice may be viewed as a negative reaction caused by anger and frustration, it has forced us to look at some fundamental assumptions about life, health, and death.

Ernest Becker writes in *The Denial of Death* of our inability to accept that our mobile, thinking minds are controlled by our frail bodies. Old institutions taught us to prepare for death; the Trappist's only spoken words are "remember death." In contrast, "modern medicine" promises us long and healthy lives. But while medical techniques may sustain body functions and sometimes prolong life, their pain, cost, and uncertainty have created frustration and anger on the part of patients and their families. In true American fashion, patients have struck back through money. We paid as long as there was hope; when hope disappeared, we retaliated—we sued. This is not the place to discuss malpractice and show how its cost has fallen back on the consumer. But it is an important development to keep in mind in any analysis of the interrelationship of health, health care, and medical care.

NO MIRACLES

It is now clear that there are no miracles for providing either good health or good health care. It is also clear that consumers, as the primary financial source for a bad system, should and must be involved in finding solutions to what has become a major problem.

A consumer's decision about how and where to exert pressure on the system in order to obtain maximum impact is invariably a complex one, involving a number of choices and based on a variety of considerations. What is called "the consumer movement" is recognized as a power force in the political system—it has even been graced with the jargonistic title, the "third sector" (the first being the public sector, the second the private sector). A brief examination of the interaction of the first and second sectors in the health/medicine field reveals how the third sector can function most effectively.

PUBLIC SECTOR

The public sector is the political establishment and the bureaucracy that serves that political establishment. The public sector refers to all levels and operations of governments—local, state, and national. The voter's general disenchantment with this sector is based on his/her inability to find correlations between his/her vote and the political decisions and public actions that affect his/her daily life. The kind of citizen involvement, concern, and action that has recently become pronounced in many issue areas is particularly important in the health care system, which has immediate impact on all our individual lives.

The key to entering the system lies in the problem of identifying the appropriate questions and knowing where responsibility for providing answers and solutions lies. For example, an individual seeking to determine how to apply pressure at the national level would need to determine which agency—and within that agency, which office—makes and implements the relevant decisions. One glance at the organization chart of the health section of the Department of Health, Education and Welfare might well induce panic in even the most determined consumer. It is easier to drive from New York to California on back roads with the help of a simple road map than to find the right office in the right corridor on the right floor of the HEW complex of buildings. HEW administers more than two hundred health programs—almost as many as there are ills of man.

THE PRIVATE SECTOR

The private sector provides a model of how to identify the points where it is possible to influence the decision-making process. It is easier, of course, for a large industry to identify its interests than it is for the single voter. Each industry knows what its interests are; it also knows its products and markets and how the government affects its every action. An industry can pinpoint those regulations that have the greatest impact and identify the actors involved, from local groups to legislators to regulatory agency officers. The industry then attempts to influence the policy-making process by producing a favorable climate, and decisions beneficial to it. The success of industry in lobbying and influencing is well known, well documented, and often condemned.

THE "THIRD SECTOR"

This same process of banding together around a defined need, identifying the appropriate sources of power and programs, and applying pressure at those points has produced the successes that forced the recognition of the consumer as the third sector. However, it was not the industrial model that first attracted the attention of the consumer advocates, but the model inadvertently provided by "Great Society" programs.

Lyndon Johnson's poverty programs, which mandated that local residents have "maximum feasible participation" in OEO (Office of Economic Opportunity) programs, provided citizens with new methods for participating in government decision-making. The experience gained through participating in these programs taught citizens that direct attacks on a nonresponsive government agency, legislator, or congressional committee brought more results than waiting passively and simply hoping for solutions to follow elections automatically. Citizens also came to realize the effectiveness of tight organization around single issues. The groups that saw the potential and perfected the method were not the poor but the well-educated middle-class, who have become the strongest consumer advocates. Those who wish to become health-consumer activists must ask themselves some questions in order to be able to define the area of interest that will provide a point of entry. While the three recent federal laws described below give some opportunities, there are many other possible approaches for the health consumer activist.

The important questions to address are the following:

1. Is involvement to be with health care or medical care?
2. Is involvement to be on the local, regional, or national level?
3. Is involvement to be focused on a specific disease? This decision is a particularly important one. Health consumers have been slow to organize, except for those connected with specific disease-oriented organizations, such as those focused on the research and treatment of heart disease, leukemia, multiple sclerosis, sickle cell anemia, and mental health. People most active in such specifically focused organizations usually have had a close family member suffer from the disease and thus have experienced the frustrations of dealing with a fragmented delivery system that makes great claims but may have little measureable effect. Many of the organizations of this type have successfully made the medical establishment more accountable in their areas since the diseases tend to be those in which doctors will admit to limitations. At the same time, they have often limited their potential effectiveness by being dominated by medical "advisers." A further problem with the organizations focused on specific diseases is that they rarely plan their own demise as a result of successful programs. Once polio was controlled, the March of Dimes began to focus on birth defects even though other organizations already existed in this same field.
4. If involvement is going to be as a general health-care activist, what are the most appropriate health advocate groups and strategies? For those who wish to be active on a national level, labor unions, Ralph Nader's Health Research Group, and Health Policy Action Committee (Health PAC) are a few of the health-consumer advocate groups that are effective and always anxious for new members. The American Public Health Association is also active and respected as a health advocate; although some professional qualifications are required for membership, these are so broad that almost anyone with an

interest in health is eligible for some class of membership. Other groups—such as the Association of Community Organizations for Reform Now (ACORN)—are concerned with a broad range of issues that include health among them.

An activist can be involved with education, prevention, or treatment. Before making this choice, it is important to become acquainted with some demographic information in order to understand what the real health needs are. Involvement in any activity or movement tends to narrow an individual's focus because the day-to-day demands of an operation make it more difficult to keep the larger picture in view. For this reason, it is important to go through this sorting prior to becoming an activist.

A study of the population will pinpoint which segments are most affected by major diseases or disorders, where these are located, and what services are available for early diagnosis, treatment, and/or prevention. It will also indicate those health problems that may be the result of environmental hazards (industrial or everyday living stresses, including housing and poverty), those that may be nutrition-related, and those that may be most responsive to direct treatment or education.

LEGISLATION MANDATING CONSUMER PARTICIPATION

Recently the federal government and some states have begun to express active concern over skyrocketing medical costs. They have also begun to acknowledge the growing need for consumer involvement in health planning. Three recent pieces of federal legislation have mandated consumer involvement. These are: 1) the Health Maintenance Organization Act of 1973, 2) the National Health Planning and Resources Development Act of 1974 (commonly referred to as PL 93-641), and 3) those sections of the Health Revenue Sharing Act of 1975 (PL 94-63), which relate to community mental health centers. Of these, PL 93-641 is the most far reaching. However, with few exceptions, citizens have not used these laws as vehicles for entering the health decision-making process. While the enactment of these laws represents progress toward greater involvement of consumers in the health field, it is not an instant answer to the frustration that seems to be an inevitable part of activism in this field. Reading the legislation demands persistence bordering on an endurance contest. Moreover, the extent to which these laws overlap creates a bureaucracy that seems to defy penetration. Yet it must be assumed that since the procedures for citizen involvement do now exist, those committed to participation will be able to make their way through the bureaucratic maze (just as those providers seeking funds from the bureaucracy are now able to).

The Health Maintenance Organization Act of 1973 Health maintenance organizations (HMOs) are membership organizations that provide prepaid medical services; that is, for a set fee, individuals and families receive all needed medical care—including preventive care, episodic care, and hospital care. Each HMO attempts to make its fees competitive with other insurance plans and then contracts with a group of doctors and hospital(s) to provide care for its members. If the doctors and/or hospital spend less than the agreed limit, they share in a performance bonus; if costs go over the agreed limit, they simply must bear them. Such a system gives the health providers (that is, doctors and hospitals) an incentive to keep people well and thus spend less than the limit. This contrasts with other health insurance plans, under which the medical establishment collects only in the case of illness.

A familiar model of this type of plan is the Kaiser-Permanente Plan started at the Kaiser shipyards in World War II (although Kaiser is unique in that it owns its own hospitals). Thus the concept has been known for over three decades, but the Health Maintenance Organization Act gave the needed incentive to the creation of other such organizations. The 1973 legislation provided that the federal government would share the costs—both planning and operational—of establishing HMOs. Moreover, it provided that where HMOs exist, employers must give their employees the option of having the industry contribute its share of health insurance costs to the HMO rather than to whatever plan is otherwise available. The act further provided that HMOs must have health consumers on their boards of directors.

HMOs, while currently not widespread, are increasing in number. Because of their inherent bias toward preventive health rather than medical repair they provide a potentially good vehicle for the health-consumer activist. Although one must be an HMO member to become a member of the board, this—along with an investment in time, effort, and probably politicking—is the only prerequisite. Once attained, board membership provides a direct line to decision-making.

PL 93-641 & PL 94-63   PL 93-641 divided the country into some two hundred Health Service Areas under the jurisdiction of the Department of Health, Education and Welfare. Each of these areas has a Health Systems Agency (HSA) that evaluates all plans dealing with health facilities and services that already do, or hope to, receive funds from the federal government. While the agencies administer various aspects of the service areas, the Health Systems Agencies provide an important mechanism for consumer input. They have real power, in part because they can prevent the granting of federal health funds, and in part because they can give technical assistance and funds for developing projects such as neighborhood health centers, HMOs, or health-education programs. The Health Service Areas are small enough to allow board and staff members to make realistic plans for the health needs of their populations. By knowing the needs and the services that presently exist, the staff can alert the board to overlapping services and thus become a major force for cost containment.

By law, a majority, but not more than 60 percent of the members of the board of a Health Systems Agency, "shall be residents of the health service area served by the agency who are consumers of health care and who are not . . . providers of health care and who are broadly representative of the social, economic, linguistic and racial populations of the health-service area and major purchasers of health care." No more than another one third can be health-care providers and the remaining are publicly elected officials and other representatives of governmental authorities in the health-service area.

PL 94-63 applies the same wording and the same concepts to the Community Mental Health Centers (CMHCs) that legislation established. In neither law, 93-641 or 94-63, is there a *procedure* for a consumer to get on the relevant board. Personal interviews and written assessments of citizen participation indicate that constant harassment of staff members is perhaps the best way to membership. Notices are distributed periodically inviting interest on the part of the public; public information meetings are held, and stories appear in newspapers—but none of these seems to be the route to board membership. Knowing the health-care providers already on the board and having the same concerns seems to be one road to membership, but hardly to being a consumer representative. Being a member of a consumer health group, particularly one of the women's groups, and constantly contacting your congressional representative may also help.

It is important to recall the lessons of OEO. Not only did members of the public community learn a great lesson from the "maximum feasible participation" wording of the OEO legislation, but so did those who represented the establishment. The name of the game became allocation of funds for programs. It literally "paid" to make sure that board members worked together. Service to the community was supposed to be the goal but this fact was lost as soon as the money came in. Community members had to be picked with care and cultivated so that they would not be disruptive as the local staff and Washington bureaucrats fought over the dispersal of funds. This is a short summary of many evaluations of one of the major breakdowns of the OEO programs; the community that was to control the programs and the funds ended up being controlled.

A similar thing is already happening to the consumer representatives on the HSA and CMHC boards. Some of the control mechanisms are easy. The use of acronyms or shorthand numerical inferences to legislation can easily be confusing to the uninitiated consumer activist, and the new member's bewilderment and embarrassment make learning and participation more difficult. It requires real persistence and a strong ego to ask constantly, "What does that mean?" The consumer who wishes to take an active part and to have an impact will find it essential to overcome these initial handicaps and to persevere.

An even more difficult part of the initiation process is that of being belittled by the health-care providers. Doctors and hospital administrators generally use abbreviations and the technological language of their discipline; disease, diagnosis, and treatment are always referred to by their scientific names. If the layperson asks what the relationship is between a particular treatment and its outcome for the general health status of the population, s/he will be ignored or answered in a long lecture on how only medical persons are able to assess the need for treatment. S/He may be asked the most pointed of all questions, "What monetary value do you put on human life; how would you respond if it were your child?" One should *never respond to that question*. It is totally irrelevant to the job on the board.*

Health-care-consumer activists should not expect the staff members of either HSAs or CMHCs to understand or represent the needs of the community. Health planning is a new discipline, mostly self-taught and almost completely without a defined structure. Therefore, the staff members of HSAs are as prone to being co-opted by the provider board members as are the community members. Few of the staff members have had experience in dealing with volunteer boards and, like the rest of us, they carry with them all of the myths about medicine and doctors. They are increasingly being pushed to consider cost, access to care, who receives care, and the actual health needs of the broad population of health consumers. However, they are, for the most part, still awed and led by the providers on the board. Strong and aware consumer members who are willing to learn about health could help to change this. Most HSA staff members are not elitists but they do need support from their boards to function effectively.

Mental-health agency staff members, on the other hand, are highly trained, not as planners but as providers of treatment. They often lose sight of their role as planners as soon as the meeting starts and the board members file in, many of whom are providers. Those board members who aren't actual providers think of themselves as at least semiprofessional by avocation. The board works as a single unit; the conflicts that do arise generally have to do with fund allocation for programs partly because most board members are there to protect a program and partly because no two members agree on a definition of mental health. It is therefore difficult to allocate among programs because no one will agree, for example, that alcoholism is a disorder with higher demands on limited funds than family counseling.

A few words of hope are in order after all of these cautions. There has been some exciting activity in a few HSAs that have encouraged true community participation. In most cases, these HSA boards have been elected rather than appointed. The result of this "from the bottom up" approach is a greater sense of ac-

* For your own peace of mind, read Victor Fuch's book, *Who Shall Live?*, and suggest your questioner do the same.

countability on the part of the board. HSAs in Los Angeles, North Central Connecticut, and Little Rock, Arkansas, all are examples of this type of community board. These groups were successful because consumer and community groups became interested in participating in health decision-making and developed their own action model. HSAs can offer a comfortable framework for consumer activity because most consumer successes in other fields have been in stopping actions and much of the HSA power is negative power. The HSA board can disapprove of proposed use of federal funds in the area, and it can stop the expansion of unnecessary health facilities. Disapproval can sometimes be a stronger weapon than approval because it forces the development of alternative plans. On the other hand, HSAs give consumer representatives the opportunity to take part in developing these alternative plans.

In summary, while good health and medical care at reasonable cost for most Americans seem far away and beyond our control, they are not. However, this is not a battle for the faint-hearted. The problem is understandable and thus manageable. It must not be left in the hands of the providers who build empires of hospitals and nursing homes and the medical practitioners who are more interested in money than lives. However, until the consumers are willing to be as dedicated as the providers, health costs will continue to rise and too many people will die before their time.

CHAPTER NINE

A Black View:
From Participation
to Anticipation

BY LAWRENCE J. AULS

On cold winter evenings in January 1975 in Columbus, Ohio, some two hundred fifty residents from mostly black neighborhoods met in church basements, school buildings, and a remodeled shirt factory to set goals and objectives twenty-five years into the future—to take a look at the year 2000. This effort was part of a larger Project 2000 conducted by the Mid-Ohio Regional Planning Commission, an organization financed by federal, state, county, and city governments.

The local Model Neighborhood Assembly (MNA) conducted the particular portion of Project 2000, an ongoing attempt to look at the long-range future of Columbus and surrounding Franklin County, described here. The MNA was a product of the federally funded Model Cities Program, which made resources available to local communities with the stipulation that citizens be given an opportunity to help determine, through planning, monitoring, and evaluating, how those resources would be spent. As in most of the other 146 cities throughout the nation that were part of the Model Cities Program, the program in Columbus enabled poor and otherwise powerless individuals to participate in making decisions that would directly affect their lives and well-being. The $23 million available through the Model Cities Program over a seven-year period gave disadvantaged communities a degree of power and influence previously unknown to them. Even though the Model Cities Program has since been eliminated, the institutions through which citizens exercised their new power are surviving—although barely.

The Columbus MNA was the logical agency to undertake the study of the black community's visions and expectations of the future and to examine the more general question of citizen participation. For the first time in our individual and collective lives we were asked on those special nights to take the giant mental leap from the more familiar participation perspective of the model cities planning process, which focused on one to five years ahead, to the anticipatory perspective of Project 2000, which focused on the next twenty-five years and beyond. This leap was an attempt to overcome a profound sense of powerlessness. Participants in the Project 2000 sessions met with some misgivings as to whether or not the exercise would be worth it.

Before *Roots,** which for black people turned out to be an intellectually defensible, eight-day, emotionally embraceable high, only a small black intelligentsia had a working knowledge of the history of black people in America; most blacks lacked a shared experience of knowing that we come from a background of immense dignity and pain. As Project 2000 demonstrated, this lack of historical understanding made it more difficult to pereceive how we would survive twenty-five more years in an environment that was, *to a large extent,* still hostile. The *Roots* experience gave us what we did not have then—a psychological foundation for the development of a black future to be shared with others, as finally our history was shared.

As one black participant later reminisced about the Project 2000 experience, "What we saw wasn't important. It was the attempt to see at all that was important. Part of our history has been so ugly, painful, and, yes, frightening and theatening that you might be considered a damn fool looking up the road."

The Model Cities Program involved communities as diverse as the poor white community of Wheeling, West Virginia; Mexican-

* Editor's note: *Roots,* the ABC dramatization of Alex Haley's book by that name, on the origins of his family in Africa and the U.S., was viewed by approximately 130 million Americans when it was shown in January 1977.

Americans in Eagle Pass, Texas; the white middle classes of Minneapolis, Minnesota; and the once riot-afflicted inner cities of Detroit and Los Angeles. The participation of citizens was its most controversial aspect because it gave a new element of power, within the existing system rather than outside it, to blacks, the most visibly alienated group in America. According to the rhetoric of the Lyndon Johnson era, it was an attempt "to bring them into the mainstream of American life." Yet the intents and motives of the program were the subject of intense debate. Leftists denounced the Model Cities Program as a pacifistic, neocolonialist tool; some on the right thought the program should have been a ruse to corral blacks into internment camps, just as Japanese-Americans were interned in California during World War II. For those in the middle, the program was something "to buy the niggers off with."

Since the legislation creating the Model Cities Program was enacted in 1966, citizen participation has had varying degrees of federal and local approval and support. But during the Nixon years, the resources available to neighborhood organizations were cut. Later their rights to hire technical assistance and to review decisions made at other levels were eliminated. Neither of these procedures was reinstated during the Ford presidency. Administrative assistance at the local level was often supplied only grudgingly, since local jurisdictions were generally nervous about giving neighborhoods the right (and the technical assistance) to write spending proposals. City governments often used their mandate to provide technical assistance to the neighborhoods as a means of keeping "eyes and ears" on what the neighborhoods were doing.

The Columbus citizens' participation organization—the Model Neighborhood Assembly—was a fifty-two-member legislative body, thirty-two of whom were elected by the neighborhoods and twenty of whom represented such organizations as the NAACP, Afro-Set, and the Welfare Department. This body focused on all issues of direct concern to the lives of citizens. Its members organized themselves into task forces to try to find solutions to problems in six areas:

1. health and social services
2. crime, delinquency, culture, and recreation
3. housing, physical development, environment, and transportation

4. education
5. employment and economic development
6. income maintenance

Each of the task forces consisted of twenty-eight members—eight MNA members and twenty local residents.

The Assembly as a whole met at least twice monthly, and often more frequently. Its executive committee coordinated its daily activities and its staff members were assigned to specific neighborhoods and to individual task forces to do much of the MNA's "leg work."

THE MNA LOOKS TO THE FUTURE

An in-depth study conducted in 1975 that involved both residents and technical experts examined the future of each of these six concerns. An extensive questionnaire was mailed to the task-force members, who were asked to articulate their views of what the future in each of the issue areas was likely to be, as well as what they hoped it would be. Because the number of returned responses was comparatively small and because the writing skills of those whose views were being sought varied, attempts were made at each of the meetings to draw out the views of those attending. The meetings—eight in all—were also open to the public.

Participants at the sessions included a highly energetic grandmother; a well-paid laborer; a successful woman entrepreneur; a Ph.D. candidate; several preachers; welfare mothers; Brothers and Sisters; one Black Nationalist with an "X" after his name who was righteously and, to more than a few, frighteningly indignant; two members of the local city council—a black man and a white woman—whom newspapers had dubbed "the Mod Squad"; and representatives of a variety of neighborhood organizations. Some at the sessions knew firsthand people who had been slaves; others had themselves been part of the generations of change that included the worst aspects of Jim Crowism; others had participated in, feared, or cheered the violent man-to-man racial confrontations of the 1940s, confrontations that contrasted with the "blacks-against-property-and-authority" happenings of the mid-1960s and early 1970s. In all, nearly two hundred fifty residents and twenty-four technical experts participated. The people in those rooms truly represented the "maximum feasible participation" called for in the Great Society legislation of the 1960s, because they reflected the varied and conflicting opinions found not only in the black community, but also in other, older neighborhoods that had problems and aspirations that cut across geographic, race, religious, educational, and, to a lesser extent, financial backgrounds.

Each of the task forces held discussions on the future of its area of concern. In addition, an executive committee discussed the meaning of citizen participation, and the project closed with a general meeting of the MNA. The findings of each of the task-force examinations were incorporated into the staff report submitted to the MNA at the final meeting. Described below are impressions from three of the task-force sessions.

1. Housing, Physical Development, Environment, and Transportation

The chairperson, a guard at the local jail, was elected to major posts within the Assembly because of his concern about honesty and integrity in money matters. The technical experts included the director and prime mover of the Housing Opportunity Center of Metropolitan Columbus, a young, white housing planner for the city whose empathy was always appreciated; a local investment counselor, again white, who headed a major effort to create a neighborhood-based and -financed real estate development company; the white president of a medium-size rehabilitation company that has a justified reputation for doing good work; a woman who knew about housing and real estate because she owned some but who functioned here in her capacity as staff member of a neighborhood review board; and the director of neighborhood-based efforts designed to deal with urban pollution.

In this task-force meeting, as in each of the others, a staff member or one of the technical experts used the previously publicized questionnaire as the basis for a presentation. A blackboard or easel was used to list the various problems, goals, and objectives suggested in the questionnaires or by the residents and/or technical experts at the meeting. In this particular task force, two of the basic questions were:

1. What should be the future of housing in the older neighborhoods in the year 2000?
2. Who should or will own the land?

(Absentee landlords owned some 73 percent of the neighborhood represented by the Model Neighborhood Assembly.)

The greatest consensus emerged around the following issues:

- conservation of existing resources;
- substantial rehabilitation and restoration of existing housing in older sections of the city;
- creation of the climate for a racial and economic mix that would allow a wholesome environment for living;
- development of private financing and better utilization of existing funds, along with necessary supportive services;
- preservation of green spaces and surrounding forestry;
- plentiful supply of fuel for homes and industry used in conformity to the best conservation techniques known and those to be explored; and
- preparation for greater population density, including increasing the supply of housing.[1]

2. Income Maintenance

The chairperson of this task force was an extremely bright and aggressive resident mother. The technical participants included the white director of a major child-care planning operation who had demonstrated the ability to be helpful and maintain her own integrity through the years of black-power rejection of white assistance, and an ebullient black woman who was director of a settlement-house day-care center.

One of the main questions addressed by this task force was, "What activities (i.e., programs) do you expect will sustain or supplement people's income in the year 2000?" The final report shows the range and depth of the participants' feelings and aspirations for the neighborhood and for society as a whole:[2]

The role of the family and its time-honored relationships has been one of the most rapidly changing phenomena of the middle of the twentieth century. The accelerating acceptance of single-parent families and the economic necessities for employment, spurred by the drive of women for equality, have accentuated the need for alternative styles of child rearing. The nuclear family in our urban areas can no longer fall back on the services of a grandmother, aunt, or sister as caregivers. Systems of Family Day Care Homes and Group Centers therefore need to be developed in an orderly fashion.

To allay fears of "Sovietizing" American children or undermining family structures it is now, and will continue to be, important to involve parents in the design and monitoring of child-care services. Since day care is a social service that is delivered in the proprietary sector more than the public, it is important to note that rising costs are increasingly threatening its profit-making capability. The future would seem to hold then either increased numbers of tax-supported programs or increasing subsidies to proprietors through contract care.

3. Crime, Delinquency, Culture, and Recreation

This task force addressed two major questions: 1) What will the cultural patterns of black people look like in the year 2000? and 2) What *should* these black cultural patterns be in the next twenty-five years?

The report emerging from this session reflected an awareness of the present position of black people and a recognition that blacks must look to themselves and their deepest needs for solutions:[3]

In twenty-five years there should be the emergence of an older and younger group of people that have established a positive track record in many fields. Through dance, the arts, movies, education, business, social work, politics, and other activities we will define common or at least respected values. The outlook will be both inward to the spirit and its impact on our everyday lives, and outward to the building of organizations and institutions that reflect our dreams and deal with our fears. A reaching out to make sure that we are international (the third world primarily), universal, and incorporate this into what we do and become.

The results of these and the other task-force sessions were submitted to the MNA, together with a staff report summarizing the exercise. The preface pointed out that thinking about the year 2000 was significant both as a reminder of the local resident's basic insecurity and as a cause for hopeful thoughts, feelings, and desires about the future.[4]

The report then noted three unique aspects of the project.[5] First, it represented the first time in Columbus's history that black citizens were asked to consider seriously the long-term future, and the first time their opinions and projections of goals were taken seriously enough to be recorded, printed, and made available for presentation to the larger Columbus/Franklin County community.

Second, it recognized that community members were "experts" whose input on the future of the older neighborhoods was important.

And third, the questions covering a broad spectrum of human services were designed to encourage pessimistic, realistic, or optimistic opinions on their needs and impact on people's lives in the year 2000.

The entire package—questionnaires, task-force reports and the overall staff report—were given to the Mid-Ohio Regional Planning Commission in order that the input of individual citizens not be diluted by a consensus report.

The reaction of the Mid-Ohio Regional Planning Association was mixed because it was the first time a predominantly black community group presented its views of the future. Although some of the objectives listed in the report are being incorporated into the Master Plan for Columbus/Franklin County, the need for other objectives involving a higher degree of community conflict are only now being recognized.

IN RETROSPECT

The Model Cities Program is dead, technically and legally, and its replacement, the Housing and Community Development Act of 1974, isn't the same thing, because the major provisions for citizen participation were gutted, although some citizen-participation projects already underway continue. Project 2000 met the same fate as many children born in poor urban and rural areas: it died early of "benign neglect." Although its death is in many ways a shame, the survival of the Model Cities Program is not as important an issue as the survival of decision-making processes that genuinely involve the affected citizenry. Racial, economic, religious, and age differences lead to differing perspectives and values, and the resulting differences in needs and desires must be accepted and taken into account in decision-making. To support the development of neighborhood-based decision-making institutions that reflect this social diversity is quite simply to master a tool for survival in twentieth-century America.

The movement is surviving in spite of setbacks. In Columbus the Model Neighborhood Assembly, after the demise of the Model Cities Program and without the funds supplied by the federal government, has diminished in influence. But the Metropolitan Human Services Commission, a new agency formed to deal with the question of human-services planning, coordination, and resource allocation in Columbus/Franklin County, is in theory committed to involving citizens at the neighborhood level. Whether or not it will actually implement anticipatory democracy is unclear.

Continuing to address the future, clear, and present danger is as critical as involving members of the community in the decision-making process. The 1975 effort was a useful one in which much was learned. And then, in the dead of winter in 1977 when *Roots* swept the land, some 130 million people shared for one brief moment in the existence of a "national village," resulting from a common view of an event and transcending separateness by open acknowledgment of the differences in how some people arrived in a Henning, Tennessee, or a Columbus, Ohio. *Roots* brought to the surface the chance to see a common future based on our ability to share and feel a widely diversified past.

"Now dreaming ain't looking," as a preacher says. When we look into the future and soberly attempt to come to grips with it, we are forced to leave behind our real or imagined fears and to come together in a circle of mutual trust—or else to perish. We did this in 1975; we could probably do it better now because of *Roots*.

The Model Cities Program introduced into the national dialogue the idea of neighborhoods sitting down together in an attempt to involve otherwise powerless individuals in the decision-making process. The Columbus experience, for one, attempted to incorporate into this process a conscious assessment of the future. Such efforts must continue and expand. Just as our use of the past can form a sound basis for coming together to create the future, so too the futures-planning techniques that were initially created for use by business and the military can be used by people who want revitalized neighborhoods and safe places to live—concerns expressed repeatedly by citizens addressing the future.

This call for participatory democracy is a further expression of the "Dream" of Martin Luther King. It is the birthright of us all.

CHAPTER TEN

Tomorrow's Technology: Who Decides?

BY BRYON KENNARD

Had people foreseen, one hundred years ago, the social and economic turmoil that would follow in the wake of the mechanization of agriculture, steps might have been taken to avert, or at least to soften, the harsh consequences of those new technologies. Instead, over the years economic necessities forced millions of rural dwellers off the land and into crowded and inhospitable cities. However one interprets these events, this much is evident: the social choices created at that time by technology were never made clear, even though the public heavily subsidized the development of agricultural technology.

Had people known sixty years ago that the automobile would bring—along with its manifest advantages—appalling environmental devastation, steps might have been taken to reduce its adverse effects.

Twenty-five years ago, when most people were hailing the advent of television, few understood that this new communications technology might be used to introduce violence into every American home and to manipulate the minds and pocketbooks of consumers, often against their best interests.

Practically every day some new technological program is

launched, usually with taxpayers' money. Many of these have as great an influence upon our lives and communities as those milestone developments mentioned above. In human biology, for example, technology is producing new social possibilities of the most fundamental sort: test-tube babies, postponement of death, mind control, genetic warfare, new life forms. How do we make decisions about options such as these? On technical grounds? Or ethical grounds?

Fortunately, we are now beginning to recognize that society ought to and can make choices about the impact of technology upon our lives. The possible social, economic, and environmental consequences of new products and technologies should be systematically evaluated in advance of their use, as should new applications of present technology, such as continued highway construction. This process is called technology assessment. Advocates describe it as an "early warning system" for society that will help avoid or reduce the undesirable consequences of technological change. We should look before we leap. It is as simple as that.

THE BEGINNINGS: THE OFFICE OF TECHNOLOGY ASSESSMENT

Although relatively new, technology assessment has quickly become fashionable in some government, academic, and corporate circles. In 1972 Congress passed the Technology Assessment Act, creating a joint committee on technology called the Technology Assessment Board. The act created an Office of Technology Assessment (OTA) to serve Congress in a manner analogous to the General Accounting Office and the Library of Congress. The act also provided for a Technology Assessment Advisory Council of twelve members to advise OTA and the Technology Board. On behalf of Congress, OTA has assessed social options in such diverse areas as food, energy, oceans, materials resources, international trade, and transportation.

In addition, the influence of citizen-advocacy groups on decisions about science and technology has increased during the past decade. The fight against the SST best symbolizes the influence of such voluntary action, but there are dozens of examples of a widespread civic revolt. Citizen opposition to highways, airports, power plants and to other forms of urban expansion has flared up in virtually every American city. Ralph Nader and his colleagues have attracted vast public support for the reform of corporate and bureaucratic institutions producing or regulating consumer goods, including everything from food and water to clothing and shelter. Minorities and feminist groups have begun to zero in on inequalities in the distribution of technology's benefits, such as jobs, income, and opportunities for upward mobility. Industrial workers have grown restive about occupational health and safety and job satisfaction and securities, all of which are increasingly determined by remote decisions about technology.

Although the response of government and corporations to the demands of citizen organizations has been belated and small, one indication that the message is getting through is the appearance of technology assessment programs within Congress, some executive agencies and state governments. Unfortunately, these tend to have serious limitations.

IN THE ABSENCE OF PUBLIC PARTICIPATION . . .

Dr. James B. Sullivan, co-director of the Center for Science in the Public Interest, has criticized technology assessment as usually practiced for systematically excluding citizens. In Dr. Sullivan's view:

- The purpose of most technology assessment is to give the go ahead for projects that have already gone ahead.
- Any technical study that criticizes a politically potent development will not see the light of day.
- Most cost/benefit studies don't tell who gets the benefits and who pays the cost.
- The hidden assumption always favors the status quo.
- Any expert who knows anything about a technological development usually works for the developer.
- Most of the information included in a technology assessment comes from the developer of the technology.

- Technologies are usually assessed by the same agencies that promote them.
- More often than not, the assessors of a technology and its developer are in cahoots.
- The greater the bulk of material in a technology assessment, the greater the intent to obfuscate the issue.
- To most assessment agencies, citizen participation, public information, and public relations are all the same.
- While agency officials are required to hold hearings for the public, they are not required to listen.[1]

If technology assessment is to protect citizens and consumers affected by technological change, it is important to alert and to inform the many voluntary organizations concerned with these issues before new technologies or new applications of existing technology are actually implemented. To this end, here are some criteria for technology assessment that citizen organizations have advocated:

- Assessment agencies should develop new concepts and methods for assessment, rather than merely gather new facts.
- New ways of assessing private sector activities are needed, for these activities do much to shape our social and physical environment. The interactions between public and private sectors should also be assessed.
- The agency should actively involve the public in the assessment process by fully publicizing each assessment as soon as conceived and by readily disclosing assessment data in easy-to-understand reports. Active solicitation of views should be accomplished at a very early stage in the study's development.
- Funds should be made available to enable nonprofit citizen organizations to participate in assessment studies.
- When contrasting opinions exist, separate assessments should be made by interests opposing the proposal. Views of experts and technicians outside the field being assessed and the views of competent generalists should also be included. Interaction should be prompted among those holding opposing viewpoints as well as those in the vari-

ous disciplines involved. The potential adverse effects should be thoroughly assessed.

· Assessments should be comprehensive in scope and well defined in detail. The interdependence of related technologies should receive adequate consideration, for to study one technology in isolation from all others can be misleading. The alternative of doing nothing at all should always be considered.

· Assessments should include a discussion of how economic costs and benefits are defined. Who will receive benefits, and who will assume the risks and costs of a proposed technology? A discussion of the effect of the technology on minority and lower-income groups should always be included.

· Hidden assumptions and areas of ignorance or lack of data should be clearly identified and discussed.[2]

CITIZENS ON THE INSIDE?

While public officials and planners have touted technology assessment as a far superior successor to cost/benefit analysis for policy research purposes, little government effort has been made to educate citizen organizations keenly interested in public policy in the use of this new tool. This is an interesting omission, since the purpose of technology assessment is to collect and evaluate hitherto neglected social data on both the advantages and the disadvantages inherent in technological change. The very groups likely to possess the best information about how social values pertain to public policy—churches, youth groups, consumer groups, etc.—have often been left in the dark instead of alerted and consulted.

For the most part, scientific researchers remain hostile to the idea that the best way to include social values in science policy is to admit nonspecialists into the process. Social values may not be quantifiable, but they must certainly be represented in policy research nonetheless. Leaders of citizen organizations ought to be included in the many boards, committees, and panels that are established to assess public policy in sciences. Citizen and consumer groups have had some success in getting citizen generalists appointed to groups, most notably at OTA, and in the process they have established an important precedent.

OTA's first major undertaking to include substantial public participation was a program examining coastal effects of offshore energy systems. It assessed oil and gas systems, deepwater ports, and nuclear power plants off the coast of New Jersey, and then held informal meetings with groups of private citizens as well as representatives of interest groups to explore citizen attitudes. More than fifteen thousand persons took part by responding to questionnaires or attending meetings.[3] The Office of Technology Assessment used the citizen comments throughout its report on the coastal effects of offshore energy systems. This report was then used by several congressional committees and executive-branch agencies in dealing with issues such as tanker safety, oil-spill technology, coastal-zone management, and offshore leasing and drilling. The citizen participation process has since been included in other OTA projects.

IT'S COMMON SENSE

The function of citizen involvement is to express values implicit in science policy. In a request asking U.S. Energy Research and Development Administration (ERDA) to include citizen leaders on the planning committee for the Solar Energy Research Institute, I wrote:

Values such as justice or beauty, by their very nature lie beyond the realm of quantification. Thus experts and technicians, acting within their disciplines, are incapable of expressing them. When it comes to values, we are all equal . . .

In our society, it has long been the function of civic and consumer leaders to assert the long-range public interest and broad social values as against narrow, short-range, technical and economic considerations. Our planners must now recognize that the involvement of citizen leaders in science policy is a way of having individuals stand in as surrogates for social values which otherwise go unexpressed and neglected.

In the past, technological innovations have frequently been introduced as toys for the rich, e.g., the automobile, television, or as tools to help those in power, e.g., the computer. Technology assessment offers us a chance to do it right: to introduce technological change with a minimum of disruption and with sensitivity for related human needs.

The extent to which government and academic researchers in science policy encourage and facilitate public participation is the extent to which technology assessment will be worth the cost and effect. Those of us in the voluntary sector are waiting and watching as the technology assessment process unfolds. It will be interesting to see whether or not we are invited inside.

IV

Anticipatory Democracy in the Workplace

Anticipatory democracy in the workplace should force a corporation to examine its impact not only upon its workers but also upon society at large. One way of making this distinction is to identify the important issues in this sphere, which range from those with the most immediate impact on the worker to those with the most significant impact on society:

1. physical working conditions
2. safety rules and practices
3. placement in particular jobs, discipline, setting work standards and pace—how the job is done
4. hiring; training
5. promotions
6. fringe benefits; collective-welfare income (for example, medical, housing)
7. job security; layoffs
8. setting salaries; management bonus plans and stock options
9. promotion of executives
10. investments in new machinery
11. investments in new buildings
12. economic relations with the company's other divisions
13. division of the profits—allocation of net earnings to reserves,

      investment, distribution to employees, outside stockholders, and so forth

14.   raising capital; economic relations to other firms, banks, government

15.   research and development

16.   choice of products, markets, pricing

Issues 1 to 7 are closest to the worker's own immediate sphere of activity; 8 to 16 move from workplace questions to the operations and goals of the company, particularly as these affect society.

In Chapter 11 Donald Conover, chief corporate planner for Western Electric, begins with the premise that the purpose of business is to produce a product or service that customers need and to make a profit doing it. Yet Conover believes that the worker must become more involved in the operations of the company that directly affect him because such participatory management is "one of the most important safeguards to the private-enterprise system and freedom in society as a whole."

George Benello, on the other hand, argues that the purpose of the company should be to allow workers to develop fully as human beings. This requires self-management or direct democracy within the economic organization. Under such a system, control over all sixteen issues listed above would rest with the workers, regardless of the form of ownership. Benello describes the movement to create self-managed economic democracy in Chapter 12.

The question of whether workers can move beyond the issues of managing the workplace conditions to the larger issues of the direction of the corporation is the subject of my own article, the last in the section. At Lucas Aerospace Company in Great Britain, the workers, including highly trained craftsmen and engineers, were faced with a continuing trend of layoffs resulting from cuts in defense spending and aircraft production. They actually devised a plan for the company to diversify into a number of new product lines that were consistent with the company's high technological capacity, yet more socially useful.

CHAPTER ELEVEN

The Case for Participatory Management

BY DONALD K. CONOVER

In a Western Electric drafting organization located in Chicago, productivity had been low. Employee turnover and absenteeism were high. The manager of two hundred or so employees decided to do something to improve morale and productivity: he would introduce participatory management.

First he met with the lower-level supervisors to explain his plan, get their support, and persuade them to go to the employees with him.

The first meeting with the employees was billed as a "what's up?" conference. There was no agenda, but rather an informal discussion about how the work was going. The result was a long list of suggestions to improve the physical facilities of the office: new paint, better coffee and food-vending machines, etc. This wasn't quite what the supervisor had hoped for, but the office did need attention, and the suggestions were reasonable. The supervisors said they would try to have the work done.

When most of the improvements had been made, a second conference was scheduled, again with no formal agenda. When the meeting started, there was a lot of talk about the improvements, and it was obvious that the meetings had made the employees feel that the supervisors were really interested in listening to what they had to say.

Finally someone observed, "The real problem around here isn't the office, it's the job. Some of the things we have to do don't make sense. We never know what's coming. The supervisor gives us a job and tells us how long it should take. Someone else checks our work when it's done, and back we go to the supervisor to get another job. The way things are organized we never know what's next, and there is always someone looking over our shoulder." As the supervisors listened, the discussion began to shift from what was wrong with the job to what could be done to improve it, and the ideas began to flow.

In the next several months, the employees rearranged the flow of work, suggested several labor-saving ideas that more than paid for the earlier office improvements, and developed a new way of handling work assignments. Instead of getting one job at a time, a supervisor laid out all the jobs for the next week. Employees chose what they thought they could complete in a week. Most employees had a high opinion of their ability and tended to take more work than the managers had expected. In most cases, they completed what they said they could do.

One of the jobs involved making charts of business results for a division vice-president. About a year after the meetings had begun, a staff supervisor for the vice-president asked that someone from the drafting unit be sent up to the vice-president's conference room to receive instructions about some new charts that were needed. The young woman who went had been doing the vice-president's charts for some time. When the staff supervisor started to tell her how to draw the new charts, she stopped him. "Tell me what information you want these charts to show, and I'll decide how to draw them," she said. "That's my job."

The first reaction from the vice-president's staff was irritation. But after the charts had been delivered it was clear that the woman knew her job. Not only did the charts show what they were supposed to, they included information the staff supervisor had overlooked.

Eighteen months after the first "what's up?" conference, the drafting unit was producing more than twice the number of drawings it had been. The unit's rate of absenteeism was among the lowest at the plant, and except for two men drafted into military service, turnover was zero.

Similar experiments are taking place in factories, warehouses, airlines, coal mines, banks, and company offices all over the United States. Individuals and groups of workers are getting the opportunity to plan, schedule, execute, and control more of their own work. They are managing and, for the most part, they like it. Managers like it too, because productivity tends to go up while personnel problems go down.

Like most ideas that excite business managers, participatory management is expected to produce practical results. It isn't the easiest way to improve results because the whole culture and tradition of business organization is contrary to the idea of enlarging the scope of work at the bottom of bureaucratic pyramids. It would be much easier if the research laboratory could come up with a machine to boost productivity. But managers have to take productivity increases where they find them, and with inflation pushing labor costs higher and higher, participatory management is one of the answers.

This may strike some readers as a mercenary way to deal with a subject that could just as easily be described as the beginning of democracy in business corporations. That general idea is where the article is headed, but I'd rather not start that way. For one thing it would be hypocritical, because I still believe that the first job of business is to produce a product or service that customers need and to make a profit doing it, not to be the architect of a Utopian society. For another, I know that changing traditions and power structure in a culture as well established as American business isn't going to be easy.

I happen to believe that the time is right for a period of substantial social innovation in business organizations and that participatory management may be one of the most important safeguards to the private-enterprise system and to freedom in society as a whole. But I also think more progress will be made if the argument for change is presented in the best light to those whose support is most important to effect the change. That means finding ways to get management, labor, and the public at large thinking on the same wavelength. Since management obviously represents a major power base, it is particularly important to convince management that its best interest will be served by supporting the change.

I recall an incident in 1975 that may illustrate the problem of different points of view. I was attending the Second General Assembly of the World Future Society in Washington, D.C. A sign on the bulletin board announced a breakfast meeting the next morning for futurists from New York City. Being a New Yorker, I decided to attend. About a dozen people showed up. They were teachers, students, and free lancers trying to make a living in future-oriented activities. After introductions we chatted about how the conference was going and tried to decide if there was anything we might do together as futurists from New York. In the middle of this discussion, someone singled me out by saying, "You work for a big corporation. What are you doing here? Aren't corporations just interested in making money? They aren't interested in the future, are they?"

I have run into this same thing many times, but it always disturbs me. The impression is that the Future (with a capital F) is to be involved with government, new technology, and new life styles. Business and the question of how the production of goods and services will be handled seems to be relegated to a secondary position; it is something to be worked in after the big questions of law and social values have been decided. Assuming that we are talking about a future that provides more, not less, democracy, the question of business and the private-enterprise system seems too important an issue to leave out of the main discussion.

There is nothing wrong with trying to improve the government. If we can find ways to regenerate democratic principles in the context of modern society and provide for greater individual involvement in shaping the course of government, we will strengthen important freedoms and have better government as well. But government isn't the whole story.

The cornerstone of American freedom has always been the combination of representative democracy in government and private enterprise in the economy. It is important to determine how goods and services will be produced. It is important to consider the role of private property and the contributions to liberty inherent in capitalism and free market competition. Assuming that people are going to continue having to work, it is important to think about how work will be organized and how trade-offs between organizational and individual needs will be restored. Most important of all, futurists must be interested in what motivates people to be productive, to assume responsibilities, and to take the personal risks necessary to be innovative. Stated another way, we need to take a systems approach to the development of social ideas for the future.

In terms of day-to-day impact, the business corporation probably does more than any other organized institution to shape the environment where we spend most of our time and exert the greatest personal effort seeking status and fulfillment. Policies and programs chosen by corporate management substantially influence our patterns of employment, consumption, and investment. Without a sense of personal involvement and control in shaping these economic dimensions of our lives, better government alone cannot produce a freer society.

When we begin to look at life in the modern corporation in terms of the individual, a mixed pattern is evident. Materially, the system continues to produce more, and the distribution of economic benefits has enriched almost everyone. However, the size and complexity necessary for that economic growth have been accompanied by a growing depersonalization of work and a widening gap between corporate and individual goals.

The size and complexity of the modern corporation, its practice of designing and organizing jobs around increasingly specialized tasks, and the geographic and product diversification of different divisions, have made it difficult for the organization to recognize the individual, and difficult for the individual to identify with the organization. In addition to the problem of finding ways to let more employees manage their own jobs, other problems have been surfacing that also need attention.

Most companies try very hard to have policies and programs that are uniform and fair in the treatment of employees. The difficulty is that in a society of free people, individual needs are not the same. When the organization gets so big that the individual is hard to recognize, the doctrine of fairness becomes the decision to treat all employees the same. For example, fringe benefits typically provide various types of insurance, such as life, medical and disability. In general, such insurance is more valuable to a married employee with many dependents than to a single employee with no dependents. In a society where life styles and family patterns are becoming more varied, business can expect increased discontent with policies and programs, designed as part of employee compensation, which are weighted in terms of personal choices not part of the corporation's business.

The issues that may need clarification include hiring, hours of work, company-paid education, job rotation, relocation, career guidance, fringe benefits, retirement, and termination. In each of these there is no question of a legitimate and important company interest. What is difficult is to balance such an array of programs in a way that satisfies both the increasingly complicated needs of the organization and the increasingly diverse needs of individual employees. As every manager knows, nothing causes more unrest and discontent than a new employee program that the employees consider tilted in favor of the company or inequitable in terms of different employee groups. Conversely, one of the most powerful motivations for effective work is the successful link between organizational needs and the personal satisfaction of workers.

One possible way to let employees decide on a better personal balance between job needs and their own preferences involves more flexibility in work hours. Various approaches are being tried: *Flexi-time* involves establishing a period in the middle of a standard workday when everyone must be at work (such as 10 A.M. to 3 P.M.), and then allowing employees to decide whether to come in early or stay late to complete a full-day's work. *Staggered work hours* is a similar idea, except that employees choose a fixed work schedule, perhaps 8:30 A.M. to 4:30 P.M., instead of 9 to 5. This has been used extensively in metropolitan areas where avoiding rush-hour crowds or arranging individual commutation schedules results in significant savings to the employee, with only minor adjustments in the organization's standard hours of work. *Permanent part-time employment* requires more elaborate job planning since, as the name implies, it involves an arrangement to work regularly on less than a full-time basis.

Some experiments have shown a direct relationship between employee control of hours of work and productivity on the job. At an auto-parts plant in Tennessee, mirror polishers were able to cut three hours or more off their workday by higher efficiency. Through a worker-management committee, agreements were reached so that employees finishing the expected amount of work early could leave or attend classes (to learn higher-level job skills such as welding or to study general-interest subjects like history).

A more complex innovation is being introduced at Material Management Centers in Western Electric. The MMCs are regional warehouses where the work involves six basic functions: receiving, handling materials, putting away, selecting, packing, and shipping. Because variations in what has to be handled and fluctuation in demand have always made it difficult to introduce meaningful time standards, this type of work is generally paid on a straight-time basis, i.e., hours worked at a certain hourly wage. Now, using computers to keep track of all the variations, a system involving over twelve hundred constant time elements and over five hundred actions that vary in the time needed to complete them has been developed. This system makes it possible to compare daily output to the number of hours a person works to generate a measure of how productive he or she is. This is essential data required to introduce a system of wage incentives.

Going a step farther, the management and the union have concluded an agreement called the *Productivity Pay Plan* in which there is a base rate of pay and an incentive bonus for each percent output above a predetermined standard ("Acceptable Productivity Level") up to a maximum of 20 percent.

The typical problem with plans of this sort has been disputes between labor and management about adjusting rates of pay so that increases in productivity are incorporated into the new expected standards of work. Management would like the new rates to reflect the improvements in methods of doing the work, and the workers would like to keep getting a bonus for doing more than the accepted standard of productivity in the past. In addition to these disputes, this situation also encourages a divisive undercurrent where productivity improvements may be held back by workers to prevent the "Acceptable Productivity Level" from increasing, thereby permanently eliminating the bonus on increased productivity.

The Productivity Pay Plan solves this problem in a unique way. When productivity has been at 17 or more percent above the standard for three consecutive months, management can offer to buy an increment of productivity and raise the base productivity level at a cost of from 5 to 10 percent of the workers' annual base salary. If the employees accept the offer, the payments are made in installments over five quarters with the first installment paid immediately.

This means that workers not only have the benefit of past productivity increases, but can now receive more bonus pay. Since this past increase approached the 20 percent limit, once it is incorporated into the base productivity level they can again be paid for increases in productivity. The decision to accept or reject such a purchase offer is made by a vote of the employees in the union. Thus, all parties have a mutual interest in improving output and sharing in the decision about how such gains will be reflected in employee compensation.

An example of the Productivity Pay Plan might work in the following manner. The employees in a particular pay group have had successive monthly outputs 18, 20, and 24 percent higher than the current Acceptable Productivity Level. They are paid an incentive bonus each month, 18, 20, and 24 percent above their base rate. The company offers to purchase a 5 percent increase in the Acceptable Productivity Level for 6.5 percent of the annual base salary (the higher amount to approximate the impact of the higher standard on the Acceptable Productivity Level to be used if the offer is accepted). The employees vote to accept. The following month their output is 17 percent above the new level. Workers receive a bonus for this and would already have received the first installment of the 6.5 percent of the yearly base salary when the company offer was accepted.

The same problems of corporate size and complexity that cause difficulties in the traditional areas of employee relations also affect employee attitudes about business as a social institution. If the employee is dissatisfied with his working conditions, news of a scandal somewhere in the company can more easily lead to the assumption that the whole company lacks integrity. At the same time, employees often are treated as if they don't understand, care about, or have an interest in the corporation. Yet today's employees are better educated than any work force in history. As consumers they are more aware, and as community residents they are more concerned. Often they are stockholders in their companies. They expect more from their employers than just a job and a pension. They are concerned about honesty in advertising, manipulation in the marketplace, protection of the environment, the use of natural resources, and the impact of corporate decisions to expand or contract jobs and facilities in their communities. When management decisions are poorly explained or appear contrary to the public interest, they challenge the employee's loyalty.

Even though confidence in government leadership has also fallen, the most frequent remedy for problems of corporate abuse seems to be government regulation or control. Yet I think most people believe that private industry is more effective when it comes to getting things done. The appeal of government control seems to be a hope that through the governmental process, the direction and control of economic resources will be more responsive to public need.

I am inclined to believe that the decline of confidence in business leadership has less to do with inequities or criminality than it does with the desire of the public, and more particularly corporate employees, to have a say in deciding what policies and rules will regulate their association with business organizations and how business will touch their lives as consumers, neighbors, or stockholders. Thus even the wisest and best management cannot refuse to share some of its decision-making power without causing resentment and ultimately rebellion.

How to accomplish greater employee involvement in decisions about corporate policy and business direction is a more difficult matter than involvement in the management of the workplace. At present there seems to be two different (and opposing) approaches. One, which is attracting support in Europe, involves putting employees, or their representatives, on the board of directors so that they have a voice in top-level decision-making. The other focuses on various programs to encourage stock ownership by employees so that their interest can be exercised as part owners of the business.

While I acknowledge that there are pros and cons to both approaches, I am not neutral. I strongly oppose the notion that an employee representative should be foisted on the Board of Directors, and I believe that a wider ownership of corporate stock is a good idea. With this bias clearly established, let us review both ideas.

The logic behind the move to require a place for employee representation on the Board seems to be that since the employee is so obviously affected by corporate policy and decisions, the employee is therefore *entitled* to have a say in such matters. In support of this logic, proponents argue that it is good for business to get the employees involved, to have them feel they are part of management in all phases of the business. It is also democratic—just as citizens have representatives to guard their interests in the government, so employees should be represented in the management of the business for which they work. Granting a significant measure of truth in each of these arguments, the nub of the issue is the word *entitled*.

It must be remembered, however, that by law the Board of Directors represents the interest of the owners of the corporation. If someone other than the owner is *entitled* to assume ownership authority, what is the owner *entitled* to? Because the decision to walk out on strike affects the stockholders, should they be *entitled* to a seat on the union's strike committee? Should taxpayers be *entitled* to help decide how large a raise municipal employees will ask for?

The plain fact is that the *entitlement* argument destroys the principle of private property. In my opinion, mandating employee representation on the Board of Directors is at best an expedient to compensate for out-of-date or improperly administered laws intended to intercede in conflicts between private property rights and the public interest. At worst, it is an attempt to eliminate differences of opinion (an impossibility) or to communize the ownership of capital (a revolution). Our problem is how to make the system work while safeguarding individual freedom. The *entitlement* argument is an attempt to make the system work at the expense of such freedom.

Beyond the philosophical objection, there are practical questions about how effective an employee representative at the Board level could be. As a manager, I realize I can't know all the details or make the judgments required to do the job of skilled craftsmen who may work in an organization I am supervising. If I tried, I would have to neglect job responsibilities that I am expected to be on top of as manager. Likewise, it is difficult to imagine how an employee who is close enough to the rank and file to represent its viewpoint could also be in touch with the complexities and details of top management issues. Also, I have difficulty understanding how a few employees appointed, or even elected, to serve on the Board of Directors would substantially increase the personal involvement of the tens of hundreds of thousands of employees in medium to large corporations. For instance, even if Western Electric were to double the size of its Board (a questionable move in itself) and have employees occupy all of the new seats, there would still not be a representative from each major factory and service organization.

The other approach to more employee involvement in top management is through expanded stock ownership. On the face of it, this approach must include solutions to economic questions of where employees are going to get wealth to buy stock in any significant amount and how to make stock ownership more meaningful in the management of today's business corporations. Both are major problems. The most powerful argument that this is the place to look for answers is the fact that only by making employees owners in the traditional way can we sustain and strengthen individual rights to private property. In other words, the problems of implementation may be great, but there is a philosophical consistency which makes the effort worthwhile.

One approach that some companies are experimenting with is called ESOP, Employee Stock Ownership Plan. The basic idea is to pay part of every employee's compensation in the form of stock in the company. The tax and capitalization issues are beyond the scope of this article, but the concept is simple enough. If employees are stockholders, they have both the legal right to exercise an owner's influence, and they have an owner's interest in the welfare of the business.

The problem of providing stockholder involvement with decisions affecting the direction or social impact of a large corporation has already been acknowledged. However, if the larger goal is the enhancement of individual involvement in decisions, it is a lot more appealing and probably more effective to search for solutions in the improvement of institutions that have already been established. This argues that the way to improve individual input to the executive suite is by expanding communication and involvement with a company's stockholders.

In companies where ESOPs have been introduced, there have been some spectacular results. The most striking example is the South Bend Lathe Company. On the verge of being liquidated, SBL got federal support for an ESOP, and the employees raised $10 million and became the new owners. After operating at a loss in 1975, productivity has increased by 25 percent and pre-tax profits were at 9 percent. ESOPs have also been introduced at such companies as the Bell System, Gamble-Skogmo of Minneapolis, Hallmark Cards, Zapata in Houston, and E-Systems, an electronic and aerospace company in Dallas. Connections between improved performance or higher employee morale and increased employee stock ownership are hard to prove. But when the employees begin to feel like owners, some of the problems of depersonalization or alienation are obviously affected for the better.

Participatory management—more employee involvement in deciding how work will be done, in deciding the policies and rules for balancing organizational and personal needs, and in deciding about the direction business may take with regard to its social impact—seems inevitable. However, there are one or two reservations before the great day arrives, and these reservations constitute the other side of the argument. They are the problems of leadership and responsibility. In presenting them I am speaking as a manager with some experience in the difference between how I might like people to act and how it is reasonable to expect they will act.

Once when I was trying to get funding for a series of television programs about the future for use within the corporation, the not-so-facetious comment of an associate highlighted this difference. We had made a pilot program dealing with problems of the city. I was taking it around the company, showing it to groups of managers and asking them to comment about its value, when another manager unexpectedly hit me with a question, "How do you want us to answer, as a manager or as a human being?"

The question reveals a lot about management. On one hand, managers acknowledge the same feelings anyone might have. However, their position as manager also entails values that may be in opposition to those relevant for dealing with certain social problems.

One of the terms managers use most frequently to describe their responsibility is *stewardship,* a term which recognizes both the private property aspect of a publicly held corporation and the balanced objectives a business must have to survive. Although today's stockholder is likely to be remote from the internal affairs of any particular corporation, the economic system and the law still regard the stock as private property. There are few circumstances where the stock is likely to be held for any other reason than the expectation of a profit. Unless we were to do away with such private property and profit seeking, everyone who exercises managerial authority is expected to have the stockholders' interest in mind when making business decisions.

Stewardship also involves questions of short- and long-term goals. Profit maximizing is often thought to be the corporation's dominant goal. Yet even if the market supported a high price today, that might not be the best way to hold a customer you hope will be back in the future. Spending money to improve quality or to develop better products or service may take something of today's profit to build a market for tomorrow. Responding to employee needs, paying a competitive wage, and offering opportunities for upward mobility have always been important in attracting, retaining, and motivating a competent work force. The net effect is that while managers may philosophically be committed to maximizing profits, time and pressure of marketplace competition force them to consider a range of short- and long-term objectives.

In addition to stewardship, management provides leadership, and in a complex world there is no way to plan, organize resources, and carry out complex tasks without leadership. Elections and committees can be very successful in assuring that different views are presented. Without a system of open communication, leadership can become remote, out of touch, and elitist. Clearly, there are ways to improve leadership, make it more responsive, provide better checks and balances. But, no way has been found to dispense with it altogether. People want more opportunity to decide how to do their own jobs. They want the satisfaction and pride of responsibility for their own labor. In the contract between the employer and employee, workers want a voice in the rules and programs defining their involvement in the organization's goals and their share of the organization's success. As employee-citizens they have a wider interest in corporate objectives and the choices that affect the impact of business on the whole of society. These are the desires shaping the trend to participatory management.

However, the more important issue is what the concept itself means to business and to a free society. Participatory management promises to reestablish the personal significance of the private-enterprise system. Finding ways to enhance individual participation in management can help eliminate the feelings of depersonalization and alienation common in an advanced industrial society. It can restore both individual incentive to make the business productive and individual responsibility about the role of business in a free society.

CHAPTER TWELVE

Economic Democracy and the Future: The Unfinished Task

C. GEORGE BENELLO

As Calvin Coolidge once commented, "The nation's business is business," and business in the United States is conducted under a system of managerialism and private ownership. This system, while buttressed by a number of myths going under the rubric of "free enterprise," is predominantly a set of large, bureaucratic corporations that are organized in a hierarchic fashion that leaves little room at any level except the top for either freedom or enterprise.

According to traditional values, the United States is the land of opportunity, exemplified in the Horatio Alger notion that anyone who works hard enough can achieve success. But the reality of mammoth organizations that employ over 80 percent of workers, the growing squalor and bankruptcy of the public sector, and the universal impact of pollution and urbanization have led to a disenchantment with the American Dream. Its failure is increasingly perceived as a failure in the chief mechanism for its achievement, the corporate system.

The corporate system purports to benefit everybody, but its inability and unwillingness to live up to this liberal claim has been at no time so clear as it is now. Official unemployment is around 8 percent, but this figure does not reflect an additional 4 percent who have stopped looking for jobs. As for those who work full time, there are many who are still unable to earn what the Department of Labor considers to be a minimal income. In 1970 the Bureau of Labor Statistics (BLS) considered $7,183 to be the minimal income for a family of four. The head of a family must earn $3.50 an hour to make this income annually. In one study, 61.2 percent of a representative sample in urban areas fell below the minimum income standard set by the BLS.[1]

In a society where income level is practically the only indication of success, these figures point to a systemic failure of massive proportions. Ceaseless efforts to placate the public via advertising, the media, and public relations are necessary to counteract the widespread disaffection that has resulted.[2] Some 14.8 million, or 7 percent of the population, exist on welfare. The present fiscal crisis of city governments has resulted in restrictions on city and state matching funds for welfare and on cutbacks in other public services—education, public housing, police and fire departments, and so on. Municipal taxes have risen and will rise more, as will utility costs. The result is that municipal crisis, while it rests most heavily on the backs of the poor, is also affecting the middle class through higher property taxes and utility rates. The base of disaffection will thus undoubtedly grow.

Another factor to be mentioned is the increasing disparity between the size and expectations of the educated class and the structure of job opportunities. Fifty percent of American youth now have some college education, but the job opportunities open to them offer only increasingly bureaucratized and fragmented work, the result of organizational growth in both the private and public sectors.

After World War II, only 16 percent of youth went on to college. But the postwar years saw the development of a system of mass education so extensive that employment in public education increased 130 percent between 1950 and 1965, while total employment increased only 21 percent during the same period.[3]

At the same time, education underwent a considerable degree of liberalization. This, combined with a more permissive upbringing ("the Spock Generation"), has vastly increased the disparity between home life and education and the authoritarian work situation. In both the public and the private sector in the last thirty years, work has become more regimented and bureaucratized than ever. The percentage of self-employed workers dropped during the sixties from 14.1 percent to 9.2 percent, while the percentage of wage and salaried workers rose by 3 percent to 83.6 percent. Although the mythology of the United States as the land of Horatio Alger still prevails, the vast majority work for wages, mainly in large, bureaucratic organizations.

The public sector is the most rapidly growing sector of the economy, employing 25 million workers. The level of political consciousness is high in some parts of these government bureaucracies. There is a new literature of public administration that recognizes the crisis resulting from the inefficiency of the welfare system and other service agencies.[4] The crisis of the public sector is exacerbated by the fact that it often serves a caretaker function, dealing with the problems created by the private sector but unable to deal directly with the causes of those problems.

In both the public and the private sectors there is widespread frustration of expectations as work has become more bureaucratized and specialized while on the output side the system has increasingly failed to deliver the amenities of life. The result has been a loss of commitment to the traditional American work ethic, and this in turn has been reinforced by the move away from a society emphasizing the values of production to one focusing on the values of consumption. What we are now witnessing in the workplace is growing inefficiency, high absenteeism, lowered quality levels and loss of productivity, corporate sabotage, and a general breakdown of the bureaucratic apparatus.[5]

A recent national survey conducted by Hart Research Associates, at the request of the People's Bicentennial Commission (now the People's Business Commission) gives some idea of the dimensions of the disaffection that has taken place.[6] Some 72 percent of the respondents believe that "profits are the major goal of business even if it means unemployment and inflation." Today 68 percent believe that corporate profits mainly benefit the stockholders, as opposed to 23 percent who believe that profits mainly create prosperity. Sixty-one percent believe that "there is a conspiracy among big corporations to set prices as high as possible," while 32 percent disagree. Fifty-eight percent believe that the corporations control public officials in Washington, as opposed to 25 percent who believe that it is the other way around. Sixty-six percent are in favor of employees owning the majority of their corporation's stock, while 52 percent also favor employees determining broad company policies, as opposed to 38 percent who believe it would do more harm than good. Sixty-six percent favor employees both owning their own stock and also appointing their own management, as opposed to 20 percent who favor ownership and control by outside investors.

The survey indicates that distrust of the present corporate system cuts across political allegiances and is exhibited most strongly in the $3,000- to $15,000-income categories. The typical proponent of economic alternatives to the present system is young —in his twenties or thirties—and a union member. It is probably true that the espousal of worker ownership and control represents more of a "no" vote for the system as it stands than a reasoned espousal of an alternative. But it does indicate that if the alternative of employee or worker ownership and control were shown to work, it could attract widespread support, and it is further evidence of the current crisis in our values and institutions.

RESPONSES TO THE CRISIS: STEPS TOWARD SELF-MANAGEMENT IN THE WORKPLACE

The 1972 government report, *Work in America,* produced under the auspices of the Department of Health, Education and Welfare, strongly criticized the current conditions of work and their effect on the worker, pointing to the continued prevalence of the managerial philosophy known as Taylorism, which seeks to reduce a job to the simplest level possible, defining each movement to be performed, so that it will require no initiative or intelligence on the part of the worker.[7] The report suggested moving away from Taylorism by job enrichment (greater on-the-job training and educational opportunities leading to advancement) and participative management. Recognizing the centrality of work to the development of identity and self-esteem, the report strongly recommended a humanization of the workplace. It received little favorable response from the Nixon Administration, and there was no official implementation of its recommendations.

In the corporate world, beset as it is by labor problems and falling productivity, the report did give rise to a spate of job-enrichment and job-enlargement programs, but the vast majority of these schemes took place in nonunionized plants, giving rise to the suspicion on the part of organized labor that the programs were being used to prevent union organizing. Moreover, while over a hundred corporations tried various job-enrichment schemes, they were carefully limited to about 1 percent of the workers, and in almost all cases were finally dropped. Management often finds its traditional prerogatives threatened by schemes which enlarge the domain of autonomy of the workers and give them a say in determining their conditions of work.[8] In the words of Edwin Hills, the director of the U.S. Productivity Commission's Quality of Work program, the democratization of work programs could ". . . open a Pandora's box from which there's no return. Pretty soon you'll have the workers managing the managers. It's a first step toward encroaching on Management's prerogatives of controlling and directing the means of production."[9]

Yet certain experiments in participation have survived, particularly where the nature of the production technology has favored worker self-determination. An example is the Teledyne Casting Company, a metal foundry near Pomona, California, employing some five hundred workers.[10] Initially, the company was run along conventional management lines and was close to failing, in an industry where failure rates are high. The technology of casting is demanding: a single crack or a failure of mold design, and the casting—very often a single copy of a large specialized piece of machinery—is ruined. Attempts to utilize traditional management methods had resulted in a situation where sixty-three percent of all parts produced were so defective they had to be scrapped. New management was brought in with a broad mandate to reorganize the work system. Workers were allowed within certain limits to set their own wage rates and their own working hours. They were given complete control of the production process, and in many cases even dealt with customers. The result was a complete turnaround, ending with Teledyne growing to a point where it became the biggest and most successful foundry on the West Coast.

In other cases, an enlightened president is the prime mover behind a switch to participatory management. One example of this is the Bolivar plant in Tennessee owned by Sidney Harman, who was appointed Undersecretary of Commerce in 1977. With the help of Michael Maccoby of the Harvard Program on Technology, Work and Character, and the participation of the union—a local of UAW—Harman developed a program to increase participation and worker involvement in the workplace. A joint committee of management and the union was established, and with their combined commitment the project has resulted in a wide-ranging redesign of the work situation, along with an in-factory school that teaches a variety of subjects that extend beyond production skills. The program has been in operation since 1973 and shows every sign of being a success.[11]

In communities faced with the closing of a local plant, efforts to maintain jobs have sometimes resulted in at least a partial democratization of the workplace. Plant closings have become more frequent because of the economic conditions caused by the recession, the search on the part of multinational corporations for cheaper labor markets abroad,[12] and the mismanagement of conglomerates that developed in the sixties.[13] Cases are increasing where the workers, aided either by a former manager or by sympathetic government agencies, buy out the plant with funds raised with the help of the community. While motivation for worker ownership has been to save jobs, it has often resulted in the democratization of decision-making, although this has not necessarily followed.

One example is an asbestos plant in Vermont, owned by a multinational corporation, which was closed down because new health regulations governing the handling of asbestos made extensive safety measures necessary. A group of workers developed community support for buying out the plant, and the Vermont government assisted. Stock was sold to both workers and to the community, and the plant managed to devise cheaper ways of dealing with the safety and health regulations, while convincing the state that some of the regulations were irrelevant. As a result of the regulations, the price of asbestos shot up, so that when the plant reopened, it immediately began to operate successfully. However, a group of managers within the plant have bought up shares from the other workers with the intention of gaining control. There is nothing in their plant constitution that prevents this from happening, and the initial experiment in democratic control may lose out to the desires of a minority seeking to capitalize on the new profitability of the operation.

In a self-managed firm, on the other hand, the right of control is vested equally in all working members, regardless of the number of shares owned. Such a firm follows the cooperative principle of one vote per person.

The worker or employee ownership model discussed above differs from the self-management model in two ways: first, while it is a step toward both employee and community control, to the extent that it employs traditional methods of stock ownership, it runs the risk of seeing shares accumulate in the hands of a few, and hence of losing its original broad base among the workers and community members. Second, and more importantly, its origins lie in the effort to maintain jobs, usually in a situation where the loss of the jobs would have a serious impact on the community. But this is a long way from a conscious effort to democratize the workplace and humanize the conditions of work. In most situations where worker ownership has developed, there has been no attempt to change the managerial system, and workers have proceeded to hire conventional management. Nor have any attempts been made to assure that ownership shares cannot be concentrated again in the hands of a few. Under a system of true self-management, control is based on membership in the working community of the enterprise. The distribution of ownership does not affect this preeminence of worker control.

The impetus to develop self-management has come largely from intellectuals and a few practicing managers and management consultants who have become thoroughly disaffected with corporate managerialism. In other words, the concept has not derived directly from the demands of the workers themselves. However, given the lack of a tradition in the United States of worker control and self-management, and the assimilation of the labor movement into the capitalist system, this is understandable.[14] The ideological hegemony of capitalism, with its emphasis on the division between mental work and manual work, its affirmation of managerialism as the only efficient means of ensuring productivity, and its success in making organized labor a partner in these arrangements has meant that the workplace is the area where that hegemony remains most strongly in force.[15] Workers' discontents are manifested in wildcat strikes, low productivity, worker sabotage, drugs and low morale, but not in any systematic attempt to build alternatives.

On the other hand, there are, here and there, disaffected managers who are finding, with the development of a movement started mainly by academic intellectuals, that there is indeed an alternative to the prevailing managerialism, and thus a partnership is being created between exponents of the theory of self-management who lack the necessary background in business practice, and people from the ranks of business whose experience has led them to seek a new theory.

If the workers still, for the most part, accept managerialism as something against which only passive resistance can be offered, managers are at least in a position to provide the entrepreneurial skills necessary to develop an alternative by imparting their skills to the workers and assisting them in developing a truly democratic workplace. The success of such an effort will depend on the extent to which managers actually engage in this sort of an educational venture.

One place where the self-management model became a reality is a Washington-based insurance company, Consumer's United Group, generally known as International Group Plans. Here, the impetus for change came from the president and founder, Jim Gibbons. Basing his efforts on the humanistic psychology of Abraham Maslow, he transformed his insurance company into a worker-owned and worker-managed company. The transition has not always been smooth.[16] The original optimism and belief in the willingness of the workers to take over the responsibility for ensuring that the work gets done has given way to a realization that this is not in all cases the way things work. Clear performance criteria are needed, and a program of both worker and management training is essential in order for the two groups to operate effectively together under a system where managers are answerable ultimately to the workers themselves. Clearer lines of authority than first existed are necessary, as well as greater selectivity in screening applicants for positions. But steps in these directions are now underway, and the prognosis seems optimistic.

The experiment of International Group Plans does not define itself as one whose validity is limited to an elite of highly trained professionals; the majority of its workers are in fact relatively untrained, and have a low level of education. Rather, it sees itself as pioneering a fundamentally different approach to work and the organization of work. The purpose of self-management at IGP is not to increase productivity or to make the workers more efficient, but rather to allow the workers to develop more fully as human beings. Human beings and their psychosocial development, rather than production and its profits, are at the center of IGP's concerns. It seeks to make radical humanism a central issue in the organization of work and in the definition of the goals of work, and to establish that this goal is feasible in a high technology industry.

THE THEORY OF SELF-MANAGEMENT

Worker-management or self-management (to use the broader term, applying to decision-making in all formal organizations) falls within the tradition of direct democracy that has existed as a minor element within Western political theory and practice since the time of the Greeks.[17] It has seen practical expression in a variety of places throughout history: the Canton of Appenzel in Switzerland has had a system of direct democracy for several centuries; the Diggers espoused it under their leader Winstanley in seventeenth-century England; some of the nineteenth-century Utopian experiments in England and America employed it; the Spanish anarchists practiced it in northern Spain before the Civil War; and lastly, the New Left and much of the civil rights movement practiced it in their organizing efforts in the sixties.

Arguments in favor of self-management fall into three categories: psychological, political, and ethical. The psychological argument, supported by contemporary humanistic and developmental psychology, stresses the importance of control over the immediate conditions of work and life as central in the development of competence and identity.[18] The development of skills, manual or mental, allows for pride in accomplishment; they set a person off from others. Forms of competence that are recognized and valued give a secure sense of personal value. Research has confirmed the Marxian notion of the centrality of "sensuous human activity" for human development by showing that psychosocial development is not merely a matter of interpersonal relations but depends on the acquisition of skills and competence.[19] Empirical studies of work indicate that the single most important guarantor of worker satisfaction is the ability to participate, while the major factor in worker alienation is powerlessness.[20] Self-actualization goes beyond survival needs. In terms of work this actualization can only take place in a noncoercive environment where a person is free to co-determine with his fellow workers the conditions and nature of his work.

The political argument for self-management is rooted in an understanding of authoritarianism and of the psychopathology of power.[21] Elitists argue that government should be left to those few most fit to govern. Yet the increased power of governments to determine questions of life and death and their failure to meet human needs and to avoid recurrent crises has rendered this theory suspect. In the private sector, managerial expertise and capitalist ideology are the basis for elitist management. Yet the Hart poll (see page 211) suggests that even these ideas are being questioned.

Direct democracy counters this elitism by arguing that one cannot delegate to others the determination of what is in one's own vital interests. It asks the ancient question, *quis custodet ipsos custodes*—who will oversee the overseers? With increasing technological complexity, the argument for elitism may have become stronger; but so has the counterargument, which points to the many ways technological and managerial elitism victimize the average person.[22]

The ethical argument for self-management is based on the doctrine of the primacy of the person—the dictum of philosopher Emmanuel Kant that human beings are never means to an end, but ends in themselves. People exist for the sake of their own development, not as raw material for someone else's. The necessary social expression of this insight is a form of organization that eschews all forms of domination or manipulation.

The psychological, political, and ethical arguments for self-management meet in the Greek concept that politics is the key to the good life. For the Greeks, the essential elements in *Paedeia,* or education, were ethics and politics.[23] The German sociologist Jurgen Habermas has noted that for the Greeks "politics was always directed toward the formation and cultivation of character; it proceeded pedagogically, not technically . . . ."[24] Viewed in this fashion, self-management is identical with direct democracy, and has inherent value not simply as a means to human liberation, but also as the immediate expression of that liberation.[25]

One of the dominant images of the future Jim Dator refers to in his article* is that of increasing scarcity, which will place severe strains on the economic system. Those who predict this future argue that a corporate state will emerge, dominated by a system of planning and control instigated by and for the benefit of large corporations in conjunction with the state.[26] What is likely to be lost in the process is the tradition of democratic government that has characterized the last few centuries in the West. A major thread in these arguments is that the present industrial system is based on the possibility of unlimited growth, and this continued growth makes the inequities and maldistribution of the system both within nations and between rich and poor nations endurable. But growth is reaching its limits, and as these are reached, the social pressures will build up, leading to explosions of discontent primarily aimed at the wealthy nations, although as industrial growth recedes, the discontent will be experienced within the wealthy nations themselves as well.

Growing resource shortages combined with population pressures are likely to result in increasingly authoritarian political systems. Added to this is the already existing tendency toward centralization exemplified both in government and business: the extensive growth in power of the executive branch of government, the growth in state and federal bureaucracy, the centralization of economic power into the hands of an increasingly smaller group of multinational corporations. The centralization of economic power is unrelated to economies of scale. Rather, it is the product of large corporations' capacity to control the market, and to obtain access to capital on a preferred basis.[27] Ecologists have seriously questioned whether the traditional laissez-faire mechanisms are capable of dealing with a world of limited resources.[28] Given this increasingly likely image of the future, the alternatives are clear: either a world governed by some sort of amalgam of corporate-state control in which the citizen has little say, or a world in which the present tendencies toward centralized control are countered by movements toward democratization and the restoration of popular control.

The goal of self-management is to humanize work. Viewed this way, it must be clearly differentiated from job enrichment and participation schemes that seek to improve the quality of working

* Chapter 19

life within the confines of the corporate structure. To the extent that these schemes do in fact result in the humanization of work, they are of value. But the corporate structure imposes a form of control by capital where workers are simply factors in the production process, the goal of which is greater productivity and profits. A recent conference on job enrichment and the quality of working life noted that where the ultimate goal was productivity, workers became aware that they were being manipulated. The goal must be the humanization of work, pure and simple, or participation and job-enrichment schemes will not work. But can a system so organized as to have profits as its goal really change those goals without altering its structure as well? Job enrichment and self-management involve significant differences in terms of their visions of economic institutions in the future. Job enrichment and participation seeks to avoid structural alterations that would affect power relations, instead enlarging the area of freedom within the system as it stands. It possesses no vision that incorporates clear ethical, political, and psychosocial alternatives. Self-management does possess such a vision, and hence it seeks to bring about a fundamental change in both the values and institutions of the society that in time would affect every aspect of the society.

Implicit in the self-management alternative is the principle of decentralism, namely, to require that all functions be carried out at the lowest level possible, leaving only coordinating functions to the highest level.[29] The American corporate system is a particularly good place to develop a movement for decentralization. Having lost its monopolistic position in the world economy and faced with increasingly organized cartels controlling the vital resources that are in short demand, the American corporate system can no longer be the guarantor of the American Dream.

The degeneration and delegitimation which is manifesting itself at the base of the society does not take a glaring or startling form. Yet each year the statistics of social pathology grow, and with it, alienation and unrest. For those able to find work, the dichotomy grows between expectations and the realities of increasingly depersonalized work in large organizations. But the system is unable to provide anything beyond subsistence-level living and unemployment or subemployment for an increasing number, somewhere between 25 percent and 50 percent of the population (depending on where the poverty line is drawn). Here expectations enter in as well: if work cannot be intrinsically rewarding, at least it must be capable of delivering the standard consumer package that represents membership in the middle class—a car, appliances, TV, a house in the suburbs.

As the mythology of the Land of Opportunity fades in the face of urban crime and degeneration, meaningless work, cynicism about Big Business and Big Government, the remaining legitimacy of the corporate system is largely negative. It may be imperfect, even dehumanizing and unjust, but there is no system that can deliver the goods any better. This view is pragmatic; the system is justified because it works, even if not very well. Criticism becomes threatening, because there is no use knocking the only game in town. But this reveals the significance of a movement for the humanization of the workplace. The technological-industrial system determines the basic thrust and nature of the United States as an advanced industrial society. The workplace is the point where that technological-industrial system confronts human social organization; it is the logical place to begin a movement toward genuine, decentralized democracy.

A movement having as its goal the creation of viable and effective models of humanized work, capable of creating useful and consumer-oriented products while utilizing a high level of technology, would strike at the heart of the corporate system in a number of ways. It could appeal to the new consumer and ecological consciousness that has arisen and that is in part responsible for the low esteem in which the corporate system is held. It could appeal to the growing group of unemployed or those employed in positions below their skill and education level. And it could appeal to the large group of organized blue-collar workers whose disaffection at present takes the form of absenteeism, drugs, and sabotage. As Andre Gorz, an economist and journalist has said, workers are hardly likely to man the barricades for a fifty-cent-an-hour pay raise. But a movement creating not only jobs but also self-determination and freedom in work, committed to producing goods possessed of both integrity and usefulness, would appeal not only to basic material needs but would also provide a live basis from which a critique of both the dehumanization of work and the falseness of consumer values could be made. In short, the actual creation of self-managed enterprises successfully creating products of integrity and usefulness could be the first step in the democratization of all institutions in the society.

ON THE ROAD TO SELF-MANAGEMENT AND DEMOCRACY

To bring economic democracy to the United States it is necessary to demonstrate concretely that a self-managed, democratic system or work organization can function efficiently and at the same time be responsive both to workers' needs and to the consumer. But establishing individual and isolated enterprises is not enough. Supporting institutions must be developed that can both assist the sound economic development of these enterprises and also link them together into a closely knit system capable of mutual support and cooperation. To some, this sounds like a scheme to develop a self-managed conglomerate, but there is a critical difference: a conglomerate is linked through centralized control and through the funneling of all profits into the central holding company, whereas a self-managed system is linked by bonds of voluntary cooperation wherein control rests with the working members of each enterprise, and there is only a voluntary contribution of profits to some central fund or bank in order to develop more enterprises.

A continuing educational effort, parallel to the economic effort, is also necessary. The present system of corporate managerialism is based on separation of intellectual skills from manual skills so that management monopolizes knowledge skills, and the production technology is deliberately specialized and limited to the most simple operations.[30] In order to humanize work and allow workers to make use of their brains as well as their brawn, there must be a training program implemented in each self-managed plant that reintegrates management and work skills through rotation of supervisory and management functions, the democratic selection of managers from the workplace, and a continuing program of education in the elements of accounting, finance, law, marketing—in short, in management skills—for those interested. At present there is a clear division between those who engage in manual work, whether blue collar or white collar, and those earmarked for management. The latter are products of a specialized education, and typically from a different class background. A democratic system of work organization must seek to counter this disparity in education by making management skills available to all.

Also needed are new sources of capital and form of capital control. Pooled risk, mutual fund-type investment vehicles would eliminate the need for single large investors, and in the process do away with the demand for external control. Such a pooled investment can possess a high-fixed interest rate to reflect the risk, or a variable interest rate pegged to worker-productivity indicators can be developed. Such an investment would in fact be safer, on a number of counts, than a conventional corporate investment, since the conditions under which a portion of the profits would be paid out could be clearly defined instead of being subject to the decisions of a self-perpetuating board of directors. Also, self-managed companies lack incentives to go bankrupt, such as tax-loss benefits, that conventional corporations have. Once control is vested in the working members themselves, there would be a maximum incentive to maintain jobs and preserve the company.

Mondragon, a Spanish network of producer cooperatives, has demonstrated for the past two decades of its existence that people can be motivated by broader goals than simply income. In Mondragon, the maximum wage differential is 1:3. Only apprentices earn at the "1" level, so the operative differential between workers and managers is 1:2, which means that workers earn an income that is at or above industry-wide levels, but they also share in the profits, while managers earn far less than conventional managers, thus keeping labor costs down.[31] Managers choose to stay with Mondragon despite the lower income level because they form part of a working community committed to values that extend well beyond profit-making. Moreover, jobs created in a self-managed system such as Mondragon are far more permanent than those in the corporate system; there have been no layoffs in Mondragon since the system first began, nor have there been any plant failures. A cooperative credit union serves as the development bank for the entire system, providing both the technical expertise as well as the funding necessary to insure that all the firms in the system (approximately fifty-five industrial firms, as well as a large number of agricultural cooperatives) maintain their economic viability.

In this country several groups have arisen in the last two or three years which have as their aim the development of cooperative, self-managed enterprises.[32] In cases where there have been plant closings—often the result of a conglomerate's decision to relocate to an area within or outside the country where labor and production costs are cheaper—these groups have been able to help workers and the community to take steps toward the development of a worker-owned and -managed enterprise. In Cambridge, Massachusetts, an investment fund has been developed that offers the possibility of investing at a fixed return in alternative-type investments that are ecologically sound, democratically controlled, and oriented toward the development of new "soft" technologies.[33]

On the West Coast, a school has been developed—the New School for Democratic Management—which offers seminars and instruction in methods of organizing and operating worker cooperatives, and in the financing and management of such organizations.[34] As yet these efforts are in their infancy, but they have prompted interest on the part of city and state governments in the possibilities that this approach offers to generate jobs and income in economically depressed areas. When enterprises are developed in such areas and are operated under a combination of worker and community control, they are not subject to the vagaries of corporations with remote headquarters, and their profits will remain within the community to ensure further local development. These efforts are far from paralleling the achievement of Mondragon, but of necessity their horizon is long term. It will be ten or twenty years before a movement that is large enough to influence national policy is likely to emerge.

It is significant, however, that in a number of cases these efforts have enlisted support from a wide range of people, including academics, drop-outs from middle- and top-level management, lawyers, and blue- and white-collar workers. This brings with it its own problems of reconciling the cultural differences of people coming from different socioeconomic backgrounds, but in many cases there are strong practical incentives to develop worker cooperatives in situations where jobs are scarce, and where both workers and local management have become fed up with management policies that are decided in corporate headquarters and that often fail to take into account local conditions and needs. With the rise of conglomerates, local operations are often viewed as exercises in corporate accounting; they may be sold or closed down for tax or financial reasons, which have little to do with the intrinsic viability of the enterprise. The return to local ownership and control thus has a strong practical and functional justification, and can contribute to the health of the local economy in ways that foreign ownership could never do.

ECONOMIC DEMOCRACY AND THE FUTURE

For a movement of this sort to have a significant impact on the American socioeconomic system, it will have to demonstrate that some of the vital economic and social needs before us can be better met by a system of self-management than by the corporate system. The labor movement will have to recognize that worker management, rather than being a threat, is probably the only way that jobs can be saved in the face of the decision on the part of an increasing number of corporations to seek lower labor costs abroad. Unions recognize the need to save jobs. At present they can only fight a holding action; developing worker management would enable them to take the initiative to maintain jobs. In addition, the American people must come to recognize that worker management is neither a Utopian pipe dream nor a communist conspiracy, but rather a profoundly democratic response to conditions of work alienation and lack of power. Ideological stereotypes are already beginning to be cast aside, as a few unions are coming to recognize that worker ownership and worker management may in the long run be the only thing that can maintain their membership.

Political initiatives to support job creation through worker management are also necessary. There must be legislation to create state development banks oriented to funding worker-managed enterprises, where the equity remains in the hands of the workers. There must be government-sponsored training programs capable of teaching management skills; every worker should know something about balance sheets, marketing, and production technologies. Unions must seek legislation allowing them to function as facilitators of worker management, rather than in their traditional adversary relationship between workers and management. Models of public corporations must be created, embodying a mix of public control and worker control, with public members sitting on boards as representatives of consumer groups, ecology groups, community groups, or utility companies.

Finally, a change in the orientation toward work must come about. The traditional approach to work, deriving from the Judaeo-Christian tradition, sees work as a necessary evil, a product of the unavoidable lower, or physical, nature of human beings. Instead of this, work must be understood as a central human activity, capable under the right conditions of fulfilling human nature and leading to a person's highest psychosocial development. Work at present is undertaken by most Americans to survive, or to earn further income which can lead to the enjoyment of leisure time. This purpose for work must be transformed. Work must become intrinsically meaningful, engaged in for its own sake. The idea must develop that every citizen has a right to meaningful work. Rather than breaking the link between work and income, as the advocates of a guaranteed annual income would have us do, the aim must be to develop meaningful work so that all those who are capable of work and who seek it are guaranteed the possibility of meaningful work in which they can develop their full humanity.[35] The technology must be redefined so as to subordinate it to the demand for meaningful work rather than allowing it to turn workers into machine tenders and robots.

CONCLUSION

Economic democracy envisions a future deeply rooted in the history of this country. The early system of representative democracy based on geographic divisions did not envision the rise of large corporate systems operating on a national and multinational level, with the power to shape the physical and social landscape, to dispose of the country's national resources, and to dictate forms of transportation, products, services, and even forms of culture. Economic decisions affecting the lives of a large number of citizens will continue to be made. The question is whether these decisions will be made by a few, without public accountability and in the interests of a few, or whether a system can evolve that is capable of ensuring that these decisions are made democratically, in the interests of the majority.

This vision of the future questions the belief in progress through technology that characterizes both Western liberalism and much of Marxism. It seeks to humanize technology and make it serve human ends. It has therefore much in common with the "limits to growth" vision of a conserver or steady-state society. But it questions the ability of even a well-intentioned elite to plan the future, believing that the critical question is the question of who plans for whom. It seeks to introduce popular and democratic control into the heart of the technological-industrial system where it affects people's lives most directly, namely in the workplace. Rather than seeking to legislate control from the outside, leaving the basic structure with its narrow orientation toward profits intact, it seeks to build in other kinds of goals, ones that will evolve integrally and organically out of the conditions of working life. The vision projected is decentralist, humanistic, and oriented toward community. Rather than creating ever-larger plants and increasing productivity, it sees work as central to human fulfillment and seeks to link work to other aspects of living, by having control over the workplace rest with those who also are the consumers and community members. In the political system, each person is equal, possessing one vote. Economic democracy would apply this same principle to the economic system, proving that technological and industrial progress need not occur only at the expense of the social values and vision embodied in the democratic ideal.

CHAPTER THIRTEEN

Lucas Aerospace: The Workers' Plan for Socially Useful Products

BY CLEMENT BEZOLD

An industrial counterpart to such political programs as Hawaii 2000, Goals for Georgia, or Alternatives for Washington requires more than the usual long-range forecasting done by outside professionals for company planners; anticipatory democracy in the workplace involves the workers themselves rather than simply managers or outside experts. Workers at Lucas Aerospace Ltd., a British-based high technology corporation, accurately forecasted a future of dwindling defense and commercial aircraft contracts. In order to avoid extensive layoffs, the Lucas workers, many of them college-educated engineers, pooled their knowledge of the company's resources and came up with an alternative-futures plan that included the production of about a hundred fifty new products designed to be more socially useful than current defense products.

Lucas Aerospace Ltd., a division of the huge multinational company, Lucas Industries Ltd., is Britain's leading aircraft company. With factories in France and Germany in addition to Great Britain, it is, by its own testimony, "Europe's largest designer and manufacturer of aircraft systems and equipment."[1] Many of its thirteen thousand employees are well-educated designers and engineers and highly trained manual workers. The company makes extensive use of highly automated equipment and does extensive research and development. Much of its work is in the commercial aircraft field, supplying equipment for Rolls-Royce engines and military aircraft for the government. Other contracts come from Common Market countries. As a consequence, the corporation is vulnerable to shifts in defense spending and changes in Common Market conditions. The elimination of nearly fifty thousand jobs since 1970, bringing the total to thirteen thousand from the all-time high of eighteen thousand, demonstrated the corporation's vulnerability and Great Britain's declining market shares.

THE SHOP STEWARDS COMBINE

In 1974 the price of oil rose and as a result demand for military and commercial aircraft fell in Great Britain. At the urging of Tony Benn, Minister of Industry (Britain's counterpart to our Secretary of Commerce), the Shop Stewards Combine decided to produce a workers' alternate Corporate Plan to reduce redundancies (layoffs), while stressing the company's potential for diversification. The Combine is comprised of one representative from each of Lucas's eleven plants and represent all thirteen unions in one voice—like a trade union Board of Directors. The Combine at first went outside the company and questioned one hundred eighty experts and institutions familiar with products more life enhancing than military aircraft. The experts turned up only three new ideas for products.

The Combine then went to the workers themselves. As is so often the case, the people on the scene in the plants and in the offices knew more than the outside experts. The Combine invited the Lucas Aerospace workers to answer a questionnaire on how the available talents and skills of the workers could combine in new ways with the existing machinery to produce alternative products. The results of this detailed questionnaire, together with outside expertise brought in to refine the suggestions, were written up and submitted as a futures proposal for the Lucas Aerospace Industries.

THE CORPORATE PLAN

The Combine presented their Corporate Plan, subtitled "A Contingency Strategy As A Positive Alternative To Recession And Redundancies," to the Lucas Aerospace Board of Directors in January 1976. Accompanying the Plan was one of the six technical volumes developed to support the feasibility of the one hundred fifty products proposed.

The Plan cited two purposes: "Firstly, to protect our members' right to work by proposing a range of alternative products on which they could become engaged in the event of further cutbacks in the areospace industry. Secondly, to ensure that among the alternative products proposed are a number which would be socially useful to the community at large."[2]

After reviewing the impact of the energy crisis on the aerospace industry, the Plan forecasted a downward spiral in military aerospace projects in the next decade. It did not decry this trend since most of the thirteen trade unions with workers at Lucas had established policies favoring decreases in defense spending. The Plan acknowledged that Lucas Aerospace would continue to be deeply involved in the aerospace industry, but it proposed alternative products that would allow Lucas to diversify into socially useful product lines:

The desire to work on socially useful products is one which is now widespread through large sectors of industry. The aerospace industry is a particularly glaring example of the gap which exists between that which technology could provide, and that which it actually does provide to meet the wide range of human problems we see about us. There is something seriously wrong about a society which can produce a level of technology to design and build Concorde but cannot provide enough simple urban heating systems to protect old-age pensioners who are dying each winter of hypothermia (it is estimated that 980 died of hypothermia in London alone last winter, which was a particularly mild one).[3]

The Combine Committee recognized that Lucas Aerospace was unlikely to become a trailblazer of social responsibility because "there can be no islands of responsibility and concern in the sea of irresponsibility and depravity." The more modest contribution of the Plan was to question corporate assumptions and to demonstrate that workers could effectively press for "the right to work on products which actually help to solve human problems rather than create them."[4]

As the *Combine News* observed:

Perhaps the most significant feature of the Corporate Plan is that trade unionists are attempting to transcend the narrow economism which has characterized trade union activity in the past and extend our demands to the extent of questioning the products on which we work and the way in which we work upon them. This questioning of basic assumptions about what should be produced and how it should be produced is one that is likely to grow in momentum.[5]

But the Plan did not abandon that fundamental economic concern. It demanded continuing education and retraining for the workers, and it refused to seek worker seats on the Lucas Board of Directors because worker jobs were not protected where such a tactic was employed (as it had been elsewhere in Europe). The Plan wanted to create a genuine solution to the problem of layoffs while simultaneously thinking about the common good.

The Plan identified one hundred fifty products. However, the Combine released only one of the six two-hundred-page supporting volumes because workers feared that Lucas management would approach the Plan as free consulting work.

The products proposed included oceanic equipment, telechiric machines,* transport systems, braking systems, alternative energy sources, and medical equipment. The Plan struck a balance between projects that would require a high capital investment and those for which virtually all capital and skills were immediately available. Some of the specific products included wind generators; a hybrid power system for cars that could cut fuel consumption in half, reduce toxic emissions by 70 to 80 percent, and greatly reduce noise pollution; a lightweight car capable of traveling through cities on normal roads and then traveling directly onto normal railroad tracks; undersea, humanly controlled robots for oil exploration and drilling repairs; and devices for remote firefighting.

---

* Telechiric machines are devices that mimic, in a dangerous environment such as firefighting, mining, and underwater work, the motions of human beings working remotely in a safe environment, thus allowing a complex series of actions in response to the immediate conditions without endangering the person directing the actions.

RESPONSE TO THE CORPORATE PLAN

The Lucas Board of Directors did not respond to the Plan until several months after it had been presented. At that time the Board observed that because civil aircraft were needed for business and pleasure activities and military aircraft for defense, the company's work *did* have social utility. The company continued to concentrate on high technology in the aerospace and defense industries, refusing to recognize either the problem of structural unemployment or the need to diversify.

The response outside the company was more rewarding for the work force: the British *Financial Times* called the Corporate Plan "one of the most radical alternative plans ever drawn up by workers for their company . . . a twentieth-century version of the Industrial Revolution."[6]

In an editorial comment, *Industrial Management* noted that strikes have been used to provide a short-term remedy to layoffs, poor working conditions and schedules, and wage differentials, yet they have rarely provided a durable solution. The Lucas Corporate Plan represented a more effective, future-oriented militancy on the part of workers: "Instead of waiting for trouble and then downing tools, workers are much more likely to anticipate issues which are threatening to produce tension. In the case of Lucas, this process has not only taken place, but manifested itself in the form of a weighty document which would do credit to a reputable management consultant." The Lucas action "is likely to be the forerunner of a development which will ultimately affect the whole of British industry. . . . The document is clearly worth consideration by management. For it clearly demonstrates that if managers don't carry out their jobs to the satisfaction of workers, then those same workers have the capability and the know-how to do it for them."[7]

Despite the reaction of the Lucas Board, the Combine has continued to encourage the company to diversify into "socially useful products" and to preserve workers' jobs. Later in 1976, when the company was considering closing its Industrial Ball Screw Division, the Combine Committee prepared a minicorporate plan that reviewed potential markets worldwide in a range of industries, including the machine-tool industry. This led the company to reverse its decision to close down the operation, though activity may be reduced in the future.[8]

Workers have also been successful in having individual plants consider aspects of the Plan. The Fabrications Group at Burnley has agreed to devote more effort to gas turbines, a more efficient generator of energy than equipment currently in use. The Combine has also convinced an energy research group to place an order with the company for two heat pumps powered by natural gas turbines that will be produced at the Burnley plant.[9]

THE FUTURE FOR LUCAS AND WORKER-GENERATED FUTURE PLANS

The Combine Committee's Corporate Plan is an impressive attempt by workers to define the future of their corporation while ensuring employment. It is significant that its workers are some of the best trained and most sophisticated in the design and development of high technology. They have, as workers, charted a path toward more "appropriate technology." While the response by the management has been discouraging, the Lucas case shows that workers can anticipate impending hardships and be both socially responsible and imaginative in their solutions.

V

Anticipatory Democracy in Citizen Movements

In addition to anticipatory democracy through the citizen/government partnerships discussed in many of the preceding chapters, citizens can shape the future in less institutionalized ways by raising alternatives not generated by the normal political system. This is particularly the case when a society is undergoing a change in values, as we are in our movement beyond an industrial and post-industrial society.

The values of the Industrial Age, which have served us well until now, pose a fundamental dilemma. As Willis W. Harman has written (in *The Futurist*, February 1977):

The basic goals that have dominated the industrial era (material progress, individualism, freedom of enterprise, few restraints on capital accumulation, social responsibility mainly the concern of government rather than other institutions, etc.) and that have been approached through a set of fundamental subgoals (efficiency, productivity, continued growth of production, consumption and technological and manipulative power) have resulted in processes and states (division of labor, specialization, cybernation, stimulated consumption, planned obsolescence, private exploitation of resources held in common), which end up counteracting human ends (enriching work roles, resources conservation, environmental enhancement, equitable sharing of the world's resources).

Harman suggests that we are headed toward a value system based on voluntary simplicity, one that incorporates the Buddhist economic principle of maximum personal satisfaction with minimum consumption. Such a system, it is said, would result in social and economic institutions that are simpler and more interdependent and thus would reverse current trends by involving more people in self-sustaining activities that incorporate the principles of harmony between human activity and the natural environment.

What does this mean for citizen participation? Many groups are emerging that have at least a vague image of what the future might hold. In Chapter 14 Hazel Henderson, a leading futurist and social critic, provides a theory of how citizens' movements are sensing the blind spots in the industrial value system and are seeking to remedy them.

CHAPTER FOURTEEN

Citizen Movements: Charting Alternative Futures*

BY HAZEL HENDERSON

A consistent theme underlying the activities of United States citizen movements has been alienation from prevailing perceptions of reality. This article focuses on those citizen groups which are moving the country away from the predominant industrial value system. These groups in effect are at the forefront of a "paradigm shift," and the implications of their approach are significant for anticipatory democracy.

While the commercial media have projected images of split-level suburban life styles conducive to satisfying the needs for a mass-consumption economy, citizen movements, whether for peace, consumer and environmental protection, or social equality, have focused on the unpublicized, the unresearched, and often suppressed information that constitutes the other side of the coin of industrial and technological development. The reason this information is suppressed is that it deals with the unintended side effects,

* This article is based on two articles by Hazel Henderson: "Information and the New Movements for Citizen Participation," *The Annals,* Vol. 412, copyright © 1974 by The American Academy of Political and Social Science; and "Ideologies, Paradigms and Myths: Changes in Our Operative Social Values," *Liberal Education,* Vol. LXII, No. 2 (May 1976), copyright © 1976 by The Association of American Colleges. Both articles are reprinted by permission.

the second-order consequences of the action of our political and economic institutions.

Institutional structures are designed to accomplish specific purposes, and in the process are designed to screen out information the people in control perceive as unwanted or irrelevant to those purposes. Thus institutions have built-in capacities for selecting, distorting, concealing, and impounding information.

A clue to the shortcomings of human institutions may be found in nature. Human institutions tend to pursue narrow purposes and single goals. Yet, as ecologist Gregory Bateson has observed, it is rare to find ecological or biological systems which seek to maximize single variables,[1] such as profit in certain products, or continued corporate growth. Since most of our institutions are limited in purpose, and hence ignore aspects of reality at the margin or beyond their operating experience, social problems which do not correspond to existing institutions are often not perceived, much less researched.

The uncoordinated activity of our major institutions is based on the Cartesian world view that we can comprehend whole systems by analyzing their parts. In academic institutions this has not only led to the growth of narrow-purpose structures and reductionism in our academic disciplines, but has also overrewarded analysis while discouraging cross-disciplinary synthesis. In economic areas it has sustained property rights while ignoring amenity rights; fostered unrealistic dichotomies, such as those between public and private goods and services; and overrewarded competitive activities while ignoring the equally vital role of cooperation in maintaining the cohesion of the society as a whole. This Cartesian view has colored all our perceptions, creating an intellectual basis for our objects and entities defined by our institutions, while ignoring other aspects of reality which lie between or across our institutional structures. It has resulted in a lag between the goals and world view of institutional leaders and those of many citizens, who do perceive aspects of the reality not defined by institutions. It is precisely in these fields that public-interest citizen movements have naturally sprung up and taken root.

These citizen groups have begun the vital task of filling in the information gaps on the effects of institutional activity which fails to consider the range of its impact on society. These groups are painstakingly documenting our growing social costs—to which economists refer, in an almost Freudian slip, as "externalities."

Several recent polls in the United States demonstrate the growing lag between the goals and models of our leaders and the average individual's perceptions of current conditions. Harris Polls, Roper Reports, and Opinion Research all testify to the drastic decline between 1959 and 1973 of confidence in our business institutions.[2] In 1975 the Gallup Poll found that for the first time Americans were coming to terms realistically with the prospect that their own futures would be less bright than they had once imagined;[3] Hart Research reported the same year that 33 percent of Americans believed that our capitalistic system had reached its peak and was on the decline, 74 percent favored plans whereby consumers would be represented on the boards of corporations, and 56 percent said that they would support a presidential candidate who favored employee control of U.S. corporations;[4] and according to Opinion Research, despite recession, unemployment, and rising fuel costs, 60 percent of Americans did not believe that the country should cut back on environmental-control programs, even if it meant they would have to pay still higher prices.[5]

The recent poll of the attitudes of corporate executives, conducted by George Cabot Lodge and William F. Martin and published in the December 1975 issue of the *Harvard Business Review* showed that 70 percent of the executives questioned preferred the old ideologies of individualism, private property, and free enterprise, but 73 percent believed that by 1985 they would have been supplanted by collective problem-solving. Furthermore, 60 percent thought that collective action would be more effective in finding solutions.[6] In a highly complex, interdependent society, individual freedom, when armed with polluting, disruptive technology, destroys the freedom of others. And, as system theorist Todd LaPorte points out, the market is no longer a valid arbiter of choices that will have "indivisible social consequences."[7]

Indeed, more Americans believe that untrammeled corporate freedoms allow big business to run the government, export capital and jobs by establishing factories overseas, despoil the environment, and waste resources. The 1974 Yankelovitch study reported that 66 percent of Americans thought that inflation was caused by business seeking higher profits.[8]

These beliefs have not as yet destroyed Americans' faith in private ownership and enterprise, however. The Cartesian world view which has given rise to such unreal dichotomies as those of "public" and "private" sectors, goods, and services[8] ignores the link between private profits and the mounting public costs they engender. It leads to a belief that as Americans we can "afford" oversize private cars, thousands of brands of patent medicines, and billion-dollar industries devoted to pet foods and cosmetics, while we cannot "afford" enough nurses, teachers, or adequate police, fire, and sanitation services in our cities.

It is not an exaggeration to suggest that today our culture is collapsing. The rise of citizen movements at those points where our current value system, or paradigm, is most deficient is one sign of this shift. As Thomas Kuhn points out in his *Structure of Scientific Revolutions,* a major shift in conceptual paradigms leads to major cultural shifts.[9] In academia and in the more philosophical of the citizen movements there are major efforts to reintegrate perceptions, to restructure our concepts, so they are closer to reality than the current institutional and social paradigm.

Yet the most imaginative researchers in this effort complain of boundary problems—they come to realize the arbitrariness of human categorization schemes as they pursue new ecological insights. Similar problems are being left in two areas where the government is making some attempt to examine the side effect of decisions before they are made—through environmental impact statements and through technology assessment.

In addition to conceptual roadblocks there are social and political ones as well. Political and corporate leaders will sometimes privately admit that they share such doubts about our goals and values. But they maintain the conspiracy of silence, reasoning: "How do I break it to my stockholders?" Political and social change is likely only when such private perceptions are widely shared and finally confirmed as a new social reality. When a critical mass of persons sharing the altered perception is reached, the political process begins and in time ratifies the cultural change that has taken place. Examples include the development of ecological consciousness since the early sixties, the women's movement, and the growth of the movement for corporate accountability. An important function of these social movements is the psychological support they provide for their members and others as values shift and government and other social institutions adapt peacefully to new conditions.

Citizen movements for peace, for social, racial, and sexual equality, for consumer and environmental protection are all primarily concerned with providing and publicizing information that will help to create new social awareness and insights that may lead to political and cultural change. They have repeatedly shown the extent to which most research is commissioned as ammunition for political manipulation. They have revealed that economics, our reigning sophistry, is value laden, not neutral in the issues it deals with, and, happily, they dare not continue to parade it as a scientific discipline. Such formerly unchallenged words as "progress," "efficiency," "productivity," and even "profits" are now part of a battle over the fundamental meaning of economic well-being.[10] As this part of the paradigm shift occurs, new information is not necessarily created, but often existing information is repatterned to provide a more effective explanation of reality.

Societies are continually adapting. These social movements represent a major adaptive mechanism as they identify aspects of new and emerging values. In this context a direct way to use their energies has been suggested by the Swedish sociologist Gunnar Myrdal. Myrdal has pointed out that citizens organized for their own purposes can often serve the same functions as costly, regulatory bureaucracies, and that even if their activities are partially subsidized, they are cheaper and more efficient than government agencies.[11]

In our new self-searching, we in the United States are developing a more humble and tragic view of ourselves and our nation's role in the world. Hubristic, machismo nationalism is crumbling as we sample the psychic relief of relinquishing efforts to police the world. As far back as 1937, psychologist Karen Horney cited the pressures on Americans of their industrial, competitive, materialistic society. She noted that three basic value conflicts had arisen: aggressiveness had grown so pronounced that it could no longer be reconciled with Christian brotherhood; desire for material goods had been so vigorously stimulated that it could never be satisfied; and expectations of untrammeled freedom had soared so high that they were in direct conflict with the multitudes of restrictions and responsibilities that confine us all.[12] As we begin to deal with the external and legitimate demands for a new economic world order, we are beginning to realize that having created a globally inter-dependent economy, we must develop the "software" to operate it cooperatively.

Neither will the spiritual and emotional dimensions of humans be denied, and we are now witnessing what might be viewed in Freudian terms as the return of the repressed on a societal scale. The human soul is determined to find meaning and cannot live by bread alone. The predominantly Cartesian, masculine-oriented, objective sytle is too limited to express our new multidimensional awareness. Intuitive "body-wisdom" is coming to our rescue in the spontaneous growth of new organizational forms, networks, rap groups, cooperatives and all the other manifestations of the human potential movement. All of these groupings bear the seeds of new cultural forms based on new perceptions.* Groups concerned with paradigm shifts such as Earthrise in Rhode Island, New York's Lindisfarne Association, and Scotland's Findhorn, and groups seeking to reconceptualize economics such as the Council on Economic Priorities, Americans for a Working Economy, the Exploratory Project on Economic Alternatives, and Environmentalists for Full Employment show a constant attempt to reintegrate goals and concepts on a higher plane of understanding. Groups such as California's Farrallones Institute, Intermediate Technology, Oregon's RAIN, and the New Alchemy Institute of Woods Hole, Massachusetts, conduct innovative research and propagate new insights: technology is *not* value-free, as we have been told, but itself creates unexpected new cultural expressions and pathologies. Similarly, the Center for Science in the Public Interest, the Union of Concerned Scientists, the Scientists' Institute for Public Information, and SPARK have helped citizens to see that science is not value-free either. All scientists must choose what phenomena to study, what they will pay attention to. After all, reality is what we pay attention to; that which we believe to be important, and for the measurement of which we design our monitoring equipment. We then find what we are looking for and the hypnotic circle is complete.

These diverse new movements for cultural change have spawned media movements for greater access, such as the Citizen's Communications Center, the National Citizens Committee for Broad-

* Editor's note: These and similar groups are listed in Appendix 4.

casting, and a proliferation of their own media and magazines: *Radical Software, Televisions.* Other counterculture journals include *Co-Evolution Quarterly, Mother Earth News, Prevention, Organic Gardening, Environmental Action, The Elements,* and a host of regional journals such as *RAIN, Foxfire, Great Speckled Bird, Doing It!* and others. In turn, the cultural ferment is affecting academia and challenging the old Cartesian disciplinary schema and the universities' slavish service to power, wealth, and the easy rewards of turning out intellectual mercenaries.

Groups such as these on the cutting edge of the paradigm shift are unlike the groups or exercises described in other chapters of this book, in that they are usually not the futures project for a city or state government, but are citizen-based. Some embrace holistic visions and others explore repressed alternatives for the future rather than explore a range of alternative futures. Some are pre-political, affecting cultural change, which lays the groundwork for later political change. While these groups may not consciously see a range of futures, they present alternative futures in many specific areas and may become a major source for cultural renewal. If these groups succeed in joining our current information/communications technology together with a critical mass of self-organizing, self-motivating, self-actualizing citizens, there is some hope for the birth of a new interlinkage of planetary consciousness as the new cultural dimension emerges.

VI
A/D Techniques

Those who seek to introduce future consciousness into the participatory process need to find systematic and effective ways of doing so. A wide range of techniques have been designed, tested, and introduced in a variety of circumstances. In Chapter 15, Jerry Glenn—a futurist who has worked for the Hudson Institute and the Committee for the Future—reviews some of these techniques and suggests criteria for determining which (singly or collectively) may be most useful in designing an A/D process. He also considers the variations and combinations that are likely to emerge.

Nan Waterman, a leader in the League of Women Voters and now Chairperson of the Board of Common Cause, addresses the question of how organizations can examine their own future. In Chapter 16 she describes a process developed by the League of Women Voters, by which any group can explore its own future after exploring the future of the nation or its local community.

CHAPTER FIFTEEN

Social Technologies of Freedom

BY JEROME C. GLENN

A NEW DEMAND

The keystone of a democracy's survival is an educated public. At the heart of anticipatory democracy is an educated public taking part in policy-making focused on the future. As developing technology accelerates change, it is necessary to keep pace with social technologies that allow genuine democratic participation in the decisions that shape the future. We need to continually refine our social technologies of freedom.

We are fortunate that people want increased involvement in the policy process, for the United States is now faced with the ending of its first dream and the making of its next. What historians came to call "Manifest Destiny" has been accomplished. We have completed our westward expansion and produced the highest average standard of living in human history. It is now time for us to create together our next image of the future or, like previous civilizations, our lack of direction will be our downfall.

Change is more rapid and social fragmentation is greater than ever before, but citizens can learn to cope with this diversity. Our methods for exploring the future have increased dramatically,[1] as has our ability to involve citizens in the process. This chapter deals with the growing range of techniques used to involve a broader base of the people in defining the future.

What are some examples of the social technologies of freedom? What aspects of a technique make participants better able to anticipate future possibilities and problems? The situations and purposes for using A/D techniques vary and thus the criteria by which to measure them vary. Many of the techniques described here are well known to planners and others involved in citizen participation.

Before looking at specific techniques, it is useful to identify some important factors that need to be addressed in order to develop an effective A/D process with genuine citizen involvement and a future consciousness:

1. *Future Orientation* Will the process effectively address long-term considerations? Those who are leading the process must maintain a high level of commitment by involving futurists, and by encouraging a long time frame as the context for current actions. Twenty-five years is a sufficient time frame to stretch the thoughts and assumptions of participants. As A/D projects set goals or suggest budget priorities the time frame may be shorter, yet it is important to remember that one purpose of A/D techniques is to put current decisions in the larger context of a range of alternative futures.

2. *Purpose of Process* Should the A/D process make decisions for direct implementation, give advice to decision-makers, or educate the public about issues? Should it be a one-shot or a continuous process? The techniques used within an A/D process will vary. Governments can use the techniques of the A/D process to disseminate information to citizens, to collect information from citizens and others, to design plans, to react to plans developed elsewhere, and to make decisions. Figure 1 matches the steps in the planning sequence (in transportation policy) to the functions performed by specific techniques.

3. *Content* Is the A/D process intended to examine one issue, such as transportation or school design, or is it intended to examine a whole range of issues? Is the conclusion to be a consensus or a range of options? Will the agenda be flexible or fixed?

4. *Participation* How many people will participate, at what

level and for how long? What kinds of knowledge and interests should participants have?

5. *Depth of Study*   Will it focus on current actions or devise alternative future scenarios and alternative policy options?

6. *Integrity*   Public suspicion of any kind of power is strongly ingrained in the American character. The whole checks-and-balances system in our Constitution reflects our understanding of the corruptibility of power. Do the leaders or institutions originating the process have preconceived goals, and will they subtly move the process towards these goals? Or will they let the process determine its own directions? The best techniques in the world will produce fraudulent results if hidden agendas are involved.

TECHNIQUES

There is a wide range of citizen involvement techniques (see Figure 1); each varies in its approach to the future. This chapter concentrates on the following techniques: polls and surveys, Delphi questionnaires, charrette, Syncon, electronic conferencing, and some possible future variations of these. In considering these specific techniques, designers of A/D processes should ask several questions. Does the technique:

1. involve the shy nontalker;
2. allow for innovation during the process;
3. create one-way, two-way, or group communication;
4. allow time to reflect and save face if an individual's mind is changed;
5. mix participants to break up cliques;
6. make people feel comfortable enough to make usually private thoughts public;
7. develop a sense of interdependency or community and common-ground sharing;
8. make necessary information available;
9. assure that people will be encouraged to think in long-range (twenty-five-year) time frames;
10. include the assessment of secondary and tertiary consequences of actions assuming alternative futures;

FIGURE 1. Using Participation Techniques in the Planning Process: An Example from Transportation Policy.

TECHNIQUES / Planning Steps	INFORMATION DISSEMINATION				INFORMATION COLLECTION					
	Public Information Programs	Drop-in Centers	Hotlines	Meetings Open Information	Ombudsman	Surveys	Focused Group Discussion	Delphi	Public Hearings	Meetings Community Sponsored
FOR ALL FACILITIES: REGIONAL OR SUB-AREA										
1. Inventory and analyze current conditions, trends, and problems	●					●	●	●		●
2. Generate preliminary definitions of development issues and policies	●							●		●
3. Forecast population and employment, based on policies										
4. Forecast travel demand, based on forecast employment and population										
5. Define transportation needs and objectives	●			●		●	●			●
6. Develop alternative transportation plans and programs	●	●	●	●	●	●				●
7. Make preliminary evaluation of alternatives	●	●	●	●	●	●			●	
8. Establish regional or sub-area priorities	●				●					
9. Select a program package	●			●	●				●	
10. Make level of action decisions					●					
11. Establish annual (or bi-annual) "action program"	●			●						
FOR EACH FACILITY: PROJECT & CORRIDOR										
12. Refine location and design alternatives	●	●	●	●						●
13. Analyze in detail environmental impacts and engineering feasibility	●	●	●	●	●					●
14. Write draft environmental impact statement	●	●	●	●	●				●	
15. Write final environmental impact statement	●	●	●	●	●				●	
16. Make decision to build or not to build facility	●				●				●	
17. Prepare final design plans, engineering plans and cost estimates	●	●	●	●						
18. Implement and construct	●		●							
19. Operate and evaluate						●	●	●		●

● Technique that may be useful at that step.

	Advocacy Planning	Charrettes	Community Planning Centers	Computer-Based Techniques	Design-In and Color Mapping	Plural Planning	Task Force	Workshops	Citizens Advisory Committees	Citizen Representatives	Fishbowl Planning	Interactive Cable TV Participation	Meetings Neighborhood	Neighborhood Planning Councils	Policy Capturing	Value Analysis	Arbitrative and Mediative Planning	Citizen Review Board	Media-Based Issue Balloting
									•	•			•	•					
			•						•	•			•	•				•	•
									•	•								•	
									•	•								•	
									•	•			•					•	•
	•	•	•	•	•	•	•	•	•	•	•	•	•	•	•	•			•
	•		•				•	•	•	•			•	•			•	•	•
									•	•			•	•				•	
									•	•			•	•				•	
									•	•				•				•	
									•	•				•				•	
	•	•	•	•	•	•	•	•	•	•	•	•	•	•				•	
	•		•				•	•	•	•			•	•				•	•
									•	•							•	•	
									•	•							•	•	
									•	•							•	•	•
	•	•	•				•	•	•	•			•	•				•	
							•											•	
							•		•	•			•	•				•	

Source: Torrey, Wayne R., and Mills, Florence W., *Selecting Effective Citizen Participation*, U. S. Department of Transportation Policy, Washington, D.C. (January 1972)

11. include all the elements of an issue represented by people from those areas;

12. have decision-makers from government and business participate with the people affected by their decisions;

13. have a clear tie to the implementation system, i.e., legislature, city council, referendum, corporate policy, etc.;

14. avoid threatening individuals and groups;

15. insist on clearly stated conclusions, preventing later misinterpretation;

16. guarantee full news-media coverage;

17. make individual participants feel equal to institutional heavyweights; and

18. create an environment such that institutional decision-makers see the process as a positive opportunity?

Voting, the main form of citizen participation in our society, is used primarily to elect public officials. It seldom indicates voters' policy preferences. Initiatives and referenda do provide policy choices but seldom in a long-term or broad context. The public hearing is another familiar public-involvement technique. It is unsatisfactory, however, because it combines the failings of many participation techniques in one. Only one person talks at a time; the more active, articulate, and self-interested individuals and institutions are disproportionately represented; it lends itself to sophistic or legal detail to obscure the feeling of the people; it often bores the officials who receive the testimony and prevents a human exchange since officials feel they should not discuss the testimony; it may be held when the working public cannot attend; it has official trappings that intimidate the average person; and it generates reams of paper but seldom any summary or conclusions.

Unfortunately, when government officials speak of citizen participation they usually are referring to the use of the ballot and the hearing stand. But times are changing, and citizens are becoming more directly involved in the policy-making process.

POLLS AND SURVEYS

Opinion polls and surveys are increasingly popular ways to include greater numbers of people in decision-making. Polls can be used to measure attitudes about the future and to determine preferred futures and specific policies as well as the price citizens are willing to pay in the form of higher taxes.

Surveys in the form of supplements to local newspapers or workbooks provided by a particular project can be used to register the ideas and preferences of those who respond. The more affluent and better educated in the community are more likely to respond, a bias that can be overcome by taking a random sample poll using the same questionnaire as employed in Alternatives for Washington.* With large enough samples, differences in the hopes, views, and priorities of different races and different income, ethnic, and neighborhood groups can be compared. Goals for Georgia, for example, showed that black attitudes toward the state's criminal justice system were not as positive as those of whites in the state. Polls are useful for exploring attitudes about the future and for registering preferences and priorities about specific sets of choices.

DELPHI

Unlike a one-shot poll, the Delphi technique consists of several rounds of questionnaires. The first questionnaire might ask respondents to forecast future events considering possible dates of occurrence, cost, future social impacts, etc. The condensed response from the first questionnaire becomes the basis for response in the second round. The average Delphi has three rounds, but it might continue for as many as five.

This technique allows the whole group to share their thoughts, and then allows individuals the chance to revise their opinions based on the collective response. Olaf Helmer and Norman Dalkey at the Rand Corporation invented the technique in the 1960s to forecast the availability of aerospace technologies. It tends to force consensus by returning information from the previous round that shows the views of the majority. The information collected can be qualitative or subjective. It is a meeting-through-the-mail that allows ideas rather than personalities to be persuasive. Delphis have been used extensively and flexibly in a variety of situations; they can be useful in allowing citizens to adjust their priorities based on those of the larger community, as well as in exploring the likelihood of trends or events in the community. The technique can show the

* Editor's note: See "Alternatives for Washington," Chapter 4 and "Goals for Georgia," Chapter 2, which discusses a similar use of a random poll.

areas in which a community is informed and those in which it is uninformed, helping planners identify community values and priorities.[2]

In general, Delphis are designed according to the following series of steps:

1. Decide what information is needed—priorities, policies, budget, future inventions with dates, impacts, etc.
2. Identify a reasonable cross section of experts or citizen respondents (usually called the Delphi Panel) who will analyze responses to the questionnaires.
3. Design and mail or print in a newspaper the first Delphi questionnaire. The newspaper method, particularly when the local media are cooperating, is one of the least expensive ways to survey the general public. The first round can ask either for reactions to events, goals, problems, etc., or for responses to a previously prepared list of questions generated by the advisory group. Figure 2 is an example of a Delphi round requesting response to a list of possible events.
4. Edit and condense written comments. Quantifiable data are usually condensed by calculating the inner 50 percent, the mean, and the median. This can be nicely laid out in the upper polygon in the year column in Figure 3; for example, 1979–1990 represents the inner 50 percent of the responses; 1986 is the mean; and 1982 is the median.
5. Lay out and mail the collected information as a second round, leaving space for the respondents to revise their previous opinions based on the thinking of others.
6. Repeat the cycle until little new information results or a predetermined level of consensus (usually defined in Delphi as distance between median and mean) is reached.

The Delphi method is popular because it is cheap and flexible, but it has serious drawbacks because its goal is consensus and consensus does not necessarily mean plausibility. Furthermore, it does not take into account the respondents' mental models—one person's 3 rating could be the same as another's 5—and its primary appeal is to the formally educated, who often have access to the policy process already.

FIGURE 2. **Round One Questionnaire for Delphi**

EVENT	YEAR	COST	INHIBITING FACTORS	ENHANCING FACTORS	SOCIAL IMPACT
1. Nuclear hijacking	(earliest) ——— (latest) ———				
2. Solar energy producing 3% of state's energy demand	(earliest) ——— (latest) ———				

CHARRETTE

Charrette is a French word meaning "little cart." During the nineteenth century in France, the charrette picked up design students' work. Sometimes students would jump on the charrette, finishing their work along the way so as not to miss the deadline. Passersby would ask to see the students' work and make comments that the students might add. Hence, charrette came to mean feverish work to meet a deadline with some public input. In the mid-1960s the Facilities Planning Division of the U.S. Office of Education decided to involve the public in school design and called that process "Charrette."

While the Delphi intentionally isolates participants from each other, a charrette is a person-to-person device for reaching a consensus. It is designed to bring people from various segments of the public, government agencies, and experts into a well-structured sequence of discussions. These intensive planning sessions have been held from one day to two weeks. Small groups focusing on aspects of the problem under discussion report periodically to the whole group which responds to their efforts. If the charrette were focusing on urban renewal of North-Central Baltimore, for example, the small groups might be devoted to land-use planning, education, health, recreation, transportation, and business. The process

FIGURE 3. Responses to Round One of Delphi Questionnaire.

EVENT	YEAR	COST	INHIBITING FACTORS	ENHANCING FACTORS	SOCIAL IMPACT
1. Nuclear hijacking	86 / 82 / 79 / 90 (earliest) 85 / 2000 (latest)	125K / 150K / 100K / 300K (cost)	Internal plant sensory devices, policy made public that no demand will be met regardless of consequences, closing plants, tightened security for transportation, more anticipatory democracy	TV shows romantic treatment of hijacking, increased political malaise, return to more authoritative government, lack of anticipatory democracy	More negative view of higher security, reevaluation of nuclear energy, more alternative energy resources, desperate backlashes at any extremes
2. Solar energy producing 3% of state's energy demand	35 / 86 / 81 / 89 (earliest) 89 / 91 / 85 / 95 (latest)	1B / 1.3B / 800K / 1.5B (cost)	Cost of materials and installation, confusion over optimal designs, fraudulent claims, social inertia, legal impediments	Another oil embargo, energy costs, cheap materials, federal and state tax benefits, public energy education, engineering breakthrough, competitive electronics industry that lowers prices	Decentralization, local autonomy, pollution reduction, job changes

pulses back and forth from these small group discussions to meetings of the entire group until the deadline is reached. The final meeting presents the consensus reached to the press, the local government officials, and the larger public drawn to the event through media coverage.

A charrette is a good process for examining a broad range of issues with decision-makers and the recipients of decisions in the same room for an extended period of time. This crucible effect has been successful in generating consensus that is likely to be acceptable to the general public and able to be implemented. Charrettes come in all sizes and shapes, but the norm is five hundred participants with about five subgroups. Since there are many issues to discuss, charts to prepare, architectural drawings to make, hall conversations to experience, and varying degrees of participation, much activity goes on outside the subgroups as well. At any given time, therefore, there are likely to be only twenty to thirty people actively working in each subgroup.

Barry Schuttler has been involved in fifty charrettes dealing with a variety of issues from school design to zoning alterations. He lists five critical factors (which also may be considered to be applicable to all A/D process techniques) in the success of a charrette:[3]

1. Include all decision-makers relevant to the planning effort;
2. Select an area for planning that has a constituency, a political base of residents;
3. Include the community residents in the decision-making;
4. Conduct the planning within the community itself and be aware of the political realities when you begin; and
5. Utilize an experienced charrette manager who has directed the process in other communities.

The charrette approach avoids electing representatives to the decision-making process because this often results in new fixed hierarchies. It is made clear that participation means representing oneself. This creates some tension and honest self-searching for government and corporate decision-makers. But the intensity of the marathon rounds of meetings soon breaks down facades and generates a sense of camaraderie that causes surprisingly healthy respect and friendship all around.

The stages for developing a charrette are (1) the pre-charrette meetings that determine the issues and participants and design the overall process; (2) fact-finding to clarify the issues and the development of support data; (3) the charrette itself; and (4) implementation of charrette conclusions.

After ten years of evaluating rural, suburban, and urban charrettes on a variety of public policy issues, Barry Schuttler has identified the benefits that can be expected from a well-managed charrette. It should:[4]

1. generate five dollars of contributed professional services for every dollar spent on planning;
2. make recommendations such that 90 percent of them or more are approved and funded by elected officials;
3. reduce the time it takes to complete a project (the time saved should range from two years for individual projects such as the building of a school, to ten years for large projects such as the redevelopment of a central business district);
4. terminate construction moratoriums and obtain public approval for previously defeated bond issues;
5. develop new programs and services that result in funded proposals for new institutions and that encourage private investment and make tax savings possible; and
6. organize previously apathetic neighborhoods, equipping them with leaders, plans, and a working agreement, with city officials approving and funding every recommendation.

The trick of a charrette is to eliminate the distinction between "them" and "us." There are no restrictions on participation except for a strict deadline. If people argue too long without reaching a consensus decision then no report is made. But when the decision-makers, private individuals, and "experts" are able to reach a consensus, it comes as no surprise that the recommendations are received favorably.

SYNCON

Created in December 1971 by John Whiteside and Barbara Marx Hubbard of the Committee for the Future, Syncon was specifically intended to bring together people from all walks of life and professional backgrounds to develop a consensus for the next step of human evolution. What image of the future could all people work for? What are the misunderstandings that need resolution? If a diverse group could come together, share their dreams for a better tomorrow, and find a common ground, a new psychological awareness might be generated that would accelerate progress toward a positive future for all.

Unlike the charrette which tends to take a local perspective within a relatively short time frame (five to ten years), Syncon takes a global perspective and looks twenty-five to one hundred years into the future. The techniques of Syncon can be applied to local issues, as they were in East Los Angeles, at Loretto Heights College, and in Jamaica; however, it is most effective as a way to generate a holistic image of the future. Approximately twenty-four Syncons have been held on such themes as the social impact of technology, energy, quality of life, crime, and information.

The size and structure of Syncons may vary, although generally they are run over the course of three and a half days. Unlike the alternation of the charrette between small and large groups, the Syncon begins with small groups which then merge first to groups of intermediate size and finally to one large group. On the average, about two hundred fifty persons meet inside a wheellike environment designed to highlight the present fragmentation of our society. Figure 4 below is the Syncon-wheel floor plan:[5]

The inner sections of the wheel—labeled social needs, applied technology, environment, production, government, and other regions (i.e., international issues)—represent functional areas of a culture. The outer sections represent areas of new potential—biology, physics, communications, political/economic theory, extraterrestrial occurrences, arts, and unexplained phenomena.

Each section is given a discussion guide to provide a framework for identifying goals, needs, and resources. Each section has a co-ordinator to facilitate the group's communication flow within the confines of modular walls. On the second day, half the walls—the ones between some traditionally antagonistic areas—come down for joint exploration; for example, the environment group and the technology group meet together. On the third day, all the walls come down, joint summaries are given, and the total group examines the impacts of its decisions and matches the goals, needs, and resources of the total body.

FIGURE 4. Synergistic Convergence in Operation

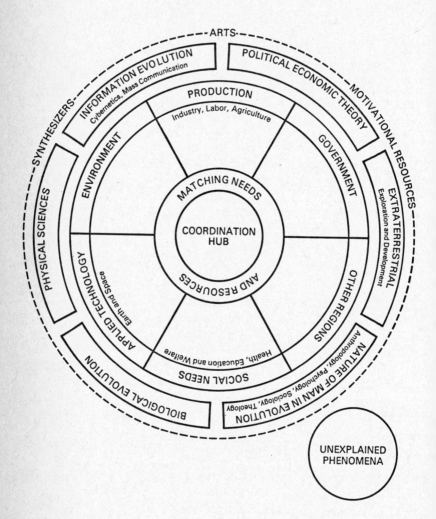

Source: The Committee for the Future, *Syncon: Washington, D.C.* (May 1973).

The whole process is intended to be made available live on television, allowing home viewers to participate by telephone. The Committee for the Future pioneered the use of live PBS television and interactive closed-circuit television for anticipatory democracy purposes. Each section has a fixed closed-circuit TV camera, microphones, two television sets, and a speaker system connected to the Syncon video console. At the console, the Syncon coordinator can watch, hear, and speak with each group. The console also allows two groups to interact audio-visually, or individual groups to see one of the videotapes in the Committee for the Future's vast collection of future-oriented tapes. A mobile television van connects as many as four color mobile cameras that put the Syncon live on the local PBS station. Such highly interactive television systems and participatory processes create a unique psychological and sociological experience, "synergistic convergence"—hence the term "Syncon."

In the evening, plays, comedies, and musical performances integrate the issues of the day artistically to give the participants both time to reflect and to relax. The whole process is something like a cross between a country fair and a think tank.

Syncons have not had the same direct legislative or policy impact as charrettes since they have developed as an educational device rather than as a method to stimulate future-oriented participation. Yet the Syncon can produce:

1. links between individuals and institutions;
2. comprehensive adult education;
3. positive, multifaceted images of the future for positive motivation;
4. strikingly future-oriented policy recommendations; and
5. projects to be carried out by the participants themselves.

Because Syncon structures involve diverse perspectives (such as unexplained phenomena and advanced physics), they usually produce broader and longer-range thinking than many other techniques. However, because they have not been as directly related to state or local policy processes, their conclusions are not often implemented.

PROBLEM/POSSIBILITY FOCUSER

Unlike Delphis, charrettes, and Syncons, the Problem/Possibility Focuser is a technique more concerned with clarifying the agreements and disagreements that surround a specific issue than with achieving consensus. The process, created by Robert Theobald, begins with a group finding all the areas of agreement and then all the areas of disagreement on the issue at hand.* The next step is to develop ideas to settle the disagreements. The last step before preparing a report on the process is to list resources that may help to clarify the nature of the disagreements listed.

Theobald sees this as a continuous process. A Problem/Possibility Focuser is generated on a particular issue, then circulated among as many people as possible to collect feedback to rewrite the original document. The process stresses the need to develop information without the distortion that accompanies systems of authority, and it is ideally suited to electronic conferencing.

ELECTRONIC CONFERENCING

As the second Space Age approaches, the benefits of the early aerospace research and development are beginning to be used to foster communications without the need to travel. Recent telephone improvements have expanded the number of people who can hear each other comfortably on conference calls. Telecopiers send duplicates of architectural plans, charts, and printed words over telephone lines. Sears is trying out two-way cable TV in Orlando, Florida. Congressman Charlie Rose (D-N.C.) has used the CTS satellite to communicate via television with his constituents in North Carolina, and Senator Adlai Stevenson, using the same satellite, held hearings in Washington while the witnesses were in Springfield, Illinois.[6] NASA's Goddard Space Flight Center is now experimenting with a hand-held, two-way audio transceiver that would dramatically increase such opportunities. Two very powerful satellites, ATS-6 and CTS, make the ground equipment less expensive.

One of the more popular electronic techniques is computer conferencing. Because the medium is the printed word, which is available instantaneously to other participants and which is stored for

* Editor's note: See Chapter 18.

later retrieval, this technique is excellent for identifying first-, second-, and third-order agreements among a geographically diverse group. It is particularly useful where the participants are unwilling or unable to interact under other circumstances. Computer conferencing can be linked with the telecopier and with videoconferencing to become the policy meeting of the future, as the technology becomes more available and accessible to the general public.

As Dr. Murray Turoff, one of the primary developers, explains:[7]

Computer conferencing is a written form of a conference telephone call . . . The computer automatically informs the group when someone joins or leaves the discussion. When a person signs off, the computer marks his location in the discussion and picks up at that point when he rejoins the conference. . . . People . . . can be both geographically and chronologically dispersed . . . everyone can "talk" or "listen" at the same time: A person can make his contribution to the discussion at his own convenience, rather than having to wait until other speakers have finished . . . Each message is assigned a number and labeled with author, date and time for easy identification and retrieval.

Anonymous comments can be made and sent to all participants or secretly to any one or more participants. Issues can be voted on secretly. Parts of texts can be readily retrieved. In addition to these, Turoff claims that one of the major advantages of computer conferencing is that it "puts unique psychological pressure on a person whose messages tend to be verbose, irrelevant, or filled with bureaucratic jargon. He will soon notice that no one is paying any attention to his messages."

STAGES IN DEVELOPING AN A/D PROCESS

How does one establish an A/D process that uses these and/or other available techniques? The obvious first step is realizing the need for involving citizens and for stretching time horizons in considering issues. A person or group of persons must take the initiative and accept the responsibility for creating that process. Usually the creation of a steering committee is one of the first steps taken.

The steering committee should be a microcosm of the people

and interests affected. James L. Creighton, a designer of futures-planning processes, suggests the following guidelines for establishing such a committee:[8]

1. it must include individuals representing the full range of values pertaining to a particular issue, rather than just those values with which the initiators are comfortable;

2. it must have a clearly defined role. A "contract" should be negotiated in order to prevent bad feelings as a result of unreasonable expectations of the role the group is to play; and

3. especially if the process is to be an ongoing one, it must have a mechanism for ensuring that the members maintain communication with their constituencies and remain, in fact, representative. Groups of this nature have a tendency (after about the third meeting) to consider themselves experts no longer in need of consulting the "uninformed public."

The work of steering committees should begin by considering the factors in process design discussed early in this article, i.e., time frame, purpose, content, participation, and depth. Having addressed these questions, the advisory group should then survey and evaluate the range of available techniques. Figure 5 below compares various techniques according to their future orientation, the resources that are required to use each of them, the extent to which the required resources are readily available to the average community, the level of participation entailed in each, the extent to which each encourages personal interchange, the extent to which each encourages candor, whether a technique contributes to community building, whether it has a tie to the policy process, and whether media involvement is likely.

Such a grid highlights the kinds of choices among alternatives that the steering committee must make. The techniques vary widely, for example, in the extent to which each calls for public participation. With such a grid, the steering committee can at least get a ready overview of the scope of choice in designing an A/D process —which not only can, but should, incorporate a number of the techniques.

Once the committee has designed the process—that is, the sequence of techniques and the issues to be addressed—an overall director is generally required. This person should be familiar with all of the elements of the process plan the steering committee has developed, be able to work in a nonauthoritarian manner, be flexible, be able to deal with ambiguity, be able to analyze the situations at hand in order to intervene when necessary, and above all, be welcomed by all camps as a person of the highest integrity. At this point, it is also useful to spread the responsibility for the various tasks to be performed. While there is not unanimity on this point, it does seem to make good managerial sense for those who have initiated the process to yield to others who will implement it. If the same group were to initiate, design, and coordinate the entire process, the "old boy clique" cultural phenomenon might undermine the public's sense of involvement in, and ownership of, the process. The steering committee should not shrivel up and die, however. Its new role is to counsel those involved in implementing the process. Thus the workload is shifted from the steering committee to others, but the overall responsibility for maintaining the sense of integrity so vital to later success remains with the initiating group.

The successful design of an A/D process includes a strategy. If the group charged with implementing the conclusions reached is distinct from the initiating group, this is an indication of a genuinely open process.

TECHNIQUES ON THE HORIZON

Advocates of participatory decision-making and public examination of alternative futures have so zealously pushed their particular techniques that little integration of methods has occurred. Such integration is one of the next steps in the growth of anticipatory democracy. One can imagine many rich combinations. For example, an advisory committee could choose to use a Delphi survey to clarify existing agreements and disagreements around an issue. The resultant Problem/Possibility Focuser could set the agenda and guide the discussion for a charrette using Syncon's interactive television techniques to provide live TV broadcasts with the opportunity for viewer response.

The current use of citizens' band radios as a participatory technique whose goal is to avoid traffic jams and speeding tickets and

FIGURE 5. Criteria For Evaluating Some A/D Techniques

	REFER-ENDUM	POLL/SURVEY	DELPHI	CHARRETTE
Future Orientation	–generally (although not necessarily) short-range	–generally present-oriented –can tap attitudes & preferences for future	–good	–2–10 years can be longer
Resources Required	–local polling mechanism	–$1–3 per household in the community	–minimal unless large sample involved	–significant time and community resources
Required Resources Readily Available to Average Community	–adequate	–yes	–yes	–yes
Participation Profile	–eligible voters	–either self-selecting or random	–self-selecting or chosen by an advisory group	–representative cross section of community interests
Results Affected by Personality Involved of Those	–has voter characteristics	–minimal	–designed to avoid interpersonal contact	–encourages airing disputes
Encourages Candor	–possible	–varies	–yes	–yes
Community Building	–possible	–possible	–possible	–yes
Policy Process Impact	–yes	–possible	–possible	–yes
News-Media Involvement	–likely	–possible	–possible	–yes

to help people in distress foreshadows large-scale use of electronic instruments for communication and participation purposes. One such futuristic possibility has been nicknamed the "Tree of Knowledge." It is envisioned as an attaché case complete with typewriter that doubles as a computer terminal, small TV monitor, camera,

SYNCON	PROBLEM/ POSSIBILITY FOCUSER	ELECTRONIC CONFER- ENCING
–25–100 years	–usually over 10 years	–usually over 10 years
–television equipment –large room –steering committee –3½ days	–minimal	–extensive
–yes (from Committee for the Future)	–yes	–rarely
–representative cross section of community interests	–self-selecting	–selected according to computer access
–positively	–positively	–based on technology
–fair to good	–yes	–yes
–possible	–possible	–not to date
–possible	–possible	–possible
–yes	–no	–rarely

telephone, and antenna to receive and transmit to satellites. Such a device could provide access to computer systems, conferences, and telephone calls to keep individuals informed on the issues of the day and to enable them to participate electronically in the A/D process. It is possible not only that such a device could become available in the next ten years but that it could become inexpensive enough to be either owned by or accessible to large numbers of citizens.

What possible combination of techniques could be used in developing the A/D process at the national level? Canada is perhaps the prime example of a country that has seriously examined the possibility of development a rational A/D process. The Canadian Ministry of State for Urban Affairs (MSUA), a counterpart to the U.S. Department of Housing and Urban Development, had various A/D approaches designed in response to Prime Minister Pierre Trudeau's expressed interest. Future Options Room, a U.S. futurist consulting firm, prepared one such approach for MSUA. It called for a combination of agency analysis and of a national public Delphi survey conducted by the news media of citizens' attitudes about present problems and future possibilities and priorities.

Figure 6 below shows how this process would work.

T_1 During the first phase, the Ministry of State for Urban Affairs (MSUA) prepares policy briefing and option sheets for a tri-level charrette (TLC) involving metropolitan, province, and federal level participants while newspapers, radio, and television conduct a public Delphi to generate public feelings for the TLC.

T_2 The second phase is a three- to six-day TLC to evaluate and synthesize policy options and public Delphi conclusions in order to evolve broad public policy criteria and/or to make policy recommendations.

T_3 During the third phase, newspapers, radio, and television disseminate and evaluate the results of the TLC while the MSUA does its own evaluation.

T_4 Next the media prepare and conduct another series of public Delphis in response to public reaction to Step 3. Likewise, MSUA prepares its issues, briefing and options sheets from its evaluation of Step 3 in preparation for the next TLC.

T_5 Next tri-level charrette.

This is a rather simplistic explanation for a complex process. It is intended to be a part of the MSUA's normal routine rather than a one-shot effort. Computer conferencing could run throughout the process to gather the input of those individuals whose advice is highly valued, but who are unable or unwilling to participate in

FIGURE 6. An AID Process Using a Combination of Techniques

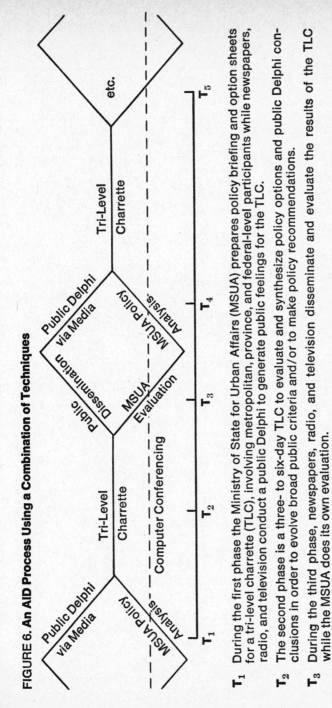

T_1 During the first phase the Ministry of State for Urban Affairs (MSUA) prepares policy briefing and option sheets for a tri-level charrette (TLC), involving metropolitan, province, and federal-level participants while newspapers, radio, and television conduct a public Delphi to generate public feelings for the TLC.

T_2 The second phase is a three- to six-day TLC to evaluate and synthesize policy options and public Delphi conclusions in order to evolve broad public criteria and/or to make policy recommendations.

T_3 During the third phase, newspapers, radio, and television disseminate and evaluate the results of the TLC while the MSUA does its own evaluation.

T_4 Next, the media prepare and conduct another series of public Delphis in response to public reaction to Step 3. Likewise, MSUA prepares its issues, briefing, and options sheets from its evaluation of Step 3 in preparation for the next TLC.

T_5 Next tri-level charrette.

any other fashion, e.g., scientists or busy executives. Computer conferencing would allow the MSUA or the media access to print-outs of sections or entire texts and add expert opinion that other-wise might not be incorporated into the process.

According to the Future Options Room plan, when recommen-dations receive a predetermined minimum level of acceptance, they should automatically become policy.

SOME TENTATIVE CONCLUSIONS

The degree to which the recipients of a decision are involved in making the decision is the degree to which the decision will be acceptable to the public. Conversely, the degree to which the decision-makers are involved in the citizen process is the degree to which the conclusions will be implemented with ease and speed. And the greater the range of alternative futures considered in the process, the more likely it is that the conclusions will have a posi-tive and lasting impact.

Once a process is put into effect, and people genuinely and ac-tively participate, it is seldom neat and tidy, especially if important and controversial issues are raised. It is important and desirable for anger to flow and for unlikely ideas to be aired. Only if this kind of free-for-all occurs—and is allowed to occur—will partici-pants come to recognize that they have neither the time nor the interest to make comments and decisions about everything. A new sense of responsibility or cooperation will follow only if the pre-vious phase runs its course. The notion that supposedly implaus-ible alternatives should be aired is not unheard of within the government. Senator Edward Kennedy (D–Mass.), for example, has proposed an Experimental Futures Agency that would fund the demonstration of some of the unlikely, unprecedented projects recommended by citizen interest groups.

Professional planners often feel threatened by the thought of greater public involvement in the making of plans. The detail in a plan from a planning department usually far exceeds the con-clusions from a public process. But the planners are often out of touch with the feelings of the people. If the public process sets the criteria for planning, then the planners can use those guidelines without feeling that their territory has been invaded. Plans can then be evaluated by the next round of the public process, creating a partnership between the planners and those for whom the planning is done.

Much work still needs to be done. Even though the range of techniques and processes is wide, we are still in the "horse and buggy" stage in terms of implementing many of them. There have been many brilliant as well as very sloppy applications of surveys, Delphis, charrettes, Syncons, and variations and combinations of these. With the aid of electronic conferencing, the variations will multiply. It is therefore important to design group processes that are not overshadowed by electronic wizardry. The electronic and social tools for communication must make people more aware and more conscious of the range of alternative futures and the means to achieve their preferred futures. Only in this way will they become the social technologies of freedom.

CHAPTER SIXTEEN

The League of Women Voters: Exploring American and Organizational Futures

BY NAN WATERMAN

Citizens and public officials are becoming aware of the increasing complexities of current problems. One has only to look at the energy crisis to see this greater awareness demonstrated. Whatever the degree of their cynicism, a great many people now understand that dealing with present and future energy scarcities involves not only economic policy but also decisions about foreign policy, controls and rationing, resource development, and environmental preservation. In addition, the time it takes to deal with complex problems demonstrates the need to identify future options early so that there will be enough time to implement a solution and to determine the means for dismantling that solution before it becomes part of the problem.

Business continually engages in planning, both long-range (twenty to twenty-five years) and short-range (three to five years). In a democratic government, informed consent of the citizenry requires a similar concern and commitment on the part of citizens for more effective long-range decision-making. Political columnist David Broder, writing about the revitalization of the American political system, put it well: "The cost of being an American citizen is going up. . . . It is going to cost us time and energy and thought diverted from our private concerns to make government workable and politics responsible again in America. . . . If we do nothing, we guarantee that our nation will be nothing."[1]

Some citizen and public service groups have begun to organize systematic efforts to look at the future of the nation, their local communities and their organizations. The League of Women Voters and its Education Fund has developed one of the most comprehensive of these. The League process is particularly interesting because of the extent to which local chapters participated in testing various formats for futures exercises as the process developed.

If one accepts the theory that the future is not pre-ordained but may perhaps differ radically from the present, then the involvement of public service groups and other organizations in decisions shaping the future is crucial. By involving their own and other constituencies, organizations can provide the popular support for decisions that move beyond passive acceptance of directions determined by current forces and past decisions.

We live in a time of fierce competition for resources, and this competition is likely to increase during the next twenty to twenty-five years. Blue-collar workers, women, racial minorities, and the poor are becoming more sophisticated about making known their demands for their share of these resources. If we are to live together in reasonable harmony, conflicting but legitimate demands on future resources must be clearly identified. Conflicts can then be resolved in such a way that people can at least accept, if not enthusiastically support, the outcomes. By helping to identify conflicts and involving League members and others in the process of compromise/consensus, the League process gives better direction to organizations and trains members in anticipating and developing consensus.

DEVELOPING THE LEAGUE PROCESS

A publication of the League's Education Fund called *Exploring American Futures* explains the process.[2] It also includes materials that any group can administer to examine its own future and that of the community or nation.

Funded by the Carnegie Corporation of New York, *Exploring American Futures* was the final product of the League of Women Voters' Education Fund's 21st Century Project. It was created in a number of stages, some planned, some growing out of preceding interactions.

The process began in January 1973 with a three-day seminar of national thinkers. Journalist Harry Ashmore, sociologist Mark Battle, development expert Lester Brown, Grinnell College President Glenn Leggett, *Harvard Business Review* editor Ralph Lewis, *Limits to Growth* coauthor Donella Meadows, and others discussed what they wanted from their world in the twenty-first century.[3] Tapes of these proceedings were used as a starting point for the next step of the process in which League groups, allied with various other community organizations, discussed what they wanted their future to be like. Groups in five cities participated. In San Diego a discussion evolved that questioned the future viability of the present structure of the League itself. That discussion led to step three.

Then, in the fall of 1973, about sixty League members from all over the state of California came together for a two-day meeting and wrestled with such questions as the composition of the League in 1990, the style of leadership most appropriate for the League of the future, and five key planning issues to be considered by the National Board of the League: finance, membership, recruitment, volunteer time, priority setting, and leadership training.

From this exercise came lessons not only about how League members saw their organization's future, but also about the best way to organize material so that a group can reach some conclusions and make decisions for future-oriented organizational change. Before an organization can decide what changes it wants to set in motion, it has to decide why they are necessary and what objectives they will help to accomplish. It has to identify its own strengths and weaknesses and the major forces affecting the organization. When a group has reached agreement on these central themes, it can begin to define how the organization will have to change to reach its goals. The next step was a two-day workshop meeting held for League leaders from eight midwestern states. Again, just as the testing of materials in San Diego touched off a statewide meeting, so too this meeting of midwestern leaders sparked a meeting of local officials to examine the future of

Madison, Wisconsin. The Madison model included sessions defining desirable national goals and the desirable Madison of the future, and a final session to begin planning to achieve that future community the participants had described.

Finally, in January 1975 the National Board of the League spent a day using the final materials exercises developed over the previous five steps as a testing exercise and to help them plan future League activities. Among the organizational priorities identified were: greater long-range planning capability, improved communications within the organization, training in organizational management skills, continued stress upon development of a sound financial base, and continued discussion of organizational restructuring. It is interesting to note that many of the priorities the National Board identified were the same ones local leaders in California had identified about a year before.

THE RESULT OF THE PROCESS— EXPLORING AMERICAN FUTURES

The final result of these stages was the publication of *Exploring American Futures,* designed to be not only a summary report but also a manual for citizens to use. The Introduction to the report notes that the process it describes is intended to involve participants in general meetings as well as in small groups of seven or eight. The small groups work to reach agreement on two alternative futures: the most probable and the most desirable. The exercise focuses on three areas: the nation, the community, and the organization. (Often, discussions focus on either the community or the nation, not both.)

The section on the nation is the most extensive. Specific information is supplied in advance; in the area of education, for example, participants choose among the following scenarios of educational institutions in the year 2000:

A. Educational institutions and their social roles have changed little over recent decades. Educational institutions place some emphasis on teaching of reading, writing, math and other skills, but in most cases serve as child-care institutions for the 5–16-year-olds in society.

B. Educational institutions are assigned the role of developing the whole person with particular emphasis on values and the personal search for meaning.

C. Education is viewed as a life-long process. People move in and out of educational situations at frequent intervals, coming back both for personal growth and training in new skills.

D. Education is viewed as essentially a practical matter. Educational institutions are therefore assigned primarily to training for a day-to-day living and vocational skills. Other aspects of learning and growth are left to other institutions (e.g., family, church, etc.) and informal social processes.

E. Educational institutions are assigned the role of preparing *well-adjusted* citizens, with major emphasis on techniques of behavior modification.[4]

If none of the above descriptions fits that of your group, compose a new one and have your recorder report it.[4]

In each group a recorder notes whether the degree of consensus around the option chosen was strong (above 60 percent) or weak (50–60 percent). The section on the nation includes twenty aspects of society, each one presented in a similar fashion. These include social mood, environmental quality, economic and political structures, government spending, status of women, etc.

The community section is not so detailed. Rather, it provides ten theme categories and cue questions to stimulate the group. The areas are similar to those covered in the nation section: community development and population, politics, government, environment, economy, values and public morality, social change, technological innovation, education, and government spending. Participants were asked for the community development and population area to "identify the characteristics of growth and population in the year 2000." They were also given the following cue questions:

- Will major growth be in urban core or suburban areas? rural? other?
- How fast is the population growing or shrinking?
- How has the age distribution changed? the racial/ethnic distribution?

- How have urban, suburban, and rural areas changed?
- What are the effects of transportation systems on population patterns?

The organization section instructs participants to assume that their desirable future will in fact develop and to do long-range organizational planning on that basis. Most of the areas of concern grow out of the League exercises in San Diego: assets, goals and objectives, activities, structure, membership, money, planning priorities, liabilities, leadership for the future. These can be adapted to suit almost any organization. To have a successful exercise, a session leader would be wise to try jarring participants out of their normal frame of mind. One technique is to send out in advance a series of questions relevant to the session introduced by some deliberately provocative statements such as: "By the year 2000 all Americans under a certain IQ will be disenfranchised and made wards of the state."

The session itself should be a satisfying experience; everyone should be allowed to speak. Decisions should be faithfully recorded, and follow-up plans laid. If the small group is homogeneous, shared values will emerge, giving the group a chance to clarify its values. If the group is diverse, consensus will be more difficult to obtain, but the sharing perceptions can create a mood favorable to united action. Above all,

The session leader should be aware and point out to participants that people often leave *Exploring American Futures* with a sense of dissatisfaction and frustration. They feel that they have not had enough time to explore all the ramifications of the issues raised, that they haven't been able to resolve many apparent conflicts, that they have no answers. This dissatisfaction is a part of the process of the learning experience, and it provides the stimulus for further thought about the future and for action to shape the future. In a sense the frustration involved in *Exploring American Futures* reflects the real world frustrations of having to make decisions with too little time and too little information.[5]

By raising issues in a future context and by identifying their preferred alternatives, citizen organizations can help define the emerging issues that should be the political agenda of the community, group, or nation. In the process, these groups can raise public consciousness and help institutionalize more effective, future-oriented citizen participation in government. Mandated citizen participation is increasingly common in federal programs, yet it seldom puts current choices in a larger context. Futures exercises enable citizens to enlarge their perspective. Citizens involved in specific programs will especially benefit from this training.

Broad-based citizen education and the creation of a constituency for long-range planning are related benefits. Futures exercises educate participants in the complexities of the issues, the difficulties of providing governmental solutions, the vast amount of information that is required for long-range planning, and the necessity for some acceptable trade-offs between groups with competing goals.

These educational lessons are particularly important. As society becomes increasingly complex and fragmented, citizens and community groups make conflicting demands on government. A consequence is that our public officials spend a considerable amount of their time acting as mediators. If, as some believe, the government is breaking down, the fault may lie more with unreasonable expectations of what our present government structure can provide than with nonresponsive and unaccountable public officials. To the extent that futures exercises can make demands more realistic, they provide a great service.*

In 1835 Alexis de Tocqueville wrote: "In a time of turbulence I maintain that the most powerful and perhaps the only means that we still possess of interesting men in the welfare of their country is to make them partakers in the government."[6] Times of turbulence reappear and require new approaches. Abraham Lincoln observed in his second inaugural address: "The dogmas of the quiet past are inadequate for the stormy present." As change accelerates and problems become more complex and interwoven, new forms of participation are necessary, and religious, ethnic and racial, educational and advocacy groups can provide a rich blend of opinion. Yet these groups must first involve their own constituencies in thinking about the probable future and the future they prefer. Only in this way will they be able to bring their hopes, priorities, and decisions to the community and to government at all levels.

While this kind of activity takes time, it is an important task. We are all passengers on "spaceship Earth," and as sociologist

---

* Editor's note: see Chapters 1 through 4.

Mark Battle said at the League's original 1973 meeting for this project, "Survival is important to me as an individual now; it's important as I look forward to the year 2000. There are a lot of people who are concerned more with their survival now than with their survival thirty years from now. But the whole issue of what happens tomorrow is based on what happens today."[7]

VII

The Future of Anticipatory Democracy

The preceding chapters have shown the first steps in recent years toward anticipatory democracy. What lies in the future? In what directions should A/D activities move?

The chapters thus far have attempted to answer questions about the A/D process that will need to be addressed further in the years to come:

1. How long a time frame is necessary to get a grasp on likely changes and possible unforeseen opportunities?
2. How can individuals and groups be encouraged to explore alternative futures with open minds, rather than making choices and decisions on the basis of a single or implicitly assumed future?
3. How can A/D processes be used to develop a wide range of alternative policies, as well as to examine the long-term impacts of those policies?
4. How can citizens be informed of the range of choices and encouraged to state their preferences in meaningful ways?
5. How can A/D processes include minorities and disenfranchised parts of the community?
6. Can those who currently hold power learn to be open to fu-

tures that are different from the situations through which they first gained power?

The concluding chapters raise a number of additional questions. Ted Becker, a political scientist and author, argues in Chapter 17 for participation in reexamining our state constitutional structures, using the latest technologies we have for rapid and effective communication. In reviewing the preparations for the 1978 Hawaii Constitutional Convention, Becker describes the "electronic town meeting" as the next step in the evolution of American democracy.

In Chapter 18 Robert Theobald, a leading futurist and author, argues that the nature of structural authority within our current institutions leads to severe distortions of information. Theobald calls for a system of "sapiential authority," authority based on knowledge and competence. As a first step toward learning how to develop and recognize this type of authority, Theobald offers the problem/possibility focuser as a technique for developing information that is necessary to effective decision-making.

In the final chapter James Dator, a pioneer in teaching futuristics and one of the designers of Hawaii 2000, argues that A/D groups should take their search for futures seriously, as it is easy to fall into premature acceptance of the predominant scenarios suggested by others. He argues that A/D groups should not let the two images of the future that are most convenient today—the postindustrial state and the conserver society—turn our attention away from the urgent questions that these "rehashed pasts" cannot answer.

CHAPTER SEVENTEEN

The Constitutional Network: An Evolution in American Democracy

TED BECKER

Right after the original Constitutional Convention, Ben Franklin was asked by a woman what kind of government the delegates had contrived. He responded, "Madam, it is a republic." That it was, and a republic is what it still resembles today. Yet we are regularly misled to believe that our form of government is a democracy.

Of course, a republic is more democratic than a monarchy or a dictatorship. And the particular system framed at the Constitutional Convention also had democratic components. In a republic, citizens elect representatives to conduct the major public business. This approach is called euphemistically "indirect democracy," but what democracy actually means is individuals voting on the issues themselves. In order to do so, they must have direct access to all important and relevant information. But Americans are well-trained to believe that such direct democracy is impossible on any scale greater than a small town meeting, a jury, or a grand jury. We are conditioned to believe that democratic processes are inconvenient and inefficient, despite the obvious fact that the present government is the very apotheosis of inefficiency and ranks high on corruption and domination by huge special interests.

Widespread disillusionment and alienation are setting in; there are clear indications that conventional electoral politics hold less and less interest and meaning. In a recent Harris Poll, 76 percent of Americans indicated that they believe that "special interests get more from the government than the people do." The number of eligible voters who vote in presidential elections has fallen for four consecutive elections. At the state and local levels, the situation is generally worse. Let's look at some cities: In Atlanta's municipal elections in 1973, 61 percent of eligible voters turned out; in 1977 that figure dropped to 42 percent. In Louisville, the decline in the same four-year span was from 74 to 47 percent. And in New York City, traditionally a hotbed of local politics, the downward trend from 1969 to 1977 was from a haughty 81 to a doleful 49 percent.

The people *know* their voice doesn't count much. Voting has become, in most elections, the functional equivalent of the rain dance, a traditional but irrelevant ritual—good only for entertainment. Many people are unable to take it seriously anymore. Does this mean that they are apathetic, apolitical, and indifferent? No, it does not. In fact, despite the fact that voter turnout is decreasing, citizens continue to rally in large numbers around such issues as abortion, laetrile, nuclear energy, environmental protection, the Panama Canal treaty, and governmental action and inaction.

Nonetheless, these citizen activists find themselves using ancient tools in an antiquated political system—one stacked to favor entrenched, powerful parties. Legislative, executive, and judicial decision-making processes (as well as the mass media) are not geared to handle true grass-roots, public pressure. Lots of effort reaps scant rewards. The result: increasing frustration with "the system."

Meanwhile, the pace of technological and scientific change is accelerating. Much of this change has worked severe dislocations —economic, ecological, psychological, familial, etc. But even as we steel ourselves for further change, we also realize that technological advances have improved the quality of life tremendously. As I will show below, a most promising way to make a place for citizen participation in American government and politics is to adapt and apply new communications and information technologies. Yes, only technology can diminish the time and distance between large numbers of private citizens concerned about and willing to work on the same public problem at the same time.

What's more, experience indicates that technological change is much easier than political change for most people to swallow. If easily usable and readily available technology could "change the system" by giving the people more muscle and a stronger voice, Americans might very well be willing to accept that—especially since such change could be accomplished without violence.

How could this be done, given the fact that Congress, state legislatures, and similar governmental bodies all representing government by the few, would surely struggle against the use of technology to diminish their power? There is already in existence in America one unique political institution that invites just such a redistribution of political power: the *state constitutional convention*.

CONSTITUTIONAL CONVENTIONS: FOR A CHANGE

State constitutional conventions are usually dull, drab fare, political meetings that fail to rouse the interest of the populace mainly because they dote on formal and legalistic issues and merely tinker with government structure. They are usually a Legislature's Legislature run by Politicians' Politicians. As such, newspapers quickly relegate them to non-front-page status and TV news coverage is usually restricted to their openings, closings, and an occasional hot item.

But if handled properly, a constitutional convention, even at the state level, can be an invitation for a peaceful revolution. The original U.S. Constitutional Convention, in 1787, was actually a *coup* pulled off by the minority Federalists. The thirty-nine men who contrived a whole new government also provided a model for all subsequent constitutional gatherings in America: anything goes as long as you get popular ratification later on.

Indeed, the only limits on the power of state ConCons are a few general ones imposed by the U.S. Constitution. For example, the U.S. Constitution guarantees American citizens some form and some degree of representative government at the state level. Also, the Fourteenth Amendment, as defined by the Supreme Court, prevents the states from abridging certain individual rights guaranteed each individual as a citizen of the United States.

Other than these checkpoints, a state ConCon may be a completely open forum, susceptible to any kind of structural change agreed upon by the delegates. And, of course, it can address itself to all sorts of important policy questions about the future of the polity. So it is nearly limitless in its potential political clout. That, however, is only one of its advantages.

Under the present system, reformers find themselves seeking major change from those most adamantly opposed to it—i.e., legislators, governors, and other incumbent officials who have little to gain from major change and much to lose. In fact, such officials realistically see reform as a personal threat. But a state constitutional convention has *no incumbents*. In elections for delegates, some people may run who have had experience at previous conventions, but no one is truly an incumbent in office, and there is no established "seniority system" for committee chairmanships.

A state constitutional convention also lacks another vested interest resistant to major political reform. Congress and all state legislatures have professional staffs and research bureaus that do legwork, data collection, and the like. Indeed, many of these staff members outlast individual legislators, becoming part of a legislative bureaucracy. A state constitutional convention is—first and foremost—fleeting, impermanent, a sometimes thing. It has no permanent staff to serve its own interests.

A FAVORABLE CONFLUENCE OF CONDITIONS IN HAWAII, 1976–78

LEGAL AND POLITICAL FACTORS

Recognizing the usefulness of state ConCons as an instrument for achieving timely and major reform in government and governance, the delegates to the 1968 Hawaii Constitutional Convention added this farsighted foresight proviso to the constitution:

The legislature may submit to the electorate at any general or special election the question, "Shall there be a convention to propose a revision of or amendments to the Constitution?" If any ten-year period shall elapse during which the question shall not have been submitted, the lieutenant governor shall verify the question, to be voted on at the first general election following the expiration of such a period.

Despite some ambiguity, this clause was interpreted as mandating the inclusion of a referendum in Hawaii's general election of November 1976: "Shall there be a convention to propose a revision of or amendments to the Constitution?" A mere eight years after the ratification of the 1968 state constitution, 76 percent of the voters voted "yes"! Why was there such a popular yearning for a new ConCon?

The Hawaii State Constitution of 1968 is much like all others in the United States: republican, three branches, a bill of rights, etc. The 1968 Hawaii ConCon was intended to bring about legislative reapportionment so as to "conform to the 'one man, one vote' rule" mandated by the U.S. Supreme Court a short time before. But no such reason could explain the people's desire for a new ConCon in 1976. What did the public have in mind?

Psychological Factors

Voter turnout in Hawaii is higher than in most states, yet the general political dissatisfaction most other Americans express also exists in Hawaii. My colleagues and I discovered this when we systematically polled Hawaiian citizens with a questionnaire based in part on the format used by pollster Louis Harris to gauge the level of confidence in the national government. We also wanted to see whether the public was willing to use the ConCon as a forum to discuss and to solve substantive problems, such as pollution, crime, and over-development.

Using a computer-generated list of telephone numbers, we interviewed 340 respondents on Oahu, Maui, and the Big Island (Hawaii). (Three hundred respondents to a survey conducted in the state of Hawaii is generally considered an adequate sample of the population if the sample is random.) We used the computer to generate numbers instead of the telephone book, since 20 percent of the telephone subscribers on the island of Oahu have unlisted numbers.

(a) Hawaii's "Alienation Index"

As anticipated, our results were much the same as those reflected in the national polls. Sixty-one percent of those respondents with an opinion agreed that "Government officials don't care what people like me think or want." Over 53 percent of our respondents felt that their state government takes the right approach to a problem less than 60 percent of the time. That's a failing grade in most circles.

We also provided our interviewees with an opportunity to rate state government in comparison with other public-service-oriented agencies, private and municipal. We asked them what degree of confidence, or lack of it, they had in the ability of each agency to "do a good and honest job." If a respondent agreed "strongly" that some agency was doing a good and honest job, we added two (+2) to its score. If the respondent only agreed "somewhat," then we added one (+1). If a respondent disagreed "strongly," we subtracted two (−2). If he or she disagreed "somewhat," then we subtracted one (−1). We then totaled all the pluses and minuses for each agency and profession. The results were as follows:

1. The Fire Department — + 509
2. Garbagemen — + 326
3. The Municipal Bus Company — + 310
4. The Telephone Company — + 196
5. Juries — + 178
6. The Medical Profession — + 131
7. The Police Department — + 130
8. University of Hawaii — + 87
9. Hawaiian Homes Commission — + 73
10. The Courts — + 23
11. The Governor — − 2
12. The Lt. Governor's Office — − 10
13. Lawyers — − 19
14. Advertising Agencies — − 61
15. The State Legislature — − 50
16. The Department of Education — − 53
17. Labor Unions — − 130

The only state governmental agency to make the top half was the University of Hawaii. All the major components of state government, including the governor, the lieutenant governor, the state legislature, and the highly centralized state Department of Education, finished with negative ratings by the public.

(b) The Public Agenda

Since the public mandated the ConCon, we thought the public ought to be asked what should be discussed and solved there. The power-brokers on the political scene and some media experts had already endorsed limited structural change, e.g., creating a unicameral legislature, electing rather than appointing prosecutors and judges, setting a new debt-ceiling, revamping the lieutenant governor's office, etc. We submitted a lengthy list of fifty items to the public, and asked our respondents to rate them as "extremely important," "important," "not too important," or "unimportant." We found the public much more interested in discussing substantive issues and problems and strongly disinclined to discuss those areas favored by the power elite.

For example, here is the public's list of the ten items considered "extremely important" to discuss and solve at ConCon:

		PERCENT OF SAMPLE WHO THOUGHT IT WAS EXTREMELY
RANK	ISSUE	IMPORTANT TO DISCUSS AT CONCON
1.	Crime	63%
2.	Public education	61%
3.	Conservation of energy	60%
4.	Welfare system	59%
5.	Unemployment	58%
6.	Political corruption	56%
7.	Environmental pollution	52%
8.	Criminal justice system	50%
9.	Housing	49%
10.	Population growth	45%

Contrast this list with those ten items that the fewest citizens rated as "extremely important":

RANK	ISSUE	PERCENT
41.	Neighborhood power in government	22%
42.	Number of houses in state legislature	20%
43.	Televising major legislative hearings	21%
44.	Historical sites	19%

45.	Public financing of elections	19%
46.	Election of prosecutors	17%
47.	The lieutenant governor's office	17%
48.	Distribution of legal services	16%
49.	Primary voting system	17%
50.	Worker participation in corporate decisions	14%

Clearly there was a schism between the public and the politicians. Our survey developed a "public agenda" that could invoke major restructuring of the government in the areas of public education, criminal justice, environmental protection, etc. This data and analysis was featured prominently in a three-article series in the state's only morning newsdaily, the Honolulu *Advertiser* (November 20–22, 1977). The overwhelming response to the article was that our survey measured the public's views with reasonable accuracy.

(c) Change the game, change the score

Meanwhile, it was clear to us that even though a state ConCon was an ideal way to make major changes in government structure and public policy, particularly if public opinion were favorable, it still wasn't likely to happen that way. After all, state ConCons are generally truncated by the powers-that-be, and the conventional structure of most state ConCons lends itself to public obscurity.

What had to be done in Hawaii was to present an alternative to the usual state constitutional convention, one that would change the rules, thereby changing the game and improving the odds for an upset. This new paradigm had to *democratize* the process dramatically. It had to capture and channel a potential surge of citizen participation.

It occurred to us again that a state ConCon was analogous to the town meeting. The problem then confronting us was how to conduct a town meeting involving nearly a half-million citizens. But this was 1977, in modern America—and it became crystal clear that such was not only possible but perhaps inevitable.

What has happened, slowly but inexorably, is that an arsenal of prodemocratic technological tools has been manufactured and stored over the past few decades. These instruments can readily remove most, if not all, the obstructions and impediments to getting millions of people together in a town-meeting type of situation. We took a number of these tools, arranged them in a new way, and came up with something we called the Constitutional Network (CN), a system of communications and information technology that establishes a comprehensive "Electronic Town Meeting" at the state constitutional convention level.

It was quite exhilarating to contemplate. At last, a system of political technology that would promote individual participation, grass-roots, issue-oriented politics, that would involve an entire citizenry in anticipating and planning its future. Almost all views of the future commonly held have Big Brother watching us; the Constitutional Network has the people watching *him!* Here's how we thought it through:

THE CONSTITUTIONAL NETWORK

Our general idea was to have a Communications Central and some twenty-odd satellite communications centers scattered around the state. In each center the following would be found:

TV Monitors

All ConCon proceedings would be broadcast live and delayed (by tape) on one CATV* channel leased by (or donated to) the Constitutional Network. This channel could be viewed either at home or at one of CN's twenty-one Centers around the state.

The second CATV channel leased (or donated) to CN would continually broadcast easily read and understandable outlines of issues being discussed at ConCon—as well as bulletins of new information and new solutions. Thus, one channel would be devoted to a *lateral* flow of information and ideas on the issues between the citizens themselves.

Videotape Cameras and Production Equipment

At each of CN's Centers, videotape cameras and production equipment and material would be available to individual citizens, interest groups, and community organizations, who would be encouraged, trained, and assisted in making issue-oriented statements for display upon the second channel. These statements would

* Community Antenna Television, more popularly known as Cable TV.

become another method of lateral people-to-people communication on the issues: a public videotape discussion.

Computer Terminals

In each Center, there would also be available for public use computer terminals—of the easily used typewriter-keyboard/display screen variety (the kind the airlines use at airports). These would be used not only to give access to relevant information a citizen might want, but also to establish a "computer conference" system between the Centers. This would be an excellent way to facilitate discussion between people around the state who want to keep in touch on certain issues of mutual interest. Citizens would be able to participate in this "computer conference" by going to one of the Centers, or by phoning a Center from their own home. Since the computer network would also be connected to local and national informational resources, citizens would have easy access to relevant data and expert opinion as well.

Telephones (With Automatic Polling Devices)

Finally, during each issue discussion at ConCon, CN would conduct random, statewide, public-opinion surveys on a nightly basis. It would utilize an automatic telephone-polling device designed to measure public attitudes on various issues. The results of these surveys would be disseminated to the ConCon delegates and to the public via the regular news media as well as Channel Two of the CN's CATV system. Moreover, the Delphi technique of polling (three rounds on each issue) would be used to help develop and formulate any latent public consensus that exists on any issue.

To facilitate a telephone conferencing system in addition to the computer conferencing system, callers would be able to call in to the various centers free of charge, or at reduced rates.

What we conceived, obviously, was a *three-way political communications system:* 1) government-to-people; 2) people-to-government; 3) people-to-people. Not only would such a system open and clear new channels of political exchange, it also would provide more and better information, thus raising the level of public discourse on vital issues. This in turn would improve the quality of public opinion eventually reaching elected (and appointed) decision-makers.

Those brimming with cynicism over the low quality of public participation in contemporary public politics have never been able to counter effectively the chicken-or-egg arguments of their pro-democratic opponents. In other words, the continuous decline of public participation in conventional electoral politics may well be traced to deep faults inherent in our present system of public information and public access and feedback to the seats of power. Systems akin to the Constitutional Network spread around the nation would challenge the present system's capacity to engage, involve, and educate the people properly on major issues.

A state constitutional convention with an operating Constitutional Network in place would not be a true town meeting since delegates make the final recommendations. But it would substantially democratize our obsolete republican system—and be a great stride in the ultimate direction of regular electronic town meetings at the state and national levels.

In our system, the public would have open access to all the data being considered by their "representatives" on all issues. Private citizens with their own "special interest" in certain social problems would be "patched into" the ongoing debate on that issue (or issues) with other interested citizens. Everyone would have an equal opportunity to furnish new alternatives and to assert their own priorities. Everyone would be working together, rather than at odds, trying to solve pressing public dilemmas. The delegates would have daily updated measurements of public opinion on selected issues, as well as forecasts on public consensuses building for certain options. Clearly, such a new communication-information interchange for policy-making and government-building has an optimum chance to hammer out novel and publicly acceptable changes in government and governance. It's enough to make anti-democratic cynics wince—and they do.

Tactics and Strategy: Incorporation and SimConCon

After developing the idea, designing the blueprint, and constructing a Styrofoam model of the Constitutional Network, our next move was to organize ourselves into a legitimate and viable organization. Thus, we incorporated ourselves into a private, non-profit corporation dedicated to the public educational process. We particularly liked this idea because it embraces the notion that a *private corporation* should be in the *public business* of *making government more democratic*. We felt that the public would have more faith in private citizens running such a system. Otherwise, they would be rightly suspicious that this three-way system would become, in truth, a more insidious version of the familiar one-way system—that is, a subtle step toward ever more efficient Big Brotherism.

Our next step was to go public. We included a broad segment of the population—community activists, corporate executives, Republicans, Democrats, liberals, conservatives—on our Board of Directors; produced and distributed literature and videotapes that described our system; appeared as speakers on pre-ConCon panels and workshops and before community organizations and neighborhood boards; and presented our views on radio and TV. Such a unique and futuristic idea about democracy-through-technology needs time to gain public support. Our present goal is to convert public support into political support by having a number of candidates for ConCon-delegate adopt some version of the Constitutional Network as part of their thinking by late spring 1978.

As we traversed the state in 1977, what impressed us most was that almost no one disagreed with the ideology inherent in the Constitutional Network. Moreover, those who supported it included an incredibly wide array of people: public-interest lawyers, libertarians, militant Hawaiian community organizers, environmentalists, techno-humanists, and small businessmen, to name a few. Most people didn't even doubt the feasibility of the system, although many potential supporters desired to see some sort of trial run. We hit upon the idea of running a Simulated Constitutional Convention (SimConCon) at the University of Hawaii in the spring 1978 semester.

The plan was to make SimConCon a "dress rehearsal" of a modern, Constitutional Network sort of ConCon. It was also decided to make SimConCon a full-time job for the participants by offering it for academic credit. (The system we devised permitted students to sign up for anywhere between six to twelve credits.) Moreover, in order to increase its visibility to the public and to increase the likelihood that ordinary citizens and potential ConCon delegates would sign up, we scheduled all our hearings, assemblies, and classes for late afternoon, evenings, and weekends. Finally, we established a computer conference, a telephone conference, and a videotape exchange system with several community colleges around the state who offered classes related to SimConCon (Simconet).

At this writing,* many potential delegates and community organizers have expressed commitments to participate in SimConCon. By using the Public Agenda, and a small-scale version of the Constitutional Network, we hope to pretest a program and process that a number of candidates for delegate will incorporate into their platforms. If that happens, then the Constitutional Network, or something like it, may become a reality in the July 1978 Hawaii State Constitutional Convention. If not, we still believe we are learning more and more about how to make this system a reality in some other political context in the near future.

Future Applications

Make no bones about it: we are attempting a new kind of politics to promote a new kind of system. If we are unable to gain sufficient public support for this system at the 1978 Hawaii ConCon, we believe we will have failed only because we, unlike Panasonic, are more than slightly ahead of our time.

We do see that a prototype like the Constitutional Network continues to gain adherents and advocates. Obviously it can be used by any group in any state in the Union. What is more, any nationwide group might use it as well (the Canadian Bar Association is now studying the possibilities of having a national ConCon in the near future in Canada). But the Constitutional Network, in whole or in part, also has relevance for political institutions other than ConCons.

For example, here in Hawaii we believe we have just begun a process that may eventually result in a Legislature-of-the-Future, the 1984 Hawaii State Legislature, when the people can look Big Brother in the eye. Perhaps a Legislative Network will evolve piecemeal, perhaps the 1978 State ConCon will help it along. We'll see.

Naturally, our system is also workable at the local level of government. In Hawaii, a network of neighborhood boards is expanding rapidly. Shortly it will become a grid of local centers that "advise" the city council and the mayor. It is but the tiniest step to

* February 1978.

convert these isolated centers into an interconnected communications and information system—yes, the Municipal Network.

Another exciting potential use of this system exists, one more ad hoc than what we've discussed so far—that is, initiatives and referenda. Indeed, initiatives and referenda, prodemocratic reforms of the Progressive Era, lend themselves to our three-way system of interaction. An Initiative-Network would provide superior, democratically derived wording for each referendum, thereby giving it far superior chances of passage than initiatives have now. After all, each referendum would be the product of an extensive public discussion, and such publicly developed referenda would not fall such easy prey to huge advertising campaigns mounted by special interests.

The Constitutional Network is an idea whose time is just about now. It is an approach to modern technology that does not lead toward more certain totalitarianism. It is a political system of communication and information that turns the tables on authoritarianism.

The Constitutional Network provides the people of America with a compact political communications system operating right out of their own homes. And what kind of exotic equipment will they need? Just their television sets and their telephones. This will keep them in touch with one another, with some paid experts, and with their representatives—in a systematic, grass-roots fashion. Such a system is bound to have powerful impact on the present republican system—it is bound to lead to more and better democracy in the future.

CHAPTER EIGHTEEN

The Deeper Implications of Citizen Participation

BY ROBERT THEOBALD

By now the reader probably has a good understanding of the issues involved in anticipatory democracy. What is the potential—and what would be the resultant stresses and strains—of a serious pursuit of anticipatory democracy? This essay will address this question and also sketch out some of the social changes that will take place if there is a successful transition between the industrial era that has nearly exhausted itself and the communications era that our society is now entering.

The transition through which we are now moving is sometimes called the Second Copernican Revolution. Copernicus enabled us to see that the earth, far from being the center of the universe, actually revolved around the sun. The communications era is teaching us that each human being is inevitably the center of his own universe—that we all perceive the world through our own unique "spectacles" determined by both our genetic inheritance and our experiences. The primary difference between the industrial era and the communications era is the perceptions that are seen as relevant within them. During the industrial era we believed that there was an objective truth that could be discovered if we struggled hard enough to find it. The primary method for this search was to divide reality into smaller and smaller segments in the belief that we would eventually find a set of incontrovertible truths. The problem is that we have found a few of them, and those that we have found are trivial in the face of the problems that confront us.

The communications era starts from a new perception: that everything is interconnected. But because no one can keep everything in mind at all times, we must learn the skills of "bounding" or of determining which factors in a specific situation are crucial enough to take into account and which can be ignored for the purpose of decision-making. Once we have discovered these patterns we can try to ensure their favorable evolution.

This approach requires a very different set of tools, institutions, and models. We have to learn to work within a communications system rather than a control system, to encourage diversity rather than sameness, to settle for "enough" instead of constantly demanding more, and to work within value patterns that have been called religious in the past: i.e., honesty, responsibility, humility, love, and a respect for mystery.

The communications era is not a set of abstractions. However, those who want to understand it must commit themselves to living in it, just as those who brought the industrial era into existence gave up the values of the agricultural era. Logic is not enough to make this choice: we must move with a leap of faith.

Any significant discussion of the issue of citizen participation, citizen involvement, or anticipatory democracy necessarily involves discussion of the sources of authority within groups, institutions, and cultures. Most Americans are profoundly uncomfortable with this subject. As a result, a series of dogmas exist that are incompatible with the ways in which society should function in the communications era. Thus, it is important to examine current assumptions and to outline an alternative vision of society.

THE INDUSTRIAL ERA AND STRUCTURAL AUTHORITY

The industrial-era culture in which we live is based on the assumption that authority—the right to make decisions and to have them stick—depends upon the position that an individual holds. A position of power can be achieved in many ways: through promotion within the bureaucracy; through appointment (as in high civil-service jobs or in certain parts of the judiciary); or through election within the present democratic process. In theory, the people who hold the highest positions in a given organization, however they have obtained them, have the right to give orders and to expect those orders to be obeyed. This type of authority might be called "structural authority."

Because we are afraid of the abuse of power, the right to command is almost always hedged by a set of constraints meant to prevent its arbitrary use. The principle of the separation of powers dominates the whole American system of government. For example, the President of the United States can bring about significant change only if there is agreement within the Congress and acceptance by the judiciary. The bureaucracy, too, frequently exercises veto power, although the Constitution does not provide for this. Similarly, presidents of organizations are subject to the control of some sort of board—when they get too far out of line they may be replaced. The consequence of this particular method of exercising power is that it effectively forces the power-holders to spend a great deal of their time trying to ensure that the actions they take are favorably perceived by those who have the ability to replace them if they become dissatisfied.

The degree of tension that exists between those who hold power and those who allow power to be exercised over them depends primarily on the degree of trust between the groups. In recent years, public-opinion polls have shown continuing decline in public confidence in all groups that hold power—government, business, labor, the media. The inevitable response has been for those in positions of power to spend even more time improving appearances and even less on the substance of necessary decisions. For example, a colleague of mine, who works in the central administration office of the higher education system of one of the larger states, informs me that quite often when a tough decision must be made, the only aspect of the problem considered is what actions might be palatable. There is often no real consideration of what *ought* to be done.

Unfortunately, a *direct relationship* exists between structural authority of the type described here and the development of distrust. Structural authority leads inevitably to distortion of information and corruption of the truth. To paraphrase Lord Acton,

"Power tends to corrupt information and absolute power corrupts information absolutely."

For example, when we work with persons or groups that have the ability to alter our lives for better or worse, the natural reaction is to provide the people in charge with the information that will satisfy them. The more direct and extreme their power over our lives, the greater the distortion of information we feel justified or compelled to create because of fear for our jobs or life styles.

The present structural authority system ensures that there will be continuing and significant distortion of information flows, independent of the people in charge of the system. So long as we preserve the present system, the concentration of power in a few hands ensures that the powerful will be bombarded with self-serving and inaccurate information. In addition, existing governmental structures lead to inertia. Every president has found that the bureaucratic system is so large and unwieldy that it can ignore even direct presidential orders. In addition, each governmental agency is so much tied up with its own area of responsibility that cross-communications often become impossible.

How can anticipatory democracy operate within this type of power structure? The nuclear-power issue, one of the most heated issues of the 1976 election, provides an example of the kind of degradation of information that can occur. In several states those who feared the long-term impact of nuclear production on the quality of life and the environment proposed nuclear referenda. Those who were convinced that the production of additional energy is essential for the welfare of the United States opposed these groups.

The referenda, of course, had the force of law—that is, the public had absolute power. Interest groups on both sides felt they were justified in distorting the truth because they believed that the "wrong" decision by the public would be disastrous. The net result was a significant distortion of information because interest groups provided that data which they thought was most likely to influence the public (in this case, those with the power) to make the "right" decision. As a result, it is now even more difficult for the citizen to make an informed decision about the direction in which the society should move and for legislators to perceive appropriate directions.

So long as we preserve our structural authority model, the belief that there can be intelligent citizen participation or anticipatory democracy is naïve and irrelevant. At the same time, pushing for citizen participation is quite often counter-productive, for two reasons: 1) the more power citizens assert through referenda and other means, the greater the distortion of information with which they have to contend, and 2) the citizen group is only one of a large number of power groups and is often among the weakest.

At present, most citizen participation increases frustration and anger. Those in charge often make decisions counter to expressed views. Citizen groups get bogged down in continuing studies and data-gathering which get farther and farther away from the real decision-making process. Even if good information has been gathered and recommendations are made to the appropriate authorities, there is no guarantee that anything will come of it.

Some groups become "successful" by growing sufficiently powerful to force other power structures to bend to their will. If these groups were previously powerless, there is certainly superficial cause to rejoice. But looked at overall, all that has been changed is the hierarchy of power, or the hierarchy of suffering in the culture.

Citizen participation and anticipatory democracy are possible only after a change in authority structures. What other models of decision-making are there?

THE INVISIBLE HAND: AN ALTERNATIVE TO STRUCTURAL AUTHORITY?

One alternative is a system in which people "do their own thing" and operate out of their narrowly defined self-interest, a model that is usually traced back to Adam Smith in economics and Jeremy Bentham in philosophy, although the true roots go back much farther. Often called the "invisible hand," this model holds that when individuals follow their own self-interest, the economy and the society flourish. In economics, the neoclassicists brought this doctrine to its finest flowering in the theory that in a completely unregulated society each person would obtain reward in whatever measure he/she was worth. In politics, the vision of the American Constitution is that of a system of checks and balances that provides for good government, if all those in the political process follow their own concerns.

Implicit in this model is the belief that the world should be perceived as a clock, would up by God, with which it would be unwise to tamper. The neoclassical economic theories of the nineteenth century that justified the existing distribution of income as reflecting immutable laws were based essentially on this belief and were one of the factors that prevented intervention to deal with social injustice.

By the end of the nineteenth century, this model had been increasingly discredited. It was clear that power groups would change the dynamics of the society to benefit themselves and that they would not hesitate to exploit those less powerful than themselves. It therefore became clear that the "invisible hand" thesis of Adam Smith and the income-distribution theories of the neoclassicists were not good descriptions of the actual behavior of the socioeconomy as the world entered the twentieth century.

However, there are still economists and business persons who believe that present-day problems could be dealt with if we were willing to apply the strict logic of Adam Smith and the neoclassicists. Milton Friedman, recently awarded the Nobel Prize, is probably the thinker who provides the best theoretical base for such an effort. Part of the attractiveness of his theorizing is that he is not totally doctrinaire. He is willing to accord the State a minimal role in those areas where this is essential—for example, providing a guaranteed income to all. He would then, however, remove all other government functions.

Also among those who still push for an invisible hand model are the cultural descendants of the hippies of the sixties, who believe that if society were freed of restraints, it would automatically become decent, and some of those involved in the self-improvement activities of the seventies, who ignore the need to change the structure of society and concentrate instead on improving the quality of individual lives. In effect, that latter group is involved in citizen-participation activities but of a style which is too limited in its impact.

I personally believe that the assumption that we can minimize decision-making on a group basis and permit the society to operate primarily on the basis of individual wishes is naïve. I therefore reject both the structural authority model and any model that assumes that no major authority systems are needed at all. What then is the real option at this time?

DECISION-MAKING BASED ON COMPETENCE

The harsh reality is that we cannot create true anticipatory democracy without a far greater shift in our understanding of socioeconomic functioning than we have yet been willing to contemplate. The way we presently understand the world and the way we think about it do not and cannot produce an approach to decision-making that is both anticipatory and democratic.

The voices contributing to the necessary rethinking are already present in our society, although there is as yet little evidence that we are prepared to listen to them. In a remarkable pamphlet entitled *New Age Politics* by Mark Satin,[1] over one hundred books are listed which together amount to an overview of the new thinking presently being done. Among the known names are Boulding, Callenbach, Commoner, Fromm, Illich, Maslow, Mumford, Robbins, Schumacher, Watts, but there are many more names which will not be known to most readers. Moreover, nineteenth-century writers such as Blake and Goethe, to mention only two, are increasingly being recognized as having stood outside the mainstream of the Western pattern of thought; they provide a backdrop for those of us who are today trying to provide a new basis for the consideration of authority.

Interestingly, more and more people are aware that the great religions, in their fundamental statements, accord with this new perception of authority. Industrial society has often dismissed the values theme of religion as hopelessly naïve, arguing that it is unreasonable to hope for morality from people. Rather we have tried, unsuccessfully, to find ways to cope with the dishonesty, irresponsibility, pride, and hatred which are inevitable when people follow their narrowest self-interest.

Today we are rediscovering the fundamental truths which are inherent in religious traditions. Cultures function when people learn to care about others. If people are not helped to understand the need for caring, the bonds which unite the society will inevitably break down, preventing intelligent decision-making. It is, in reality, impossible to achieve citizen participation in the absence of honesty, responsibility, humility, love, and a respect for mystery. The fact that many now believe that a commitment to religious values is not infeasible is, in effect, a chilling reminder of the extent of the decay in our culture.

What then can we hope for? It appears to me that those in favor of citizen participation and anticipatory democracy tend to overplay their hand disastrously and to suggest that development of citizen participation and anticipatory democracy would lead to a Utopia. This burdens such activities with expectations that cannot be realized, which inevitably leads to frustrations. All we can hope for is that increased citizen involvement will lead to more appropriate decision-making. This appropriate decision-making might make it possible to "manage the world"—a new level of competence would be reached that the scope of present technologies makes essential.

There is an alternative to the structural authority and invisible hand models. *This new view states that people must make decisions in those areas where they are competent, set up communication between interrelated areas of competence, and work cooperatively together throughout the whole thinking and decision-making process.*

Hidden within this statement is an assumption that needs to be made explicit. I am arguing that there are some people who are more competent than others to make decisions and that it is essential that these people are provided with decision-making power. There are generally contradictory reactions to this statement.

One group argues that this model implies that there will be no change in the present society—that the present elite will continue in power. Yet there is a great deal of evidence that the people who hold structural authority are not necessarily competent in the areas in which they exercise authority, and that they would be rapidly replaced if tests to determine competence were applied.

A second group argues that there are no tests that can effectively determine competence. However, we know that in real situations where real problems must be solved, it is fairly easy for people to perceive their relative competencies and to set up systems that reflect them. The reason that this does not happen more often at the present time is that a truly competent individual or group is deeply threatening to an incompetent structural authority system.

Third, there are those who fear that the long-run result of vesting authority in competence would indeed result in the emergence of a different elite, one that would be just as difficult to dislodge. I believe that such a fear is based on two major misreadings of reality. First, in a world built on competence—or sapiential authority—people would be aware that power interrupts good communications. Thus, while there would always be an elite at any moment in time (for this is inevitable), the elite would be a constantly changing one, and no group such as the young, the old, those of particular racial groups, or particular sexes would be systematically excluded.[2] Second, those who object to elites do not recognize that in a society based on competence it will be essential for all individuals to be educated so that they can make decisions about their own lives. People will have to be far more self-sufficient than they have been throughout the industrial era, both in the physical and the intellectual sense.

Citizen participation is only feasible or desirable if we can replace the norms of the industrial era with those of the communications era. To this end, it is useful to consider the parallels and the differences between the shifts that took place in moving from the agricultural to the industrial era and those that are required in moving from the industrial to the communications era. In the former move, change developed largely on a generational basis, with each generation having a different vision of how the world should be organized; this led to great tensions between generations. The present situation is quite different. We do not have time to wait for generational change; each of us is confronted with the need to re-examine our own criteria for success in the light of the widespread changes taking place in the culture. Most of us are finding this task exceptionally difficult because we have no model for it; no culture so far as we know has completely rethought its models, as we must.

But it does appear that the values we are now called upon to adopt are more human, and therefore more acceptable, than the ones we need to give up. As J. M. Keynes wrote in his famous essay, "Economic Possibilities for our Grandchildren":

. . . we shall be able to rid ourselves of many of the pseudomoral principals which have hag-ridden us for two hundred years, by which we have exalted some of the most distasteful of human qualities into the position of the highest virtues . . . All kinds of social customs and economic practices affecting the distribution of wealth and of economic rewards and penalties, which we now maintain at all costs, we shall be free to discard.

However, even though these values are more human than those that presently prevail, we may not be able to change rapidly enough. Responsible human behavior is difficult to achieve; there are times when even those who are most committed to it long for an easier task. In addition, as yet there is no coherent, consistent body of knowledge available to guide those who wish to behave with more intelligent maturity.[3]

THE COMMUNICATIONS ERA AND SAPIENTIAL AUTHORITY

What we need is a new understanding of human behavior. We can start from the tautological statement that "People act in their perceived self-interest at the moment when they act." It is not being argued that people necessarily know what is in their best interest, nor that the actions they take are necessarily best suited to achieve their goals, nor that people act consistently: they may strive for one goal at one point in time and for another at a different moment. It is simply being stated that people define success differently and that these definitions are based on their perceptions of their past personal experiences and their genetic potentials.

Given the fact that people necessarily act in their perceived self-interest, any sucessful attempt to change behavior will involve three processes:

1. helping people to re-evaluate the meaning of their past experiences;
2. enabling people to discover visions of the future that will change their goals in more desirable directions; and
3. enabling people to learn skills so that the statements they make and the actions they take are more likely to achieve the directions they value.

As individuals learn to re-evaluate their past, to imagine their future anew, and to act in the present, they will inevitably begin to try to affect the society of which they are part. This in turn will lead to effective anticipatory democracy. However, it is not reasonable to expect rapid change because all societies have enormous inertia, and bureaucratic structuring makes change even more difficult.

True citizen participation requires profound shifts in the ways we govern ourselves. First, we need to recognize that there are few conflicts where one side is completely right and the other completely wrong. The trouble with our existing legal system is that it struggles to distort shades of gray into extremes of black and white; in so doing it often distorts the truth beyond recognition. We need to develop further the arbitration, conciliation, and facilitation techniques that already exist to create more ways to compromise conflict rather than aggravate it.

Second, we need to develop new structures that will enable people to develop and state their views as clearly as possible. We need in the future to search for the surprising and the unexpected. The ability to perceive directions before they have developed fully is one of the scarcest and the most desirable skills in our culture.

It is my conviction that listening to the views of the public is particularly important at the present time. There is an extraordinary gap between the "public" rhetoric to which people believe they should give lip service and the "private" discussions that the same people have with their friends and colleagues. Novel ways of polling need to be developed that give the people the psychic freedom to respond with what they feel, rather than with preconceived categories.

We need to create a new mechanism for clarifying existing disagreements and options. This process—which may be called a "problem/possibility focuser"—would ideally have four parts:

1. one that describes the agreements existing around a particular issue, especially those factors that cause people to believe that this is an issue deserving attention;
2. one that describes the disagreements existing around a particular issue, the reasons behind the disagreements, and the types of knowledge needed in order to reach agreement;
3. one that explores the range of scenarios implied by different

perceptions of the issue under consideration and suggests the various policy measures needed in order to take account of the various views;

4. one that suggests the resources available for further study: print, video, audio, computer based, etc.

So that problem/possibility focusers would be revised and updated constantly, a continuing team with revolving membership would create them. The object of a problem/possibility focuser is to increase the agreements and to limit the disagreements surrounding an issue so that those who make policy have the best possible guides to understanding the world within which they must act.

A change in any portion of the culture necessarily alters the other parts. Thus, a restructuring of the system of authority entails a total alteration of the society, and change of such magnitude cannot be described in an essay. I have written many books and articles trying to find a good way to describe the nature and the requirements of the communications era, yet I am still looking for the proper handle.

My thesis is that those who would really advance the cause of anticipatory democracy can only do so if they insist that it bring about a fundamentally changed social order. Most of those who write about citizen participation and anticipatory democracy do not share this perspective. From my point of view, therefore, the first task of the careful reader of this book and other such writings is to determine if it is enough to add anticipatory democracy techniques to our present style of government or whether we must hasten the transition between the industrial era and the communications era.

CHAPTER NINETEEN

The Future of Anticipatory Democracy

BY JAMES A. DATOR

"All human beings are futurists, but some people may be more futuristic than others."

This is a contention I want to explore in the following pages. The essence of anticipatory democracy is, as I understand it, to do something about the fact that while most futurists are not very democratic, most democratic, participatory, citizen-based, and ethnic-revitalization groups are not very futuristic. The aim of anticipatory democracy is to democratize futures research (and futures researchers) and to futurize democratic processes (and democrats).

It seems to me that a great deal of what is wrong with A/D groups is that they have failed to address, let alone overcome, the basic dilemma that anticipatory democracy desires to resolve.

Choosing a group of citizens from all walks of life and asking them to determine the futures goals of their community is an excellent thing, but doing so does not necessarily make the people involved an "A/D group." Instead, it often merely makes them a group or subgroup of people who have a better idea of some techniques of social forecasting than they previously had; who understand better their own goals and the character and argument of people who have different futures goals than they do (and perhaps thus have a better notion of who "the enemy" is, and how to "defeat" him); and who have a stronger desire and ability than before the A/D exercise to realize their image of the future.

Whether they actually know much more about the future—or about genuinely alternative futures—is much more problematic, it seems to me.

Let me try to justify what may seem to be an autocratic and decidedly non-A/D statement.

My own interest in what is now called futuristics (or futures study or research, futurology, etc.) grew from a combination of six personal factors:

1. My father died shortly after I was born, and I was brought up to be independent and self-reliant by three independent and self-reliant women who never encouraged me to do much looking back at my heritage or ancestry. For example, I have no idea at all what the origin of "Dator" might be, and I am not much interested in reflecting on what I have, or might have, been.

2. In high school and college I was unusually interested in questions of social ethics. Studying how the ancients answered the question, "What is the good life?"—in both Utopian and real terms —occupied a great deal of my scholastic time. I have always been interested in making the world "a better place." There is very little that I wish to conserve *merely* because it has been around for a long time or even merely because it works fairly well now. I can always imagine that *anything* can be better than it is—especially, of course, myself. On the other hand, I find I have an atypically high regard for the opinions of others. I cannot believe that I am "right" and that others are "wrong" in matters of difference between us: I can only assume that we all see through a glass darkly, and that we each see out of our own highly personal and limited experiences. In fact, though I feel very strongly about many things, I tend not to "stand up for my rights" because I often can easily see the value of doing things differently from the way I happen to prefer now.

3. Since the end of my undergraduate college work—and lasting throughout graduate work to the present—I have been (in addition to the above ethical concerns) extremely interested in two other matters: the application of scientific method to the study,

prediction, and design of society, and understanding the forces that cause societies to change over time. In the context of my education, this meant, on the one hand, trying to do such things as predict elections, or legislative roll calls, or Supreme Court decisions, and on the other, understanding the process of "development" or "modernization" or "industrialization."

4. In 1960 I went to Japan and lived in Tokyo for six years, partly in order to understand how that country "modernized" so easily and rapidly compared to most other non-Western countries. In the process of trying to discover the answer I came to have an even keener interest in attempting to both predict and shape the future of America and other "developed" societies. I also learned even more deeply than previously what personal independence and individuality meant: Japanese society is so closed and tightly knit that there was no way that I (or any other non-Japanese) could ever become a fully integrated member of it. On the other hand, Japanese society is extremely tolerant of the behavior of foreigners. No matter what I did or how I behaved—whether I was acting out of my most unconscious American socialization experiences or out of an outrageous whim—I was viewed the same by most members of Japanese society with bemused tolerance and curiosity. I learned therefore *not* to expect or desire or fear social support or censure, but rather to create and live by my own values, recognizing, of course, that I would always be in a social situation where others would have values of their own.

5. During my stay in Japan, I began to spend more and more of my teaching and research time on "the future" of whatever it was I was teaching/researching. When I returned to the United States in 1966 and began teaching at Virginia Tech, I discovered for the first time that there were others who were becoming interested in the future, and I read with great excitement the writings of Marshall McLuhan, Theodore Gordon, Arthur C. Clarke, and Alvin Toffler (especially his revelatory *Horizon* article of 1966 entitled "The Future as a Way of Life"). I joined The World Future Society in 1967 and began to teach a course called "Political Futuristics" at Virginia Tech. My future in the future was set.

6. In 1969 I had the opportunity to go to the University of Hawaii, and—happy to get out of the mountains and snow, back to the beaches and sun that I prefer—I went to teach Japanese politics and to further my interest in futuristics. I knew absolutely

nothing of the Organizing Committee of the Governor's Conference on the Year 2000 which held its first organization meeting the week I arrived in Honolulu. Thus, it is entirely because of Glenn Paige—who was both a member of the Department of Political Science of the University of Hawaii, as was I, and a member of the Organizing Committee—that I was invited to do what every scholar should always do (and few futurists certainly have had the chance to do): to put my personal reputation where my academic mouth was; to test out my ivory-tower notions about the future on the business people and politicians who were the members of the Organizing Committee. And learn I did, from so many people, especially George Chaplin, Keiji Kawakami, Glenn Paige, and the former State Senate President, David McClung.

It is absolutely clear to me that my designation as a "futurist" is due entirely to my interaction with the committee and its work, and to the fact that my name kept appearing in George Chaplin's Honolulu *Advertiser* as "Jim Dator, University of Hawaii, futurist . . ." I never knew I was a futurist before (I thought I was a political scientist), and I know it to be true now only because I have seen it in print so often.

Why have I spent such an embarrassingly long time on these personal remarks? Because I think it is important, partly to understand the comments that are to follow, and partly to see what ordinary people some of us futurists are. (Others, especially the many who came to futuristics from engineering or business backgrounds, are no doubt more filled and extraordinary than I.)

The point is, I have spent a great deal of the past fifteen years trying to find out 1) what the most likely alternative futures are; 2) what various people *think* the future will be; and 3) what I personally want the future to be. During this time I have taught more than five formal, semester-long courses on the future (and various aspects of futuristics) at Virginia Tech, the University of Hawaii, and the University of Toronto. I have conducted scores of short courses for teachers, administrators, business groups, service organizations and the like; I have delivered hundreds of lectures on futuristics literally all around the world, and I have served as a consultant for many governmental and business organizations. I have tried at these times (along with more formal research projects and discussions with my fellow futurists) to clarify each of the above three points.

It would be helpful to our understanding of A/D groups, perhaps, if I were to describe what I have found to be various people's thoughts of the future. This is significant, I believe, because much of what the future becomes depends upon what people think it will be. Willing doesn't make it so, of course, but people tend to act (or don't act) in the present partly on the basis of their image of the future. Hence, from my desire to understand what the most likely alternative futures are, I need to know—among other things —what various people think the future will be.

It might be helpful if I label and briefly describe the ten categories of images of the future that I have encountered, commenting in more detail on several of the more popular ones.

1. *Que sera, sera.* Many people, having what I call the "Doris Day image of the future," believe "Que sera, sera. Whatever will be, will be; the future's not mine to see, que sera, sera." They believe that there is no discernible pattern to history or the future— events simply "happen"—or they contend that since everything is in the hands of God, it is not for humans to know, or to worry, about things to come.

2. *As it was in the beginning is now and ever shall be, world without change, amen.* For hundreds of thousands of years, until only about ten thousand years ago, all humans lived in environments that changed so imperceptibly that the past was a near-perfect predictor of the future. Though the advent of agriculture and the establishment of civilizations fundamentally changed this as a universal characteristic, many people throughout the world have only within the last hundred years had their stable tribal ways challenged by the destructive dynamism of "civilization." Even more developed societies, with established stable patterns, have been challenged by the destructive forces of industrialization.

Thus, most of us are only a few generations away from the experience of traditional or agricultural societies where the basic social and personal patterns of the future were largely prefigured by present and past patterns, and where only occasional major events or catastrophes changed the course of history. In traditional society, only "weird" people and clairvoyants concerned themselves with the future. Normal, well-adjusted folks knew all there was to know about the future if they conformed to the present and past ways.

3. *If Winter comes, can Spring be far behind?* One variant of the traditional image of the future, a variant which is especially strong in agriculturally-based societies of the temperate zone, and a view which pervades almost all religions (coincident as they are with the transformation from tribal, hunting, and gathering societies to stable agricultural ones) is a cyclical view of social change. Everything has its season: there is a time to laugh, and a time to weep, a time to sow and a time to reap, a time to wake and a time to sleep, and if you want to predict the future, all you need to know is what time it is—where you are in the cycle; where you are on the wheel. Things are not stable and "flat" as in the traditional view; but change for the good (or ill) is not continuous either, and neither growth nor decline goes on forever. To understand the future you must understand cycles and be able to determine when and to what extent the actual situation you are experiencing relates to the general law of the cycles that govern it.

4. *Why don't you make something of yourself?* But such is not the official view of the future of the industrial society in which we presently live. We are "developed," and the essence of development is to have found a way to break *permanently* out of the traditional cycle, and to grow endlessly. This is the meaning of progress: to live in a society where every day in every way things are getting better and better, where we know that tomorrow could be better than today, because today is better than yesterday.

Some would say that the official dogma of the past one hundred years (possibly the last 250–300 years) has been this belief, and that many institutions were invented to inculcate and support it. The most important of these was the public school system, created about a century ago to promote social progress and personal upward mobility. If one went to the right school, studied hard (and studied the right things, which is to say science, technology, and management), then one would be able to find a place at or near the top of the ship of state as a captain of industry. If one did not study hard enough, or studied the wrong things (or went to the wrong school), then one found oneself in the middle, or at the bottom, taking orders from the top and being a hardworking cog in the great, over-progressing industrial machine-state.

This view of the future is adhered to by most people in modern industrial society, as tenaciously by those at the bottom as by those at the top. In fact there is good reason to believe that the lower and working classes hold these values even more strongly than do the upper-middle and upper classes. For most people the whole point of life is to acquire the proper attitudes and skills so that they can get the proper job that will give them access to the proper goods and services made possible by their contribution to industrial society.

5. *After the Revolution . . . !* A variant of this "developmental" image of the future—a profoundly important one ideologically, politically, and personally—is the Marxist view of the future.

Some Marxists believe that though the permanent era of communism will be a high-technology society of abundance and social transfer, with all the desirable characteristics of a steady-state, the period prior to communism is marked by economic growth and material development. Whether a desirable steady-state is achieved depends on whether a true socialist revolution occurs: capitalist states can only grow past their environmental resources and social limits and thus *must* collapse under the weight of their contradictions. Only if capitalist industrial states are transformed by revolution into socialist industrial states can the subsequent transformation to the communist steady-state be accomplished. Capitalism can have only quantitative change, which is ultimately destructive; for qualitative change to occur, the revolution is necessary.

6. *We are entering a new Dark Ages.* But more and more people in industrial society are coming to believe that the present industrial state—whether capitalist or socialist—is about to reach, if it has not already actually passed, its limits to growth. Industrial society is coming apart at the seams, and the harder we try to keep on trucking down the same old road, the more certain do we hasten its end. The immediate future is thus bleak indeed: wars, famines, internal strife. And after that, a new and lengthy Dark Ages—a return to the awful steady-state of primitive society and warring bands of savages.

7. *Toward a steady-state for spaceship Earth.* Given the choice between unsustainable continued growth and undesirable global destruction, growing numbers of people are arguing that we must seek to stop growth now; that we must dismantle the industrial

state before it collapses about us; that we must return—or create anew—more decentralized, more ecologically balanced, less highly technological, more human and stable communities.

This view is rapidly becoming the major alternative to the developmental image of the future indicated in Item 4. At present, it is only a minority view, and (as with development itself, of course) there are many important variations. But within the establishment of most industrial states it is now respectable, if not obligatory, to encourage a serious search for a viable alternative to industrial society in order to ward off probable doom.

8. *Let's return to the Garden of Eden.* At the far end of the environmental or ecological image of the future are a small number of true back-to-nature advocates; persons who question not only the desirability of industrial science and technology but of all "progress" of the past 2,000 to 10,000 years. Pointing to the many cautionary tales against objective knowledge and technologies found in world literature (warnings against Prometheus and fire, Eve and the Apple of Knowledge, and all such Faustian bargains), some people feel that humans must return to something approximating the state of nature before the advent of "civilization." Most people who hold this view do not believe that humans will voluntarily choose to take this step backwards, and thus they are extremely pessimistic about the chances for human survival.

9. *I think I'm going out of my head.* All the images of the future which I have mentioned thus far are public, or sociopolitical images, with programs of sociopolitical action. But there are some people who believe all reality is subjective, that the future has no objective reality other than those images that are within each person's individual consciousness. Prayer, meditation, consciousness-expanding exercises, or special beliefs, etc., are all that are needed —or possible. The external world is illusory, or a diversion from the true purpose of life, which is contemplation and self-realization. What is required is adherence to revealed doctrine—certainly not political action.

Though this view is not likely to be strongly represented in most A/D groups in the United States at the present time—and is not widely found in our culture generally—strong advocates of variations on this position are found everywhere, and we should recognize that just as entire societies were dominated by forms of this belief in the past, it is entirely possible that it could—or should—become dominant again.

10. *Machines of Loving Grace.* My own view of the future does not fit comfortably into any of the ones mentioned above. Instead, I see the future of the world (especially of industrial societies) being shaped by three forces: the first is the conflict between those who desire and encourage continued industrial growth (and they are presently more numerous, older, and in positions of power) and the growing number of people who favor some form of low-technology, low-energy, humanistic, and decentralized conserver society. I find the major conflict within any group of persons concerned about the future to exist somewhere between these two positions. I expect this conflict to increase in importance. I do not think one or the other will "win," but the conflict itself will be a characteristic of the future, with two other forces, mentioned below, playing a greater role in affecting the outcome.

The second major force shaping the future, in my view, will be new technologies, especially those in electronic, communications, biology, and space. In the beginning of the futurist movement in the United States (in the early 1960s) the focus was on the manner in which technology shaped societies. At that time, this shaping was viewed as basically positive, and the task of the futurist was to help humans adjust to technologically-induced change. The environmental/humanistic/conserver society movement, however, has tended more recently to focus attention on the negative aspects of new technologies—the fact that the production of new technologies generally enriches the producers while the consumers must endure, among other things, the destruction of past institutions, values, and modes of behavior. Thus, there is a tendency of the conserver-society advocates to want to choose only those technologies which preserve old ways and values, and to avoid those which are different from either the present or the past.

There are many conflicting views about the relationship between humans and their technologies. Some feel the relationship is trivial or casual. They believe that technologies are mere tools that do not significantly alter human behavior or values. Human nature is essentially unchanged and unchangeable by technology. Moreover, there is no such thing as "good" technologies or "bad" ones; it is all a question of the way humans use their technologies. Thus it is humans who are at fault if technology is misused, not the tools themselves.

Others differ profoundly. Some, as we saw in the image of the future I labeled "Let's return to the Garden of Eden," believe that with every step in the development of new technologies the human condition has worsened. Technology, in this view, tends to dehumanize us, and some technologies (many of recent, industrial vintage) dehumanize us absolutely. It is only those tools that have stood the test of time—around which have developed carefully time-tested rules of use and sanction—that should be incorporated into any decent society. It seems to me that much of the environmental/humanistic/conserver-society movement adheres to some variation of this view, with perhaps the more "establishment" among them also believing it is possible to retain some things from modern technology, while giving up most of it.

For myself, I am absolutely convinced that the truth of the relationship between humans and their technologies is found in Marshall McLuhan's dictum: "We shape our tools, and thereafter our tools shape us." That is to say, we have become the humans we are now by interacting with ourselves and the environment through our tools. Thus significantly different technologies, as they have in the past and do in the present, will in the future contribute to a continual redefinition of what it means to be human.

This is not to say, of course, that humans thereby have no control over their future, that there is a "technological imperative" which determines all. To the contrary, it is very much within our abilities to attempt to see how technologies have shaped our past; and with thorough public understanding of that relationship and public discussion of evolving values, as well as new technologies, we can choose to develop those tools that will help us live the way we want to live. If, after *this* process, we choose to live like agricultural villagers or neolithic tribesmen, then so be it. But just as I am not convinced that the present is the best of all possible worlds, neither am I persuaded that we have descended from a Golden Age superior to our own. Given a choice between the present and any past I know of, I'll take the present. But given a choice to defend the status quo or invent a better world, I enthusiastically choose for the future.

I should add that by the term "technology" I mean more than hardware alone. I also mean "software," which determines the use of technology. Every tool has its rules for use. The rules may differ from culture to culture, or time to time; they may be long-lasting and culturally approved, or they may be transitory and ad hoc. But even the *naming* of a tool often implies correct and incorrect usage, though popular use often overrides the intention of official rules.

In addition, because hardware-defined technologies often compete with and may replace or restructure human institutions, I also find it very helpful to include human institutions (in the sociologist's sense) among the technologies, and thus to distinguish between "physical" technologies and "social" technologies. Slavery thus was an example of agricultural technology, eventually rendered obsolete by industrial agriculture, telephones replaced messenger boys, and mothers, an invention of necessity, may (or may not) be replaced by what are popularly termed "test-tube babies."

Vast segments of our society are blind to (or dispute the existence of) the functional interchangeability of physical and social technologies. We are unnecessarily defensive of social technologies (which often are not particularly worth defending) when they are threatened by new physical technologies. Similarly, one of the biggest deficiencies of the present is that while we have invented meta-technologies (namely, research and development) for inventing physical technologies, we have no easy way, and often do not even see the possibility, of inventing new social institutions to replace our old ones, or of inventing a new blend of social and physical technologies to replace or modify some modes of human interaction held over from the past.

I am convinced by my study and observations that one of the major shapers of the future will be the unfolding impact over the years of new technological developments in space, electronics, communication, human management, biology, and other areas. Moreover, I believe that we should welcome the improvements to human existence which they may make possible, rather than dwell on their potentialities for evil (or, worse, their potentialities for present profit). What is urgently required is that attention be given to the important questions related to technology and human values.

And, finally, to the third major force which I believe will shape the future of America and most of the rest of the world. It is what I call "The Decline of the West and the Rise of the Third World."

By this I mean not only the recognition of resource and energy limitations (or at least profound and multiple challenges), which is slowly sinking in to the Western consciousness, but the even more significant recognition that much of the development of the West has been dependent on the underdevelopment of the rest of the world: that imperialistic and otherwise exploitative relationships have been the basis of much of our wealth, and that changes of consciousness, aspirations, and abilities on the part of many people in the non-Western world make it highly unlikely that we can expect to have such cheap and easy access to global resources as we have in the past.

Even more profoundly, as much of the environmental/humanistic/ conserver-society movement indicates, growing numbers of our population are dissatisfied with much of "the American Way of Life" (part of which is grave concern over its exploitative nature) and ardently desire to find a mode of life based upon less materialistic values. I should point out, by the way, that this concern and complaint has been a part of "the American Way of Life" from the beginning. Much of American history is the record of the victory of a developmental image of the future and the environmental/humanistic image: the settler over the Indian/ hunter-trapper; the Federalists over the Anti-Federalists; the North over the South; urbanism over agrarianism; the establishment over the counterculture; and science and technology over art, culture, and the humanities. Thus a great deal of the battles between developers and conservators today is simply a renewal—by the formerly defeated—of an age-old conflict. It is not clear at all that the oft-vanquished will lose this time, though it is not likely that they will win either.

Richard Rosecrance has recently edited a book entitled *America as an Ordinary Country* (Cornell University Press, 1976). Without necessarily endorsing everything in it, I suggest you consider the title. It is an indication of the changed situation I am referring to. More and more people are recognizing that America is not—or may soon no longer be—the dominant superpower it once was. For some this is a cause for rejoicing; for others a cause for despair and fear.

But this would not be enough to be the potent harbinger of a transformed future were it not for the fact that at the same time much of the rest of the world is gaining a new vision of its future:

no longer (or less and less) do people feel that they must catch up with the West. Marx said that the developed countries show the developing countries their future. If that is the case, many developing countries, viewing the current chaos and collapse in much of the West, are pausing to consider whether they too want to endure such hardship, and whether it is not possible for them to choose a different future, based upon their own resources and heritage, rather than upon an imitation of the West.

It is my experience that, increasingly, non-Western parts of the world are developing the leadership and cultural vision which makes such an alternative future possible. As recent fascination with China on the part of many Americans makes clear, large segments of our population, too, are quite willing and eager to look to some other country as a model of our future as well.

I do not think China is at all an appropriate model, nor do I believe that there exists anywhere in the world today or in the past an adequate model for our future. The conflict between those favoring continued growth and supporters of the environmental/humanistic/conserver society, the impact of new technologies, and the decline of the West paralleled with the rise of the Third World—all these factors combined lead me to conclude that neither a refurbished present nor a revitalized past indicate with great clarity the path toward our preferred futures.

That, too, is why I think anticipatory democracy is so important, but I will indeed be discouraged if it comes to mean being demagogically panicked into ostrichlike fear of the future and adoration of either a linear extension of the present or a Utopian vision of another time or place.

I said this was to be a very personal essay. It may be that it is entirely eccentric—that I totally fail to see what is important about the future for the present, and that the only real or important choices lie between the super postindustrial state and the conserver society. Certainly the overwhelming evidence from my students, my consultancies, my lectures, and my readings is that with only a few gratifying exceptions, we are being offered a choice of essentially two futures by our A/D experiences so far, and these two futures turn out to be rehashed pasts.

Perhaps that judgment is wholly inadequate—a product of extended dichotomous thinking by the left (or is it the right) hemisphere of my masculine brain. Or perhaps the judgment is correct, but the real options open to us are really only these, and I am being academic or Utopian to want something else from A/D groups.

For myself, I can easily see the future of anticipatory democracy meaning the establishment of more and more groups such as those we have had in the past, with the membership being balanced between the two dominant ideologies of the present (the post-industrial state vs. the conserver society), some token "others"—the religious future freaks, the science-fiction buffs, the disbelievers in the whole futuristic enterprise, the doomsdayers, and me.

And having such groups established, and hearing of the controversy, we can once again ignore the future, content that it is under advisement, and turn our attention away from the urgent questions that defy (it seems to me) conventional understanding, such as, "How can there be 'the rule of law' in a society without consensus, without community, and—may I say it—without precedent?" "Can we help people put an end to the expectation of permanance in interpersonal relations, and encourage them to find deep satisfaction in transitory encounters?" "Can we find a way to permit people finally to be free individuals without being destructive to others or themselves?" "Can we devise a way to live in a world where there will be the widest possible diversity of values and aspirations; where people holding diverse views cannot be kept apart but must be encouraged to live together in tolerance—in fact, to prefer interpersonal value difference over interpersonal value conformity?" "Can we, in fact, find a way to help people dream undreamt dreams—and to realize them—instead of rehashing the same old nightmares and empty boasts?"

I believe we can and we must, and the future of anticipatory democracy that I prefer—if not the one I see—lies in this direction.

Notes
and Bibliographical
Addendum

CHAPTER ONE

STATE, REGIONAL, AND LOCAL
EXPERIMENTS IN ANTICIPATORY DEMOCRACY:
AN OVERVIEW

David E. Baker

1. Report of Dimensions for Charlotte-Mecklenburg staff as cited in: Keith Alan Bea and Cynthia Elmer Huston, *Citizen Futures Organizations: Group Profiles* (Washington, D.C.: Congressional Research Service, 1976), Report #76-260, p. 50.

2. Report of the Commission on Minnesota's Future (St. Paul: January 1977), p. 82.

3. This number of groups was derived from a composite analysis of the following sources: "Tomorrows and 2000s," *Earthrise Newsletter,* Vol. I, #6 (Earthrise, Providence: October, 1973); William W. Simmons, *1974–75 Exploratory Planning Briefs* (Hamilton, New York: American Management Associations, 1975), pp. 20–36; Keith Alan Bea, Dennis L. Little, and Sandra S. Osbourn, *The States Look to the Future: A Survey of Tomorrow/2000/Goals Organizations* (Washington, D.C.: Congressional Research Service, 1975), publication # CB 150 A/75 203 SP, 40 pp.; Keith Alan Bea and Cynthia Elmer Huston, *op.*

cit., 116 pp. In addition, the author is grateful to Robert Lamson, Program Manager, Communications Programs, Division of Inter-governmental Science and Public Technology, National Science Foundation, for the use of his extensive files on A/D groups. With the multitude of groups of varying sizes and purposes now or recently active in the A/D field, it is virtually impossible to keep up with them. Therefore, this listing is representative of the major groups whose life span and amount of activity are of particular note.

4. Most states and regions have developed some form of planning and development capability. Below are the names of some of the more adventurous and unique of these programs. They differ from the A/D projects in that direct citizen involvement is less.

> Alaska: State Planning Strategy (now having greater citizen involvement)
> Arizona Trade-Off Model
> Connecticut Plan for Conservation and Development
> Florida Growth Plan Element/Florida 2000
> Ohio 2000—Choices for Today
> Utah Process
> Wisconsin State Department Policy Process
> New England River Basin Commission

5. The participants also learned the value of the spirit of harmony and consensus in a uniquely Hawaiian way. At the major conference in August 1970 there had been conflict and tension around a number of issues, including the implications of the Vietnam War, and the tension over the present-action concerns and the future orientation of Hawaii 2000. When the existence of these tensions led newcomers to question the existence of the Aloha Spirit, another participant replied:

> I would like you all to understand that the "Aloha Spirit" is the coordination of mind and heart . . . it's within the individual—it brings you down to yourself. You must think and emote good feelings to others.
> Permit me to offer a translation of the word "aloha":
> A stands for *akahai,* meaning kindness, to be expressed with tenderness,
> L stands for *lokahi,* meaning unity, to be expressed with harmony,
> O stands for *'olu'olu,* meaning agreeable, to be expressed with pleasantness,
> H stands for *ha'aha'a,* meaning humility, to be expressed with modesty,
> A stands for *ahonui,* meaning patience, to be expressed with perseverance.

These are the traits of character that express the charm, warmth, and sincerity of Hawaiians. It was the working philosophy of my ancestors. . . .

"They handed it down to me and I wish to give it to you," Mrs. Paki concluded. There was a momentary hush in the theater and then several hundred of us began to applaud and to stand together in a prolonged ovation. One participant said, "We've been muddling around for four days trying to find directions for Hawaii's future. . . . No one else even thought of what that woman said. She's got the answer." George Chaplin and Glenn D. Paige, *Hawaii 2000: Continuing Experiment in Anticipatory Democracy* (Honolulu: U. of Hawaii Press, 1973), pp. 70–71.

6. *Ibid.*
7. Edward Lindaman, in a telephone conversation with the author, September 1975.
8. Nicholas Lewis, in a telephone conversation with the author, September 1975.
9. Minnesota State Planning Agency, *Minnesota's Future, Proceedings of a Seminar on Minnesota's Future, February 10, 1973* (St. Paul: Minnesota State Planning Agency, September 1973), p. 2.
10. Nelson Rosenbaum of The Urban Institute estimates that intense involvement of all affected households in a particular area can cost from $.70–$1.00 per household. Thus, for a state with 100,-000 households, this would amount to a publicity budget of $70,-000 to $100,000. Surveys can cost from $10–$15 per respondent or up to $15,000 for a sample of 1,000 persons. See Nelson Rosenbaum, *Citizen Involvement in Land Use Governance: Issues and Methods* (Washington, D.C.: The Urban Institute, 1976), p. 76.
11. Georgia Planning Association, *Goals for Georgia, What the People Said* (Atlanta: January 1972).
12. William B. Shore, *et al.*, *Listening to the Metropolis, An Evaluation of the New York Region's Choices for a '76 Mass Media Town Meeting and Handbook on Public Participation in Regional Planning* (New York: Regional Plan Association, 1974), p. 96. This handbook provides an excellent and well-documented description of the complete strategy utilized in gaining support from the media for the project.
13. The full results are reported in "The Metropolis Speaks, Report on the Vote of the People," *Regional Plan News,* August 1974, #95.
14. State Planning Agency, *Minnesota Horizons,* St. Paul, 1975, p. 36.

15. State Senator David Huber, in a telephone conversation with the author, October 1975.

16. Georgia Planning Association, *op. cit.*, provides the summary tables of citizen responses on goals for the state, and methods to pay for new services.

17. *Goals for Dallas: Proposals for Achieving the Goals* (Dallas: Southwest Center for Advanced Studies, 1965). *Goals for Seattle 2000* (Seattle: Seattle 2000 Task Force, 1973).

18. Edward Lindaman, *op. cit.*

19. Boulder Area Growth Study Commission, *Exploring Options for the Future, A Study of Growth in Boulder County,* Vol. X, pp. 89–94 (November 1973).

20. Nicholas Lewis, *op. cit.*

21. Keith Alan Bea and Cynthia Elmer Huston, *op. cit.*

22. *Ibid.*

23. *Minnesota Rev. Statutes,* Chap. 341, Sect. 4.

CHAPTER TWO

THE GOALS FOR GEORGIA PROGRAM

Newt Gingrich

1. *Atlanta Magazine* (December 1970).

2. *Ibid.*

3. Governor Jimmy Carter, in his inaugural address (Augusta, Georgia, 1971).

4. *Focus on the Future of Georgia 1970–1985* (Georgia State Department of Education, Atlanta, 1970).

5. *Ibid.,* p. 365.

6. *A Blueprint for Action: Goals for Georgia in the Seventies* (Georgia Business and Industry Association, Atlanta, June 1970).

7. *The Challenge: Active Participation by Citizens of Georgia in Determining State Directions, Goals, and Priorities for the Coming Year,* Carter Administration memorandum, May 14, 1971.

8. Jimmy Carter, "Why Not the Best," *Atlanta Magazine* (September 1971).

9. *Goals for Georgia: What the People Said* (Georgia Planning Association, January 1972).

10. Tim C. Ryles, *Citizen Perspective on Goals for Georgia* (School of Urban Life, Georgia State University, 1973).

11. Interviews conducted by the author in preparing the article.

12. In 1972 a state and local government study committee released some seventy recommendations, some of which became part of Carter's legislative agenda. Governor Carter summarized his Administration's activities in 1974 in *A Blueprint for Action: Goals for Georgia in the Seventies,* in which he gives the progress on 61 programs, most of which were based on the Goals recommendations.

13. Ryles, *op. cit.,* p. 2.

CHAPTER THREE

GOALS FOR DALLAS

Robert B. Bradley

1. Thomas Muller, *Growing and Declining Urban Areas: A Fiscal Comparison* (Washington, D.C.: The Urban Institute, 1976), p. 18.

2. R. D. Norton, "The Political Economy of City Growth and Decline," University of Texas at Dallas (January 1977, mimeographed), p. 8.

3. Richard Smith, "How Business Failed Dallas," *Fortune,* Vol. 70 (July 1964), p. 159.

4. *Norton, op. cit.,* Table 1–2.

5. Richard Forstall, "A New Social and Economic Grouping of Cities," *The Municipal Yearbook* (Washington, D.C.: International City Management Association, 1970), p. 125.

6. David Craigie, "Socioeconomic Cause and Consequences of Change in Racial Residential Differentiation: A Longitudinal Study of 74 American Cities," Dissertation, University of Arizona (1977), Appendix I.

7. *Ibid.*

8. The history of racial segregation and the political experiences of the Dallas black community are detailed in *Lipscomb v. Wise,* a court case in which Dallas was ordered to implement single-member districts for local council elections.

9. Richard Murray and Arnold Vedlitz, "Political Organization in Deprived Communities: Black Electoral Groups in Houston, Dallas, and New Orleans." Paper delivered at 1975 Annual

American Political Science Association meeting, August 29–September 2, 1974.

10. Dallas Citizens Council, "Summary Statement: Characteristics and Purposes of Dallas Citizens Council (January 10, 1973, mimeographed).

11. Smith, *op. cit.*, p. 160.

12. *Lipscomb v. Wise*, 399 F. Supp. 782 (N. D. Tex. 1974).

13. Murray and Vedlitz, *op. cit.*, p. 26.

14. *Lipscomb v. Wise, op. cit.*

15. Erik Jonsson, "Days of Decision," reprinted in *Goals for Dallas: Submitted for Consideration by Dallas Citizens* (1966), p. 301.

16. Peyton Davis, "J. Erik Jonsson: No Longer Mayor, But Still a Leader," *Dallas Times Herald,* Sunday Magazine (September 26, 1976), p. 17.

17. *Ibid.*

18. *Dallas Times Herald,* "City Goals Hailed as Nation's First" (February 2, 1966).

19. Smith, *op. cit.*, p. 211.

20. *Ibid.*, p. 159.

21. *Ibid.*

22. William Schultze, *Urban and Community Politics* (North Scituate, Mass.: Duxbury Press, 1974), p. 360.

23. *Ibid.*, p. 361.

24. Smith, *op. cit.*, p. 216.

25. Jonsson, *op. cit.*, p. 302.

26. Bryghte Godbold, director of Goals for Dallas, in an interview with the author (1976).

27. *Dallas Times Herald,* "Concept of Future Dallas Born in Planning Session" (December 4, 1965).

28. *Dallas Times Herald,* "Goal Committee to Begin Studies" (January 4, 1966).

29. Goals for Dallas, *Goals for Dallas: Submitted for Consideration by Dallas Citizens* (Dallas, Texas: July 1966), pp. 4–27.

30. *Ibid.*, pp. 12–13.

31. Goals for Dallas, *Goals for Dallas: Proposals for Achieving the Goals* (Dallas, Texas: August 1969), p. vi.

32. Goals for Dallas, *Goals for Dallas: Achieving the Goals* (Dallas, Texas: August 1970), p. xii.

33. *Ibid.*

34. Goals for Dallas, *op. cit.* (August 1969), p. xi.

35. Goals for Dallas, *op. cit.* (August 1970), p. xii.

36. Goals for Dallas, "Summary Report: Achievements (1974, mimeographed).

37. The Goals for Dallas program is now in its second cycle. Analytically, the two rounds can be considered distinct. But because the second cycle is only now (1977) beginning, its effects, to a great degree, are as yet unfelt. Thus, for convenience I will consider both efforts as one. However, the changes manifested in the current effort serve as a useful barometer of the internal criticism percolating through the Goals organization of the first cycle.

38. Goals for Dallas, "Goals for Dallas: Leadership Dallas, Survey of Goals for Dallas Task Forces." Presented to Goals for Dallas by Sandra Cole, Jerry Kelley, Dennis Lathern, and Lupe Martinez (Dallas, Texas: 1975, mimeographed).

39. J. R. Nininger, V. N. Macdonald, and G. Y. McDiarmid, "Goals for Dallas, 'A': An Experiment in Community Goal Setting," Local Government Project, Ministry of Treasury and Intergovernmental Affairs, Ontario, Canada (May 1975), p. 10.

40. Goals for Dallas, *op. cit.* (1975), p. 4.

41. Bryghte Godbold, *op. cit.*

42. Nininger, Macdonald, and McDiarmid, "Goals for Dallas. 'B': An Experiment in Community Goal Setting," Local Government Project, Ministry of Treasury and Intergovernmental Affairs, Ontario, Canada (May 1975), p. 10.

43. *Ibid.*

44. Jonsson, *op. cit.*, Preface to the 3rd edition.

45. Goals for Dallas, *op. cit.* (August 1970), p. 275.

46. *Dallas Morning News,* "Goals Program Criticized" (March 12, 1968).

47. Bryghte Godbold, *op. cit.*

48. *Ibid.*

49. *Ibid.*

50. *Ibid.*

51. Smith, *op. cit.*, p. 159.

52. Rabbi Olan, Goals participant and religious leader, in an interview with the author (December 1976).

53. Peyton Davis, "His Honor and His Wife: Bob and Margaret Folsom," *Dallas Times Herald,* Sunday Magazine (September 26, 1976), p. 15.

54. Rabbi Olan, *op. cit.*

55. Nininger, Macdonald, and McDiarmid, *op. cit.* (Goals for Dallas, 'B'), p. 10.

56. Nininger, Macdonald, and McDiarmid, *op. cit.* ("Goals for Dallas, 'A'), p. 15.

57. Goals for Corpus Christi, *Choices Facing Corpus Christi* (Corpus Christi; 1975).

CHAPTER FOUR

ALTERNATIVES FOR WASHINGTON

Robert L. Stilger

1. *Alternatives for Washington*, Vol. 1, Office of Program Planning and Fiscal Management, Olympia, Washington (May 1975).
2. "Washington Asks its Citizens to Choose the State's Future," in *State Growth Management*, Council of State Governments (May 1976), p. 80.
3. *Ibid.*, p. 79.
4. *Ibid.*, p. 80.
5. In an interview with the editor, June 27, 1977.
6. *Ibid.*

CHAPTER SIX

CITIZENS AND LEGISLATIVE FORESIGHT

Clement Bezold and William Renfro

1. Roger K. Davidson, "The Struggle for Congressional Committee Reform" (Paper presented at the 1974 annual meeting of the American Political Science Association), p. 4.
2. Quoted in Clement Bezold, *Strategic Policy Assessment and Congressional Reform: The Future in Committee*, Ph.D. Dissertation (Ann Arbor: University Microfilms, 1976), p. 6.
3. *Ibid.*
4. See the poll taken by the People's Bicentennial Commission, *Common Sense*, Vol. 3, pp. 11–17, 1976; and *Consumerism at the Crossroads*, A National Opinion Research Survey of Public,

Activist, Business and Regulator Attitudes toward the Consumer Movement, for Sentry Insurance, 1977; and, *Confidence and Concern: Citizens View American Government,* A Survey of Attitudes by the Subcommittee on Intergovernmental Relations, Senate Government Operations Committee (Government Printing Office, 1973).

An important finding of the *Confidence and Concern* poll was the support for more participation, noted on p. 143:

"The people also want to see themselves and the citizens groups they feel could represent them have a much more important place in the governmental process. The public feels deeply that it can and would participate much more than now in a more open and inviting process."

5. The foresight provision and related developments are described in Clement Bezold, "Congress and the Future," *The Futurist* (June 1975), pp. 132–142.

6. Center for Governmental Responsibility, "Congressional Committees and National Growth Policy," in *Forging America's Future,* Report of the Advisory Committee on National Growth Policy Processes of the National Commission on Supplies and Shortages, Appendix II.

7. *Toward a Modern Senate,* Report of the Commission on the Operation of the Senate (Government Printing Office, 1976), p. 44. The Commission also had papers prepared on foresight techniques and options by Marvin Kornbluh, Dennis L. Little, and William L. Renfro, "The Tools of Futures Research: Some Questions and Answers"; Clement Bezold, "Senate Committee Foresight"; and William L. Renfro, "Foresight in the Senate"; all in *Techniques and Procedures for Analysis and Evaluation,* Commission on the Operation of the Senate (Government Printing Office, 1977).

8. "Foresight Options for the Senate," by William L. Renfro and "Comments on Senate Foresight," submitted to the Select Committee by Clement Bezold, *Operation of the Senate Committee System: Staffing, Scheduling, Communications, Procedures, and Special Functions* in Appendix to the Second Report with Recommendations of the Temporary Select Committee to Study the Senate Committee System (Government Printing Office, 1977), pp. 49–72, 72–73.

While the foresight concerns of the Congress are growing, this interest is not unique to the federal level—a number of state legislatures have also increased their foresight activity. For instance, in 1975 the leadership of the Massachusetts legislature called for foresight, as a complement to oversight, noting that "as legislators oversee how well executive agencies carry out old mandates, they should also foresee what new mandates should be given and what old mandates should be discontinued." The Massachusetts legislature has since developed an organization to provide relevant foresight information. With the aid of the National Science Foundation, several states have improved their ability to use information technology to generate futures information. Some states, most notably California and Hawaii, have developed methods for forecasting the impacts of major bills after they have been introduced but before they are acted on by a legislative committee. David Baker in Chapter 1 of this book points out the use of A/D exercises to provide futures information to legislatures—particularly in Minnesota through the Minnesota Horizons Program. See *Networking,* quarterly newsletter of the Science Resource Network, Science Resource Committee, Massachusetts State House, Boston, Mass.; and Irwin Feller, *et al., Sources and Uses of Scientific and Technological Information in State Legislatures* (Pennsylvania State University Institute for Research on Human Resources, 1975); Peter Wissel, "The Hunting of the Legislative Snark: Information Searches and Reforms in the U.S. State Legislatures," *Legislative Studies Quarterly,* Vol. I (May 1976), pp. 251–267.

9. Rules of the House of Representatives, Rule X 2(b)(1) in *Jefferson's Manual* (Government Printing Office, 1977).

10. *Ibid.,* Rule X (2d).

11. *Ibid.,* Rule XI (e)(4). For a discussion of the implementation of this inflation impact requirement see Center for Governmental Responsibility, *op. cit.,* pp., 30, 52, 62.

12. *Committee Reform Amendments of 1974,* Report of the House Select Committee on Committees, to accompany H. Res. 988, Rept. #93-916, Part II (Government Printing Office, 1974), p. 65.

13. See footnotes 7 and 8 above.

14. Marvin Kornbluh, "Legislative Implications of Socio-Economic Models," Congressional Research Service Multilith No. 77-128SP, 1977; see also "Futures in the Political Process," by William Renfro and Marvin Kornbluh, in *Handbook for Futures Research,* Jib Fowles, editor, Greenwood Press, Westport, Connecticut.

15. *Paley Commission Report—President's Commission on National Materials Policy,* William S. Paley, Chairman (Government Printing Office, June 1952).

16. Based on the Mandate in Public Law 91-510, Legislative Reorganization Act of 1970. For a discussion of the use of this CRS emerging-issues service see Bezold "Senate Committee Foresight," *op. cit.*, p. 43.

17. Based on the mandate in Public Law 92-484, The Technology Assessment Act of 1972, Section 3(c).

18. Programs designed to monitor trends on a continuing basis include the Trends Analysis Program of the Institute of Life Insurance in New York City, the trends program of the Center for Policy Process in Washington, D.C., the work of Willis Harman and his associates at the Stanford Research Institute, and that of Herman Kahn and his associates at the Hudson Institute in New York.

19. Adapted from "Foresight: Congress Looks to the Future," Congressional Research Service Issue Brief #77007 by William Renfro, Library of Congress, 1977.

20. *Forging America's Future, op. cit.*, p. viii.

21. Bezold, "Comments on Senate Foresight," *op. cit.*

22. Renfro, "Foresight Options for the Senate," *op. cit.*

23. The Impact Forecast Chart also appeared in *What's Next*, August 1977, p. 1.

24. Joseph Coates, "Life Patterns, Technology, and Political Institutions," in *Changing American Lifestyles*, Valparaiso University, 1977.

25. David K. Hartley, Janet W. Patton, and Lucia B. Findley, "The Regional Impacts of Federal Policy," in *A National Public Works Investment Policy*, Background Papers, House Public Works Committee (Government Printing Office, 1974) p. 114.

26. Congressional Budget Office, *Budget Options for Fiscal Year 1977* (Government Printing Office, March 15, 1975), pp. 369–379.

27. For a discussion of this idea see Nelson M. Rosenbaum, "Citizens and the Federal Budget," Urban Institute Working Paper, 1977.

28. For Florida see Clement Bezold, "Citizens and the Constitution," Testimony to the Florida Constitution Revision Commission, August 31, 1977, and in Hawaii, the work of Democracy Hawaii '78, and Constitutional Network. This later Hawaii group, which includes Jim Dator and Ted Becker, has proposed using the latest in communication processes and electronic technologies—cable TV, satellites, video film, computer conferencing, and automated telephone polling to involve the entire population of the state in the activities of the 1978 Constitutional Network in Hawaii.

29. S.3050. The Balanced National Growth and Development Act of 1974. 93rd Congress.
30. *Forging America's Future, op. cit.*

CHAPTER SEVEN

THE ORIGINS OF CITIZEN INVOLVEMENT IN FEDERAL PROGRAMS

Nelson M. Rosenbaum

1. James Bryce, *The American Commonwealth* (1888), quoted in Theodore Lowi, *The End of Liberalism* (New York: W. W. Norton, 1969), pp. 128–129.
2. James Landis, *The Administrative Process* (New Haven: Yale University Press, 1938), p. 46.
3. See, for example, A. Wolfe, "Will and Reason in Economic Life," *Journal of Social Philosophy*, 218 (1936); R. Cushman, *The Independent Regulatory Commissions* (New York: Oxford University Press, 1941); Herman Finer, "Administrative Responsibility in Democratic Government," *Public Administration Review*, 335 (1941).
4. Major and early examples of the "subgovernment" literature are Marver Bernstein, *Regulating Business by Independent Commission* (Princeton: Princeton University Press, 1955), and Samuel P. Huntington, "The Marasmus of the ICC: The Commission, The Railroads and the Public Interest," *Yale Law Journal* (1952). For a similar indictment of land-use regulatory agencies, see Richard Babcock, *The Zoning Game* (Madison, Wisc.: University of Wisconsin Press, 1966).
5. One of the most prominent contemporary advocates of strict legislative standards is Theodore Lowi. See Lowi, *End of Liberalism*, pp. 287–312. See also Henry Friendly, *The Federal Administrative Agencies* (Cambridge, Mass.: Harvard University Press, 1962), pp. 163–175. This school of thought derives, of course, from the older legal tradition of concern about improper delegation of legislative power. See E. Freund, *Legislative Powers Over Persons and Property* (Chicago: University of Chicago Press, 1973).

6. Major works in this tradition include Richard Neustadt, *Presidential Leadership* (New York: John Wiley & Sons, 1950); Charles Hyneman, *Bureaucracy in a Democracy* (New York: Harper, 1950); Paul Appleby, *Policy and Administration* (University, Ala.: University of Alabama Press, 1949); Roscoe C. Martin, ed., *Public Administration and Democracy* (Syracuse, N.Y.: Syracuse University Press, 1965).

7. On the background of demands for direct citizen involvement in government, see Carl Steinberg, "Citizens and the Administrative State: From Participation to Power," 32 *Public Administration Review* 190 (1972); John Strange, "The Impact of Citizen Participation Upon Public Administration," 32 *Public Administration Review* 457 (1972); Herbert Kaufman, "Administrative Decentralization and Political Power," 29 *Public Administration Review* 3 (1969); and Alan Altshuler, *Community Control* (New York: Pegasus, 1970).

8. On the general evolution of public participation rights in administrative law, originating in the Administrative Procedure Act of 1946, see K. Davis, *Administrative Law Treatise* (St. Paul, Minn.: West, 1958); E. Gellhorn, "Public Participation in Administrative Proceedings," 81 *Yale Law Journal* 359 (1972); and Richard Stewart "The Reformation of American Administrative Law," 88 *Harvard Law Review* 1669 (1975).

9. James Q. Wilson, "Planning and Politics: Citizen Participation in Urban Renewal," 29 *Journal of the American Institute of Planners*, 242 (1963); J. Clarence Davies III, *Neighborhood Groups and Urban Renewal* (New York: Columbia University Press, 1965).

10. The voluminous commentary on citizen participation in the Community Action and Model Cities programs is reviewed, cataloged, and analyzed in John Strange, "Citizen Participation in Community Action and Model Cities Programs," 32 *Public Administration Review* 655 (1972). See also "Symposium on Citizen Action in Model Cities, CAP Programs," 32 *Public Administration Review* 377–470 (1972).

CHAPTER EIGHT

CONSUMER ACTIVISM IN THE FUTURE OF
HEALTH CARE

Rosemary H. Bruner

BIBLIOGRAPHY

Beauchamp, Dan E., *Health Policy and the Politics of Prevention: Breaking the Ethical and Political Barriers to Public Health,* Report to American Public Health Association Meeting, Chicago, Ill., 1975.

Becker, Ernest, *The Denial of Death* (New York: The Free Press, 1973).

Department of Public Affairs. "The Emerging Health Care Environment: Selected Issues," (unpublished internal document, Hoffman-LaRoche, Inc., Nutley, N.J., 1976).

Dudley, James R., "Citizens Board for Philadelphia Community Mental Health Centers," *Community Mental Health Journal,* (1975). pp. 2, 4.

Fuchs, Victor, *Who Shall Live?* (New York: Basic Books, 1974).

Goodman, William, M.D., *Development of an Integrated Mental Health Delivery System,* Report to Butley Hospital, Providence, R.I. (May 23, 1975).

Group Health Association of America, "GHAA Q and A," *Group Health and Welfare News* (May 1976).

Group Health Association of America, "Legislative Summary of the HMO Amendments," *Group Health and Welfare News* (September 1976).

Health Research Group, *Trimming the Fat Off Health Care Costs: A Consumer's Guide to Taking Over Health Planning* (1976).

Hyman, Herbert Harvey, *Health Regulation—Certificate of Need and 1122* (Aspen Systems Corporation, Germantown, Maryland, 1977).

Kazis, Richard, "Toward Local Control of Health Care Planning," *Self Reliance* (May–June 1977), pp. 13–15.

Landsberg, Gerald, and Hammer, Roni J., and Neigher, William D., *Consumer Feedback as a Mechanism for Humanizing Mental Health,* Report to National Conference on Social Welfare, Washington, D.C. (June 1976).

Levitt, Theodore, *The Third Sector* (AMA CON, a division of American Management Association, New York, 1973).

Molner, S. M., "The Distribution of Health in America," (unpublished internal document, Corporate Planning, Hoffman-La Roche, Inc., Nutley, N.J., 1972).

Molner, S. M., "Trends in Public Control of Healthcare," (unpublished internal document, Corporate Planning, Hoffman-La Roche, Inc., Nutley, N.J., 1975).

Musto, David F., "Whatever Happened to Community Mental Health," *The Public Interest,* 39 (Spring 1975), pp. 53–79.

Pecarchik, Robert, and Ricci, Edmund, and Nelson, Jr., Bardin, "Potential Contribution of Consumers to an Integrated Health Care System," *Public Health Reports,* 91, 1 (January–February 1976) pp. 72–76.

Powles, John, "The Medicine of Industrial Man." *Ecologist,* 2 (1972), pp. 24–35.

Reissman, Frank, ed., "Special Health Issue," *Sorial Policy,* 6, 3 (November/December 1975), pp. 2–3.

Spiegel, Hans B. C., "Citizen Participation in Federal Programs: A Review," *Journal of Voluntary Action Research,* Monograph No. 1 (1971).

U.S. Congressional & Administrative News, "Special Health Revenue Sharing Act," Vol. 1, 94th, 1st Session, 89 Stat 304 (July 1975).

U.S. Department of Health, Education & Welfare, "Citizen Participation, Request for Public Comments," *Federal Register,* XLI, 218 (November 10, 1976), pp. 49772–81.

U.S. Department of Health, Education & Welfare, "Health Systems Agencies, Proposed Rulemaking," *Federal Register,* XL, 202 (October 17, 1975), pp. 48802–12.

Woodham-Smith, Cecil, *Florence Nightingale* (New York: McGraw-Hill, 1951).

CHAPTER NINE

A BLACK VIEW:
FROM PARTICIPATION TO ANTICIPATION

Lawrence J. Auls

1. "Project 2000," A Staff Report of the Model Neighborhood Assembly to the Mid-Ohio Regional Planning Commission, 1975.
2. *Ibid.*

3. *Ibid.*
4. *Ibid.*
5. *Ibid.*

CHAPTER TEN

TOMORROW'S TECHNOLOGY: WHO DECIDES?

Byron Kennard

1. James B. Sullivan, from a speech before the American Association for the Advancement of Science, 1974.
2. *Public Assessment of Technology,* National Council for the Public Assessment of Technology, pp. 6–7.
3. A report on the New Jersey Coastal Development assessment which describes the public participation program in detail may be obtained from the Government Printing Office, Washington, D.C. 20402. Stock No. 052-003-00245-1. Price $4.45.

CHAPTER TWELVE

ECONOMIC DEMOCRACY AND THE FUTURE: THE UNFINISHED TASK

C. George Benello

1. Harry Braverman, *Labor and Monopoly Capital* (Monthly Review Press, 1974), p. 400.
2. Amitai Etzioni, "Basic Human Needs, Alienation and Inauthenticity," in Glass and Staude (eds.), *Humanistic Society* (Pacific Palisades, California: Goodyear Publishing Co., 1972), p. 91.
3. *Liberation,* June 1972, p. 26.
4. See, for example, Frederick C. Thayer, *An End to Hierarchy! An End to Competition!* (New Viewpoints, N.Y., 1973), or W. N. Dunn and B. Fouzoni, *Toward A Critical Administrative Theory*

(Sage Publications, Administrative and Polity Studies Series, California, 1975).

5. Introduction by James O'Toole, in O'Toole (ed.), *Work and the Quality of Life* (Cambridge: M.I.T. Press, 1974).

6. Jeremy Rifkin, *Own Your Own Job: Economic Democracy for Working Americans* (New York: Bantam Books, 1977), Appendix.

7. *Work in America*, U.S. Dept. of Health, Education and Welfare (Cambridge: M.I.T. Press, 1972).

8. Andrew Zimbalist, "The Limits of Work Humanization," in *The Review of Radical Political Economics*, Vol. 7, No. 2 (Summer 1975).

9. *Ibid.*

10. James B. Shuman, "Democracy Comes to the Factory," unpublished manuscript.

11. Michael Maccoby, "Changing Work: The Bolivar Project" *Working Papers for a New Society*, Vol. 3, No. 2 (Summer 1975).

12. Richard Barnett and Ronald Muller in *Global Reach* give an account of the multinationals' search for cheaper labor markets in Taiwan, Hong Kong and elsewhere. The last manufacturer of color TV tubes in the United States closed its doors (in New York State) and moved to Taiwan in 1976.

13. My own experience as a consultant to plan managers in New York State and Massachusetts indicates that conglomerates have, in their rush for acquisitions, taken on companies in industries they knew little about, and have caused these companies which were previously successful to fail.

14. G. William Domhoff, Chapter 6, "How the Power Elite Shapes Social Legislation," in *The Higher Circles* (New York: Vintage Books, 1971).

15. *Ibid.*

16. Lee Ranck, "Corporation of the Future," in *Engage/Social Action*, Vol. 2, No. 9 (September 1974).

17. For a history of political experiments in direct democracy, see George Woodcock's "Democracy, Heretical and Radical," in *The Case for Participatory Democracy*, ed. by C. George Benello and Dimitrios Roussopoulos (New York: Viking, 1972).

18. Charles Hampden-Turner, *Radical Man: The Process of Psychosocial Development* (Cambridge: Schenkman Publishing Co., 1970).

19. See the work of Erich Fromm, esp. *The Sane Society* (Rinehart, 1955), and the work of his pupil, Michael Maccoby. See also the introductory chapters of *Work in America, op. cit.*

20. See Paul Blumberg, *Industrial Democracy: The Sociology of Participation* (Schocken paperback, 1973), esp. Chapter 5.

21. See Adorno *et al.*, *The Authoritarian Personality* (Harper, 1950), and the subsequent literature by Christie and Jahoda, Milton Rokeach, and Harold Lasswell.

22. Paul Goodman, *People or Personnel: Decentralizing and the Mixed System* (New York: Random House, 1963).

23. Werner W. Jaeger, *Paideia,* Vol. 1 (New York: Oxford University Press, 1945).

24. Jurgen Habermas, *Theory and Practice* (Boston: Beacon Press, 1973), p. 42.

25. See Murray Bookchin, "The Forms of Freedom," in Benello and Roussopoulos, eds., *op. cit.*

26. See the articles by Geoffrey Barraclough, "The Coming Depression," *New York Review of Books,* June 27, 1974, "The World Crash," *N.Y.R.,* January 23, 1975, and "The World Economic Struggle," *N.Y.R.,* August 7, 1975. Also Robert L. Heilbroner, *An Inquiry Into the Human Prospect* (New York: Norton, 1974).

27. Barry Stein, *Size, Efficiency, and Community Enterprise* (Center for Community Economic Development, Cambridge, 1974).

28. See, for example, Garrett Hardin's well-known article, "The Tragedy of the Commons," *Science,* Vol. 162, December 13, 1968.

29. E. F. Schumacher, *Small Is Beautiful* (New York: Harper & Row, 1973).

30. Harry Braverman, *Labor and Monopoly Capital* (Monthly Review Press, 1974).

31. Little has been written in English about Mondragon, unfortunately. See "The Mondragon Movement: Worker Ownership in Modern Industry," by Campbell and Foster, I.C.O.M. Pamphlet No. 5, Industrial Common Ownership Movement, England.

32. A loose coordinating organization, the Funding and Educational Development Organization (FEDO), has its headquarters in Washington, D.C. and publishes an occasional newsletter on activities in the field. In Cambridge, Massachusetts, the Workers' Cooperative Association, developed out of the New England office of the American Friends' Service Committee and affiliated with the FEDO, has a staff of business and organizational consultants which has been working actively with a number of enterprises whose workers wish to develop worker cooperatives.

33. The fund, called the Community Investment Fund, plans to obtain SEC registration in order to offer securities nationally. Its

investment interests extend to land trusts, worker cooperatives, community-development corporations, and investments in appropriate technology alternatives. It is associated with a number of groups active in these areas, including the Workers' Cooperative Association.

34. The New School for Democratic Management, a project of the Foundation for National Progress in San Francisco, has held a summer session in 1977 and is planning sessions in 1978 in various parts of the country. The Workers' Cooperative Association is planning a similar program, oriented toward bringing people together with common interests and skills who wish to seek work in worker cooperatives.

35. This suggestion is put forward in Schumacher, *op. cit.* "Technology with a Human Face," p. 144.

CHAPTER THIRTEEN

LUCAS AEROSPACE: THE WORKERS' PLAN FOR SOCIALLY USEFUL PRODUCTS

Clement Bezold

1. Lucas Aerospace Combine Shop Steward Committee, "Corporate Plan: A Contingency Strategy as a Positive Alternative to Recession and Redundancies" (January 1976), p. 3. See also: Dave Elliott, "Beyond the Wage-Labour Bargain: The Lucas Aerospace Workers Campaign," Young Fabian Pamphlet, 1976; "Dole Queue or Useful Products," *New Scientist* (July 3, 1975), pp. 10–12; Walter Patterson, "Redundant Swords, Plowshares Needed," *Environment* (April 1976), pp. 2–3; Patrick Wintour, "Lucas—Most British of Companies," *New Statesman* (May 27, 1977), pp. 706–707.

2. Corporate Plan, *op. cit.*, p. 5.

3. *Ibid.*, p. 7.

4. *Ibid.*, p. 8.

5. *Ibid.*, p. 9.

6. *Financial Times,* as cited in *Combine News* (September 1976), p. 1.

7. "Editorial Comment: What Industry Can Learn From the Lucas Affair," *Industrial Management* (July 1976), p. 4.
8. *Combine News* (September 1976), p. 2.
9. *Combine News* (January 1977), p. 1.

CHAPTER FOURTEEN

CITIZEN MOVEMENTS: CHARTING ALTERNATIVES

Hazel Henderson

1. Gregory Bateson, *Steps to an Ecology of Mind* (New York: Ballantine, 1972), p. 501.
2. *Bell Magazine* (January–February 1975), p. 10.
3. *New York Times* (October 26, 1975), p. 1.
4. *The Progressive* (October 1975), p. 13.
5. Opinion Research Corporation, Report to Management (Princeton, N.J.: August 1975).
6. George Cabot Lodge and William F. Martin, "Our Society in 1985: Business May Not Like It," *Harvard Business Review*, (December 1975).
7. Todd LaPorte, *Organized Social Complexity* (Princeton, N.J.: Princeton University Press, 1975), p. 19.
8. Hazel Henderson, "No To Cartesian Logic," in *Futurology* (June 1975).
9. Thomas Kuhn, *The Structure of Scientific Revolutions* (University of Chicago Press, 1962).
10. Hazel Henderson, "Limits to Traditional Economics," in *Financial Analysis Journal* (May 1975).
11. Gunnar Myrdal, *Beyond the Welfare State* (New Haven, Conn.: Yale University Press, 1960).
12. Karen Horney, *The Neurotic Personality of Our Time* (1937). Cited by Hazel Henderson in "The Decline of Jonesism," *The Futurist* (October 1974).

CHAPTER FIFTEEN

SOCIAL TECHNOLOGIES OF FREEDOM

Jerome C. Glenn

1. The World Future Society, *Introduction to the Future* (WFS 1977).
2. For an example of the use of a Delphi survey to identify community development goals, see Harold Becker and Paul de Brigard, "A Framework for Community Development Action Planning," Institute for the Future, Report for the Connecticut Department of Community Affairs (February 1971).
3. Barry Schuttler, *Citizen Participation Artification for Community Development,* National Association of Housing and Redevelopment Officials (February 1977).
4. *Ibid.*
5. The Committee for the Future, *Syncon: Washington, D.C.* (May 1973).
6. Luther J. Carter, "Videoconference via Satellite: Opening Congress to the People?" *Science* (July 1, 1977).
7. Murray Turoff, "The Future of Computer Conferencing," *The Futurist,* August 1975, pp. 182–83.
8. James L. Creighton, *Alternative Futures Planning,* Bureau of Reclamation, U.S. Department of Interior, Denver, 1976, p. 28.

CHAPTER SIXTEEN

THE LEAGUE OF WOMEN VOTERS: EXPLORING AMERICA AND ORGANIZATIONAL FUTURES

Nan Waterman

1. David Broder, "The Party's Over," *Atlantic* (March 1972).
2. *Exploring American Futures,* League of Women Voters Education Fund, Pub. #592, 1975 (Hereinafter abbreviated *EAF*). Originally, this material was copyrighted in 1972 by Pacific House, adapted with permission by Western Behavioral Sciences Institute

for the League of Women Voters Education Fund. (This publication is available from the League office at 1730 M Street, N.W., Washington, D.C. 20036.)

3. The others present at the workshop were Lucy Wilson Benson, former President of the League of Women Voters; Lawrence D. Cohen, former Mayor, St. Paul, Minn.; Charles Hamilton, Professor of Political Science, Columbia University, coauthor of *Black Power;* Constance Baker Motley, Judge, U.S. District Court, New York; William Simon, program supervisor in Sociology and Anthropology, Institute for Juvenile Research in Chicago.

4. *EAF*, p. 6.

5. *Exploring American Futures: A Leader's Guide,* League of Women Voters Education Fund, publication #566, 1975.

6. Alexis de Tocqueville, *Democracy in America.*

7. *21st Century USA—If We're Going to Play the Futures Game,* League of Women Voters Education Fund, publication #457, 1973.

CHAPTER EIGHTEEN

THE DEEPER IMPLICATIONS OF CITIZEN PARTICIPATION

Robert Theobald

1. Mark Satin, *New Age Politics* (Fairweather Press, 2344 Spruce Street, Vancouver, British Columbia, 1976).

2. Those who doubt my flat statement about the necessity of an elite at any particular moment in time should read "Sociality" from *The Parable of the Beast* by John N. Bleibtrau (New York: Macmillan, 1968).

3. For bibliographic and other material, write to Futures Conditional Information Service, Box 5296, Spokane, Washington 99205.

Appendix

1. The Work of the Committee on Anticipatory Democracy

Much of the work reported in this volume was encouraged by the Committee on Anticipatory Democracy and its members. The committee, a group of more than fifty futurists, planners, and future-oriented citizens (listed at the end of this Appendix) was formed on an ad-hoc basis at the suggestion of Alvin Toffler in the spring of 1975 to congratulate members of the House of Representatives for the passage of the foresight provision the previous year, and to inform Congress of the citizen futures efforts developing around the country.

Encouraged by the enthusiastic response of members of Congress, the group undertook a series of activities with Congress, the executive branch, and state and local governments, which in turn led to the creation of the Congressional Clearinghouse on the Future and the Institute for Alternative Futures.

The Clearinghouse, described by Congressman Charlie Rose in Chapter 5, grew out of a presentation by Alvin Toffler and Ted Gordon, president of the Futures Group and a member of the Committee for Anticipatory Democracy. The Institute for Alternative Futures grew out of discussions between Toffler and William Birenbaum, president of Antioch University and also a member of the Committee. A unit of Antioch University housed at its School of Law in Washington, D.C., the Institute provides educational services to the various units of the university while encouraging anticipatory democracy through education and research in a variety of settings. The Clearinghouse and the Institute are two of the major centers for information and innovations in the areas of legislative foresight and citizen futures efforts.

The tone for much of the work of the Committee on Anticipatory Democracy was set by the addresses at the plenary session of its September 1975 conference, the first legislative seminar on futurism, entitled "Outsmarting Crises: Futures Thinking in Congress."* Senator John Culver, speaking for himself and the more than twenty-five other members of Congress sponsoring the conference, noted that legislators every day face decisions whose outcomes will affect our lives and the quality of our existence over many years. Futures techniques, while they will not remake Congress, can offer real possibilities.

Alvin Toffler spoke to the audience of nearly four hundred members of Congress and their staffs on the crisis of parliamentary democracy. Industrial society, around which our legislative institutions have developed, is undergoing a phenomenal transition or transformation, and parliaments around the world are feeling the strain and are being forced to think ahead. Toffler described the efforts of the citizen futures projects and their significance as an indicator that the future is becoming a political question. He recommended that Congress be cautious of forecasters and their predictions—as they should of any narrowly focused expert—but encouraged Congress to seek more imaginative proposals and to develop sets of alternatives for problems before crises arise.

Hazel Henderson described futurism as an evolutionary response to the side effects of our earlier decisions. We are experiencing an explosion of unanticipated second-order consequences —much of it negative and alarming. To do futures research requires a consideration of values and the widest possible participation of all segments of our society, both in formal futures-research projects and in formulating alternative futures. She included in the ranks of futurists those political and social activists who are

* For the text of the speeches by Senator John Culver, Alvin Toffler, Hazel Henderson, and others, see *The Congressional Record*, Sept. 26, 1975, S16826-28; Sept. 29; and Sept. 30, E5112.

operating with new or different images of the future.* Henderson ended her talk by noting that the most imaginative of the
futurists around us are urging that we look up from our preoccu-
pation with retooling the world and try retooling ourselves. Futures research is societal learning in its broadest sense.

* Many of these groups are listed in Appendix 3.

a. Ad Hoc Committee on Anticipatory Democracy

(SIGNATORIES, LETTER TO CONGRESS, APRIL 28, 1975)

John W. Abbott
California Tomorrow

Roy Amara
Institute for the Future

Lawrence Auls
Model Neighborhood
  Assembly

Wendell Bell
Yale University

Clement Bezold
Center for Government
  Responsibility

Craig Bigler
Assoc. State Planning
  Coordinator, State of Utah

William Birenbaum
Staten Island Community
  College

Paul O. Bofinger
Society for the Protection of
  New Hampshire Forests

Elise Boulding
University of Colorado

Willard Boyd
Iowa 2000

Lester Brown
Worldwatch Institute

Rosemary Bruner
Health Planner

Irving Buchen
Fairleigh Dickinson
  University

Thomas Carlton
Futures Lab.

F. Scott Carpenter
Astronaut

George Chaplin
The Honolulu *Advertiser*

Richard B. Cobb
Office of Planning & Budget
State of Georgia

Donald Conover
Western Electric

Magda Cordell
State University of New York

Edward Cornish
World Future Society

Richard Cornuelle
Author

James Dator
Hawaii Futures Research
 Center
Ontario Educ. Comm.
 Authority

Stuart C. Dodd
University of Washington

Maryjane Dunstan
College of Marin

F. M. Esfandiary
Planner

Amitai Etzioni
Center for Policy Research

Betty Friedan
Feminist

R. Buckminster Fuller

Newt Gingrich
West Georgia College

Russell Goings
1st Harlem Securities

David Goldberg
Vermont Tomorrow

Theodore Gordon
The Futures Group

Willis Harman
Stanford Research Institute

Hazel Henderson
Princeton Center for
 Alternative Futures

Russell Kolton
Earthrise

John McHale
Center for Integrative
 Studies

Carl Madden
Economist

Margaret Mead
Anthropologist

Donald Michael
University of Michigan

Arthur Okun
Economist

Billy Rojas
Futurist

William Ruckelshaus
Attorney

Jonas Salk
The Salk Institute

Arthur Sears
Writer

Harold G. Shane
Indiana University

Norman Shavin
Atlanta Magazine

W. W. Simmons
Applied Futures

Robert Stilger
Northwest Regional
  Foundation

Harold Strudler
Institute for the Future

Robert Theobald
Participation Publishers

Alvin Toffler
Author

Lee Udall
Center for Arts of
  Indian America

Carol van Alstyne
American Council on
  Education

Robert E. Weber
Project on Human
  Potential & Year 2000

Warren Ziegler
Syracuse University Research
  Corporation

b. Federal Government Support of State Goals and Futures Groups

As David Baker showed in Chapter 1, funding is an important issue for the goals and futures groups. Funding is usually obtained from a variety of sources, including corporations and foundations as well as local, state, and federal governments. Senator John Culver (D–Iowa), one of the originators of Iowa 2000 and a leader in the area of congressional foresight, has proposed that federal support be increased for citizen participation in planning.

Culver has sought to avoid the proliferation of additional agencies or large programs. Instead, he has looked for opportunities to expand or to readjust existing programs. Culver's amendment to the Environmental Research, Development, and Demonstration Authorization Act of 1979 (H.R. 11302), passed first by the Subcommittee on Resource Protection and then by the full Committee on Environment and Public Works, is likely to become law during this session of Congress. It provides $3 million for use by "citizens groups in determining how scientific, technological, and social trends and changes affect the future environment and quality of life of an area, and for setting goals and identifying measures for improvement." To obtain funds, groups must demonstrate a prior record of interest and involvement in goal-setting exercizes and studies concerning the quality of life and must receive the endorsement of their state governor.

While the amount of funding available for citizens' futures groups is relatively small (75 percent of each program's cost up to a maximum of $50,000), Culver's environmental authorization amendment is a positive step toward raising the visibility of citizen involvement in planning.

Culver is considering other approaches to additional sources of funding. These include amending the major federal planning assistance program—the "701" program for comprehensive planning by cities and states through the 1954 Housing and Urban Development Act—to include a broader definition of participation and a longer time horizon.

c. What Is Anticipatory Democracy*

BY ALVIN TOFFLER

Anticipatory democracy is a process—a way of reaching decisions that determine our future. It can be used to help us regain control over tomorrow.

Two crucial problems endanger the stability and survival of our political system today.

First: *Lack of future-consciousness*   Instead of anticipating the problems and opportunities of the future, we lurch from crisis to crisis. The energy shortage, runaway inflation, ecological troubles —all reflect the failure of our political leaders at federal, state, and local levels to look beyond the next election. Our political system is "future-blind." With but few exceptions, the same failure of foresight marks our corporations, trade unions, schools, hospitals, voluntary organizations, and communities as well. The result is political and social future shock.

Second: *Lack of participation*   Our government and other institutions have grown so large and complicated that most people feel powerless. They complain of being "planned upon." They are seldom consulted or asked for ideas about their own future. On the rare occasions when they are, it is ritualistic rather than a real

---

* First appeared in *The Futurist*, published by The World Future Society, Washington, D.C. (Vol. 9, October 1975). Reprinted with permission.

consultation. Blue-collar workers, poor people, the elderly, the youth, even the affluent among us, feel frozen out of the decision process. And as more and more millions feel powerless, the danger of violence and authoritarianism increases.

Moreover, if this is true within the country, it is even more true of the world situation, in which the previously powerless are demanding the right to participate in shaping the global future.

Anticipatory democracy is a way to tackle both these critical problems simultaneously. It connects up future-consciousness with real participation.

Thus the term "anticipatory" stresses the need for greater attention to the long-range future. The term "democracy" stresses the need for vastly increased popular participation and feedback.

There is no single or magical way to build a truly anticipatory democracy. In general, we need to support any program or action that increases future-awareness in the society, while simultaneously creating new channels for genuine, broad-based citizen participation. This means, among other things, an emphasis not on "elite" or "technocratic" futures work, but on mass involvement. We certainly need experts and specialists; they are indispensable, in fact. But in anticipatory democracy, goals are not set by elites or experts alone. Thus, where futures activity exists, we need to open it to all sectors of society, making a special effort to involve women, the poor working people, minority groups, young and old —and to involve them at all levels of leadership as well. Conversely, where participatory activities exist at community, state, or federal levels, or within various corporate or voluntary organizations, we need to press for attention to longer-range futures.

A/D ACTIVITIES TAKE MANY FORMS

Anticipatory democracy may take many forms, including the following:

1. Creation of city or statewide "2000" organizations. These bring thousands of citizens together to help define long-range goals. These goals are sometimes then embodied in legislation. Examples include Hawaii 2000, Iowa 2000, and Alternatives for Washington—all three at the state level; Seattle 2000 at the city

level. Some sort of "2000" activity has been identified in over twenty states.

2. Certain important movements in American society are inherently proparticipative: they work to open the society to the full participation of women, ethnic minorities, the elderly, the poor, or others who are frequently excluded from decision processes in the system. Working with these movements to introduce greater future-consciousness, more attention to long-term goals, awareness of new technologies or social trends that may impact on them, contributes to the spread of A/D.

3. Media feedback programs. Radio and TV audiences are seldom given a chance to voice their views—particularly about the future. The use of TV, radio, cable TV, cassette, the print media, and other communications systems to present alternative futures and provide channels for audience feedback, simultaneously increases both participation and future-consciousness.

4. Congressional reform. Passage of a "foresight provision" (H.R. 988) in the U.S. House of Representatives now for the first time requires that most standing committees engage in futures research and long-range analysis. By strengthening the Congress vis-à-vis the executive branch, it increases the potential for democratic participation as well. For example, anticipatory democracy organizations like Alternatives for Washington or Iowa 2000 could systematically feed citizens' views on the future into foresight discussions in Congress. We need "foresight provisions" in the Senate, and in state legislatures and city councils as well.

5. Community Action Programs. Nearly nine hundred CAPs exist in all parts of the nation. Aimed at combatting poverty, they all involve some form of participatory planning, often neighborhood based. Attempts to strengthen participation and to extend planning beyond the short term also help the move toward anticipatory democracy.

6. Referenda. There are many ways to link referenda to long-term future issues. (The British just made a long-range decision to stay in the Common Market, and relied on the referenda to tell Parliament how the country felt on the issue.)

7. Steps aimed at involving workers, consumers, minorities, women, and community groups in decision-making in industry and government—when linked to long-term planning—further the process of A/D. The Congressional Office of Technology Assessment,

for example, has an active Citizens Advisory panel that becomes deeply involved in decisions about the very long-range effects of new technologies. Movements for worker participation or self-management in industry, for consumer-watchdog agencies, for participatory management, can all be encouraged to become more future-conscious. Unless participation affects the planning process, it has little impact.

8. Futurizing the programs of organizations like the Young Women's Christian Association, the Red Cross, or the National Education Association—to choose three at random—helps spread the necessary awareness through the network of existing voluntary organizations.

9. Opening up global or transnational organizations to greater participation and future-consciousness. The United Nations conferences, especially the informal meetings that occur simultaneously with them, are opportunities for introducing A/D on a global scale. Such conferences as those devoted to the law of the sea in Caracas, population in Bucharest, environment in Stockholm, food in Rome, women in Mexico City, and the forthcoming one on human settlements in Vancouver are events at which globally oriented people and nongovernmental organizations with local constituencies can get together to exchange information and strategies, and to influence formal policy.

10. Creation of participatory planning mechanisms within community organizations. For example, bringing the entire membership of a church; or a broadly representative group of parents, teachers, and students in a school; or patients, medical staff, and service employees in a hospital into the planning process advances anticipatory democracy. Provided the process is truly participatory and the time horizon reaches beyond, say, ten years, it strengthens A/D and helps educate people to play a more active role in the national political system as well.

11. Democratizing The World Future Society through expanding its membership to include groups now underrepresented, and to assure fully democratic internal procedures is yet another step in the direction of A/D. Preventing futurism from becoming prematurely academicized or super-professionalized helps avoid its use as a tool for mystification of the public.

These are all examples of A/D activity. They are not given in any order of precedence, but they reflect the diversity of possibilities. Dozens more could no doubt be cited. We need to *invent* many additional kinds of A/D activity. This will require the help of millions of people from every discipline, from every walk of life, every profession, ethnic and class background. A democracy that doesn't anticipate the future cannot survive. A society that is good at anticipating but allows the future to be captured by elites is no longer a democracy. As we move into the future, anticipatory democracies will be the only surviving kind.

2. Possible A/D Programs

More specific A/D activities include those on the following list. These are some possibilities—not necessarily recommendations. It is up to *you* to decide whether any of them are appropriate. You may want to adapt them or, better yet, invent your own!

· Visit your city council or state legislature and urge passage of a "foresight provision" modeled after H. R. 988 in the House of Representatives.

· Set up future-consciousness teams to attend political rallies and meetings. These teams would ask speakers to explain what effect their proposed programs might have on, say, the year 1985 or 2000. By pressing for a discussion of long-range consequences, the entire political discussion is raised to a higher level. Another question that can be asked: "If we don't really know what effect your proposals will have by 1985, what procedures ought we to be following to find out?"

· Phone a radio talk show and suggest a program on the future, inviting listeners to suggest goals for the community over the next fifteen- or twenty-five-year period. Such shows have already been tried out in San Diego, Dallas, Atlanta, New Orleans, and other cities. A good response can be used to get interested listeners together to form an A/D group.

· Contact the city or state planning agency and suggest citizen-participation activities like Alternatives for Washingon. Provide the agency with the names of individuals who will take the initiative in organizing these activities, and sources of information on previous activities of this kind.

· Get a group of futurists to visit the nearest Community Action Agency or Community Action Program and ask: 1) What the futurists can offer in the way of methods, insights, perspectives; 2) What the futurists can learn from community experiences with public participation in planning.

· Organize speaking teams for community groups that express an interest in A/D or futurism.

· Arrange for an anticipatory democracy booth at local events. Use booth to distribute A/D literature, but also to get ideas and criticism about the future of your community from the public.

· Approach major companies in your area and ask them to make public in at least a general sense their plans for new investments, jobs, technologies, etc. Publicize their reactions as well as their plans. Ask to what degree consumers, employees, or public officials were consulted in drawing up the plans.

· Place ballot boxes in local supermarkets, shopping centers, or movie theaters, with ballots asking passersby to check off the three things they most like and the three things they most dislike about the community. Pass findings to local press and relevant officials. What are they doing now to preserve the good and eradicate the bad by 1985?

· Organize an open discussion of long-term goals in a church or synagogue to define its purposes in relation to the community over a ten- to twenty-five-year period.

· Working with doctors, the nursing association, and other community health groups, try to organize a community-wide "health plebescite," asking, through the mass media and other channels, for ordinary people to tell what they think is wrong, and what they think will be needed to improve health services by 1985. Compare their priorities with the local health budget.

· Approach parent-teacher associations, teachers' organizations, and students about running an Education 1985 or Education 2000

Conference, where parents and teachers, as well as professionals, would have a chance to voice problems, hopes, and fears about the future and where they may suggest ways of futurizing education.

Anticipatory democracy is not a single "thing"—it is a process. It can be created in a wide variety of ways. It's up to you to create your own.

3. List of State, Local, and Regional A/D Groups

STATES

An asterisk indicates a program that was discontinued prior to 1977. Listing gives last known contact.

Alaska

Alaska Growth Policy Council

Lt. Governor Lowell Thomas, Jr., Chairman
Office of the Governor
State Capital, Pouch A
Juneau, Alaska 99801
(907) 465-3500

California

California Tomorrow*

Monadnock Building
681 Market Street
San Francisco, California 94105
(415) 391-7544

Connecticut

Commission on Connecticut's Future

(Mrs.) Chase Going Woodhouse, Chairperson
Commission on Connecticut's Future
Auerbach Service Bureau
G. Fox and Co. Building
Hartford, Connecticut 06115
(203) 249-9711

Delaware

Delaware Tomorrow Commission

David Hugg
Principal Planner, Natural Resources Section
Office of Management, Budget and Planning
Townsend Building
Dover, Delaware 19901
(302) 678-4271

Georgia

Goals for Georgia*

Office of Planning and Budget
270 Washington Street, S.W.
Atlanta, Georgia 30334
(404) 656-3861

Georgia 2000

Georgia 2000
P.O. Box 7731
Station C
Atlanta, Georgia 30357

Hawaii

Hawaii 2000/Commission on the Year 2000

Gerald Sumida
Carlsmith, Carlsmith, Wichman and Case
Suite 2200
Pacific Trade Center
Honolulu, Hawaii 96813
(808) 524-5112

Idaho

Idaho's Tomorrow

Paul Card
Division of Budget, Policy, Planning and Coordination
State House
Boise, Idaho 83720
(208) 384-3900

Illinois

Illinois 2000

David Baker
Executive Director
20 North Wacker Drive
Chicago, Illinois 60606
(312) 372-7373

Iowa

Iowa 2000

Penny K. Davidsen
Program Coordinator
IOWA 2000 Program
c/o Institute of Public Affairs
University of Iowa
Iowa City, Iowa 52242
(319) 353-3270

Louisiana

Louisiana Priorities for the Future & Wake-Up Louisiana

Robert Wall, Executive Director
2714 Canal Street, Suite 302
New Orleans, Louisiana 70119
(504) 821-6422

Maine

Commission on Maine's Future*

Commission on Maine's Future
184 State Street
Augusta, Maine 04333
(207) 289-3261

Massachusetts

Massachusetts Special Legislative Commission on the Effects of Growth on the Quality of Life in the Commonwealth

Senator Robert Wetmore, Chairman
State Senate
State House
Boston, Massachusetts 02133
(617) 727-1540

Massachusetts Tomorrow

David Dodson Gray
President
Massachusetts Tomorrow
61 Chestnut Street
West Newton, Massachusetts 02165
(617) 235-5320

Minnesota

Commission on Minnesota's Future

Neil Gustafson
Executive Director
Commission on Minnesota's Future
101 Capitol Square Building
St. Paul, Minnesota 55101
(612) 296-3852

New Hampshire

New Hampshire Tomorrow*

Society for the Protection of N.H. Forests
5 South State Street
Concord, New Hampshire 03301
(603) 224-9945

North Carolina

Board on State Goals and Policy

Dana Heering
Division of Policy Development
Office of State Planning
Administration Building, Room 502
Raleigh, North Carolina 27603
(919) 733-4131

Vermont

Vermont Tomorrow

Dave Goldberg
Executive Director
Vermont Tomorrow
5 State Street
Montpelier, Vermont 05602
(802) 223-6067

Washington

Alternatives for Washington

Floyd Argersinger, Executive Director
Alternatives for Washington
Office of Program Planning and Fiscal Management
House Office Building
Olympia, Washington 98504

LOCALITIES

Akron, Ohio

Goals for Greater Akron Area

Barbara Hiney
Executive Director
Goals for Greater Akron Area
One Cascade Plaza, 8th Floor
Akron, Ohio 44308
(216) 375-2176

Atlanta, Georgia

Atlanta 2000

Dr. Robert Hanie
Executive Director
Atlanta 2000, Inc.
1320 Healey Building
Atlanta, Georgia 30303
(404) 577-5654

Austin, Texas

Austin Tomorrow

Luther Polnau
Advanced Planning Supervisor
City of Austin Planning Department
P.O. Box 1088
Austin, Texas 78767
(512) 477-6511

Charlotte-Mecklenburg County, North Carolina

Dimensions for Charlotte-Mecklenburg

Jane Beggle
Director
Institute for Urban Studies and Community Service
University of North Carolina at Charlotte
Charlotte, North Carolina 28223
(704) 597-2307

Clarinda, Iowa

Clarinda Citizens Involvement

Anna Smith
Executive Director
Box 57
Clarinda, Iowa 51632
(712) 542-2200

Corpus Christi, Texas

Goals for Corpus Christi*

Bruce W. McLendon
Senior City Planner
City of Corpus Christi
Box 9277
Corpus Christi, Texas 78408
(512) 884-3011

Dallas, Texas

Goals for Dallas

Goals for Dallas
Suite 825
1 Main Place
Dallas, Texas 75250
(214) 741-1738

Fort Worth, Texas

Sector Planning Program

George Human
Director
City Planning Department
1000 Throckmorton Street
Fort Worth, Texas 76133
(817) 355-7211

Galveston, Texas

Goals for Galveston

Kenneth Wellborn, Director
2 Moody Plaza
Galveston, Texas 77550

Hartford, Connecticut

Greater Hartford Process

Peter Labissi
President
Greater Hartford Process
100 Constitution Plaza
Hartford, Connecticut 06103
(203) 249-1331

Los Angeles, California

Los Angeles Goals Program

Calvin S. Hamilton
Director of Planning
Los Angeles Department of City Planning
Room 561-C, City Hall
Los Angeles, California
(213) 485-5073

Lynchburg, Virginia

Central Virginia Tomorrow

Haywood Robinson
Central Virginia Tomorrow
412 Madison Street
Lynchburg, Virginia 24501
(804) 846-2278

Nashville, Tennessee

Citizens Goals 2000 Committee

Victor S. Johnson
Citizens Goals 2000 Committee
P.O. Box 7235
Nashville, Tennessee 37210
(615) 255-5800

Norwich, New York

Citizens Unlimited

Rodney S. Morris, Coordinator
CITIZENS UNLIMITED for Community Involvement
(Citizens Involvement Center)
13 South Broad Street
Norwich, New York 13815

Raleigh/Wake County, North Carolina

Goals for Raleigh/Wake

Betty Doak
Executive Director
Box 17022
Raleigh, North Carolina 27609
(919) 781-5736

Santa Barbara, California

ACCESS*

William R. Ewald, Jr.
Principal Investigator
The Lugo Abode, Studio 4
114 East de la Guerra Street
Santa Barbara, California 93101
(805) 963-0428

Seattle, Washington

Seattle 2000*

Phil Sherburne
Office of Policy Planning
Department of Community Development
400 Vesler Building
Seattle, Washington 98104
(206) 624-3600

Sherman, Texas

Goals for Sherman

Steve Avard
Goals for Sherman
209 West Houston
Sherman, Texas 75090
(214) 893-7411
(214) 465-4641

* Discontinued prior to 1977. Listing gives last known contact.

REGIONS

Delaware Valley

Year 2000 Plan—Delaware Valley Regional Planning Commission
(Pennsylvania, New Jersey)

Richard Nalbandian, Coordinator
D.V.R.P.C.
Penn Towers Building
1819 J. F. Kennedy Boulevard
Philadelphia, Pennsylvania 19103
(215) 567-3000

Great Lakes Region

Great Lakes Tomorrow*

Richard Robbins
c/o Lake Michigan Federation
53 West Jackson Boulevard
Chicago, Illinois 60604
(312) 427-5121

New York City Regional Area

Choices for '76
Regional Plan Association (New York)

William A. Shore
Regional Plan Association
235 East 45th Street
New York, New York 10017
(212) 682-7752

Pleasant Hill, Oregon

Bend in the River Project*

Ken Kesey
85829 Ridgeway Road
Pleasant Hill, Oregon

* Discontinued prior to 1977. Listing gives last known contact.

Rocky Mountain States

Federation of Rocky Mountain States, Inc.

Philip M. Burgess
Vice-President and Executive Director
Federation of Rocky Mountain States, Inc.
Suite 300-B
Denver, Colorado 80211
(303) 458-8000

The South

Commission on the Future of the South*

E. Evan Brunson
Southern Growth Policies Board
P.O. Box 12293
Research Triangle Park
North Carolina 27709
(919) 549-8169

Trident 2000

Herbert McMurphy
Trident 2000
114 Wentworth Street
Charleston, South Carolina 29401
(803) 577-2006

The Upper Midwest

Critical Choices for the Upper Midwest: The Next Ten Years

George Thiss, Executive Director
Upper Midwest Council
Federal Reserve Bank Building
Minneapolis, Minnesota 55480
(612) 373-3724

4. List of Information Sources on A/D Groups

Institute for Alternative Futures
Antioch School of Law
1624 Crescent Place, N.W.
Washington, D.C. 20009
(202) 265-0346

The Congressional Clearinghouse for the Future
3692 House Office Annex #2
U.S. House of Representatives
Washington, D.C. 20515
(202) 225-3153

Futures Research Group
Congressional Research Service
Library of Congress
Washington, D.C. 20540
(202) 426-6498

Earthrise, Inc.
P.O. Box 120 Annex Station
Providence, Rhode Island 02901
(401) 274-0011

The World Future Society
4916 St. Elmo Avenue
Washington, D.C. 20014
(301) 656-8274

NorthWest Regional Foundation
P.O. Box 5296
Spokane, Washington 99205
(509) 455-9255

5. List of Citizen Groups on the Cutting Edge of Alternative Futures

ACORN
Governor's State University
Park Forest South, Illinois 60466

Alternative Christmas Catalogue
1924 East 3rd Street
Bloomington, Indiana 47401
(812) 339-5205

Americans for a Working Economy
1620 I Street N.W.
Washington, D.C. 20006
(202) 296-1970

Center for Science in the Public Interest
1757 S Street N.W.
Washington, D.C. 20009
(202) 332-4250

Citizens' Communication Center
1914 Sunderland Place N.W.
Washington, D.C. 20036
(202) 296-4238

Co-Evolution Quarterly
Box 428
Sausalito, California 94965
(415) 332-1716

Conference on Alternative State and
    Local Public Policies
1901 Q Street N.W.
Washington, D.C. 20009
(202) 234-9382

Council on Economic Priorities
84 Fifth Avenue
New York, New York 10011
(212) 691-8550

Council on Public Interest Law
1250 Connecticut Avenue N.W.
Washington, D.C. 20036

Earthrise
Box 120, Annex Station
Providence, Rhode Island 02901
(401) 274-0011

The Elements
1747 Connecticut Avenue N.W.
Washington, D.C. 20036
(202) 234-6485

Environmental Action
1346 Connecticut Avenue N.W.
Washington, D.C. 20036
(202) 833-1845

Environmentalists for Full Employment
1785 Massachusetts Avenue N.W.
Washington, D.C. 20036
(202) 265-2250

Exploratory Project on Economic Alternatives
2000 P Street N.W.
Washington, D.C. 20036
(202) 833-3208

Findhorn
The Park, Forres,
IV 36 OTZ,
Scotland
Phone: Findhorn 311

Foxfire
Eliot Wigginton
Foxfire Fund, Inc.
Rabun Gap, Georgia 30568
(404) 746-2561

Great Speckled Bird
Box 54495
Atlanta, Georgia 30308

Initiative America
606 3rd Street N.W.
Washington, D.C. 20001
(202) 393-3939

Institute for Local Self Reliance
1717 18th Street N.W.
Washington, D.C. 20009
(202) 232-4108

Intermediate Technology
556 Santa Cruz Avenue
Menlo Park, California 94025
(415) 328-1730

Lindisfarne Association
50 Fishcove Road
Southampton, New York 11968
(516) 283-8210

Mother Earth News
Asheville Highway
Hendersonville, North Carolina 28739
(704) 693-0211

National Citizens' Committee for Broadcasting
1028 Connecticut Avenue N.W.
Washington, D.C. 20036
(202) 466-8407

National Council for the Public Assessment of Technology
1785 Massachusetts Avenue N.W.
Washington, D.C. 20036
(202) 462-3338

Organic Gardening
33 East Minor Street
Emmaus, Pennsylvania 18043
(215) 967-5171

Public Citizen
1200 15 Street N.W.
Washington, D.C. 20036
(202) 659-9053

Prevention
33 East Minor Street
Emmaus, Pennsylvania 18043
(215) 967-5171

Radical Software
51 Fifth Avenue
New York, New York 10003

Rain Magazine
2270 N.W. Irving St.
Portland, Oregon 97210
(503) 227-5110

Scientists' Institute for Public Information
49 East 53rd Street
New York, New York 10022
(212) 688-4050

Spark
Box 4729
Baltimore, Maryland 21211

Spark
Box 1274
Detroit, Michigan 48231

Televisions
National Citizens Committee for Broadcasting
1912 N Street, N.W.
Washington, D.C. 20036
(202) 331-1566
   Media Access—(202) 785-2613

The Union of Concerned Scientists
1208 Massachusetts Avenue
Cambridge, Massachusetts 02139
(617) 547-5552

Worldwatch Institute
1776 Massachusetts Avenue N.W.
Washington, D.C. 20036
(202) 452-1999

(We recognize that this list is incomplete; we hope to hear from
other groups around the country.)

Index

Notes about the Authors

LAWRENCE J. AULS is president of Mainway Wholesale Supplies, Inc., one of the first black electrical wholesale distribution firms in the country. A civil-rights activist and community organizer in Columbus, he has been involved in the development of minority futures programs and, as a member of the board of the National Association of Black Manufacturers, chairs a committee on energy-focused venture capital for minority small business.

DAVID E. BAKER is currently the director of Illinois 2000, a futures project of the Illinois Chamber of Commerce. For several years he was the director of a project on state growth policy at the Population Institute, a position from which he was able to study and encourage the development of anticipatory democracy projects in a number of states. He has served as consultant to several government agencies and congressional committees on the long-term implications of population and growth policy.

TED BECKER is professor of law and political science at the University of Hawaii. The author of several books on law and the judicial system, including a textbook: *American Government: Past, Present, and Future* and *Unvote for a New America*. He was one of the founders of the Hawaii Constitutional Network aimed at making the 1978 Hawaii constitutional convention an Electronic Town Meeting.

C. GEORGE BENELLO has taught sociology at Goddard College and was a fellow of the Cambridge Institute, where he directed research on new-town development. He is editor of both *Our Generation* and *Current Magazine*. He has written several articles on social theory and is the author of *Wasteland Culture* and editor of *The Case for Participatory Democracy*. He is also one of the developers of the Federation for Economic Democracy and the Foundation for Educational and Development Organization, whose goal is to create self-managed firms.

CLEMENT BEZOLD is director of the Institute for Alternative Futures. A political scientist and public-interest activist, he has advised several state and local citizen futures projects. A recognized expert in legislative foresight, he has been a consultant to several congressional committees. He has taught at Antioch University's School of Law and Maryland Graduate Program, and at the University of Florida where he was assistant director of the Center for Governmental Responsibility.

ROBERT B. BRADLEY is a professor of political economy at the University of Texas at Dallas. An expert on urban policy and politics, he has authored several reports and articles on city government. He has taught courses on Texas politics and the Future of America and in 1978 designed a science and technology information system for the Nevada legislature.

ROSEMARY H. BRUNER is a strategic planner for the pharmaceutical firm of Hoffman-La Roche, Inc. A community activist, she has organized and held positions in local and state chapters of the League of Women Voters and the National Organization of Women. She has also worked as a health advocate for community organizations and as a human-services analyst and administrator.

DONALD K. CONOVER is the director of Corporate Planning at Western Electric where he has been employed for twenty years, holding a variety of engineering and manufacturing management positions. He has been an officer in various professional societies, such as chairman of the Organization Development Council and vice-president of the North American Society for Corporate Planning. He is the author of numerous papers on the subjects of organization and planning.

JAMES A. DATOR is a professor of political science and futuristics at the University of Hawaii. A leading futurist, he taught one of the first courses on the future at Virginia Polytechnic Institute in 1966. In Hawaii he was one of the developers of Hawaii 2000 and has acted as adviser on long-range planning to the judiciary and to the state legislature. He has published numerous articles and edited several books. He has also produced television programs on the future in Hawaii, Canada, and Great Britain, and is currently working on a major television series on the future.

JEROME C. GLENN is executive director of the Futures Option Room in Washington, D.C. He has worked for the Committee for the Future, the Hudson Institute, and The World Future Society. His articles on the future of education and forecasting have appeared in several national journals. He has taught futures research at the University of Massachusetts, Antioch Graduate School of Education, and the Smithsonian Institution.

NEWT GINGRICH is a professor in environmental studies at Georgia State University in Carrollton, Georgia. An historian by training, he has actively encouraged anticipatory democracy in Georgia, and has been a candidate for Congress. He is the author of a major study on NATO military preparedness in Europe.

HAZEL HENDERSON is an author and co-director of the Princeton Center for Alternative Futures. She is a leading advocate of greater public participation in governmental decision-making and serves on the board of several public-interest organizations, including the Council on Economic Priorities, the Environmental Action Foundation, and Worldwatch Institute. She has been a guest lecturer at Columbia, MIT, Dartmouth and several other colleges and universities. Her articles have appeared in the *Harvard Business Review, The Public Administration Review,* as well as in numerous other journals. She is the author of *Creating Alternative Futures: The End of Economics.*

BYRON KENNARD is a community organizer and co-director of Environmentalists for Full Employment. One of the principal organizers of the May 1978 Sun Day, he was formerly the chairman of the National Council for the Public Assessment of Technology. He frequently consults with government agencies and other organizations on public participation and appropriate technology.

WILLIAM L. RENFRO is an analyst in futures research with the Congressional Research Service of the Library of Congress. An attorney and physicist, he has worked in the futures-research area for several years, in both the private and government sectors. Mr. Renfro has published numerous reports and articles in such areas as congressional foresight, energy, and office information systems, and has worked with citizen goals and futures groups in Georgia and Connecticut. The views expressed in his article are his own and not necessarily those of the Congressional Research Service or of the Library of Congress.

CONGRESSMAN CHARLIE ROSE, a representative from the Fayetteville, North Carolina, area since 1970, is a leader in citizen participation and foresight in Congress. As a member of the North Carolina legislature, he introduced the reforms that allowed for the use of computers, which has greatly expedited the legislative process. In Congress he is Chairman of the Computer Subcommittee of the House Administration Committee. He was the leading force among the fifty members of the House who founded the Congressional Clearinghouse on the Future.

NELSON M. ROSENBAUM, an analyst at The Urban Institute, is an expert on citizen participation. He has written extensively on this subject as well as on the redevelopment of inner cities. His most recent book is *Citizen Involvement in Land Use Governance.*

ROBERT L. STILGER is the executive director of the Northwest Regional Foundation, a Spokane-based nonprofit educational corporation which publishes *Futures Conditional Magazine* and which specializes in citizen participation in community and neighborhood development. He was partially responsible for the design of segments of Alternatives for Washington's Phase II Program.

ROBERT THEOBALD, an economist, writer, speaker, and consultant is the author of *The Rich and the Poor, The Challenge of Abundance, Free Men and Free Markets,* and *Habit and Habitat.* Among his writings most directly relevant to anticipatory democracy are *Beyond Despair: Directions for America's Third Century,* and, with J. M. Scott, *Teg's 1994.*

ALVIN TOFFLER is author of *Future Shock* and *The Eco-Spasm Report,* and editor of *Learning for Tomorrow* and *The Futurists.* Articles by him have appeared in many periodicals, ranging from *Life, Horizon,* and *Playboy* to the *Annals of the American Academy of Political and Social Science.* He has taught at the New School for Social Research and has been a visiting scholar at the Russell Sage Foundation and a Visiting Professor at Cornell University.

NAN WATERMAN is a member of the board of trustees of the League of Women Voters, where she guided the development of the League's futures program. In 1977 she succeeded John Gardner as chairperson of the board of Common Cause.